Flow charts for the

Term Service Contract

This contract should be used for the appointment of a supplier for a period of time to manage and provide a service

An NEC document

April 2013

Construction Clients' Board endorsement of NEC3

The Construction Clients' Board recommends that public sector organisations use the NEC3 contracts when procuring construction. Standardising use of this comprehensive suite of contracts should help to deliver efficiencies across the public sector and promote behaviours in line with the principles of *Achieving Excellence in Construction*.

Facilities Management Board support for NEC3

The Facilities Management Board recognises that the NEC Term Service Contracts support good practice in FM Procurement in the public sector.

Cabinet Office UK

supported by

BIFM
ADVANCING OUR PROFESSION

BIFM recommends the use of NEC3 Term Service Contract and NEC3 Term Service Short Contract for all types of Facilities Management and maintenance contracts.

NEC is a division of Thomas Telford Ltd, which is a wholly owned subsidiary of the Institution of Civil Engineers (ICE), the owner and developer of the NEC.

The NEC is a family of standard contracts, each of which has these characteristics:

- Its use stimulates good management of the relationship between the two parties to the contract and, hence, of the work included in the contract.
- It can be used in a wide variety of commercial situations, for a wide variety of types of work and in any location.
- It is a clear and simple document – using language and a structure which are straightforward and easily understood.

NEC3 Term Service Contract is one of the NEC family and is consistent with all other NEC3 documents. Also available are the Term Service Contract Guidance Notes.

ISBN (complete box set) 978 0 7277 5867 5
ISBN (this document) 978 0 7277 5923 8
ISBN (Term Service Contract) 978 0 7277 5891 0
ISBN (Term Service Contract Guidance Notes) 978 0 7277 5921 4
ISBN (how to write the TSC Service Information) 978 0 7277 5925 2
ISBN (how to use the TSC communication forms) 978 0 7277 5927 6

First edition June 2005
Reprinted with amendments 2007
Reprinted 2010, 2011, 2012
Reprinted with amendments 2013
Reprinted 2016, 2017

British Library Cataloguing in Publication Data for this publication is available from the British Library.

Typeset by Academic + Technical, Bristol

Printed and bound in Great Britain by Bell & Bain Limited, Glasgow, UK

CONTENTS

The number of each flow chart is the same as the number of the clause in the NEC Term Service Contract to which it primarily relates.

FOREWORD

I was delighted to be asked to write the Foreword for the NEC3 Contracts.

I have followed the outstanding rise and success of NEC contracts for a number of years now, in particular during my tenure as the 146th President of the Institution of Civil Engineers, 2010/11.

In my position as UK Government's Chief Construction Adviser, I am working with Government and industry to ensure Britain's construction sector is equipped with the knowledge, skills and best practice it needs in its transition to a low carbon economy. I am promoting innovation in the sector, including in particular the use of Building Information Modelling (BIM) in public sector construction procurement; and the synergy and fit with the collaborative nature of NEC contracts is obvious. The Government's construction strategy is a very significant investment and NEC contracts will play an important role in setting high standards of contract preparation, management and the desirable behaviour of our industry.

In the UK, we are faced with having to deliver a 15–20 per cent reduction in the cost to the public sector of construction during the lifetime of this Parliament. Shifting mind-set, attitude and behaviour into best practice NEC processes will go a considerable way to achieving this.

Of course, NEC contracts are used successfully around the world in both public and private sector projects; this trend seems set to continue at an increasing pace. NEC contracts are, according to my good friend and NEC's creator Dr Martin Barnes CBE, about better management of projects. This is quite achievable and I encourage you to understand NEC contracts to the best you can and exploit the potential this offers us all.

Peter Hansford

UK Government's Chief Construction Adviser
Cabinet Office

PREFACE

The NEC contracts are the only suite of standard contracts designed to facilitate and encourage good management of the projects on which they are used. The experience of using NEC contracts around the world is that they really make a difference. Previously, standard contracts were written mainly as legal documents best left in the desk drawer until costly and delaying problems had occurred and there were lengthy arguments about who was to blame.

The language of NEC contracts is clear and simple, and the procedures set out are all designed to stimulate good management. Foresighted collaboration between all the contributors to the project is the aim. The contracts set out how the interfaces between all the organisations involved will be managed – from the client through the designers and main contractors to all the many subcontractors and suppliers.

Versions of the NEC contract are specific to the work of professional service providers such as project managers and designers, to main contractors, to subcontractors and to suppliers. The wide range of situations covered by the contracts means that they do not need to be altered to suit any particular situation.

The NEC contracts are the first to deal specifically and effectively with management of the inevitable risks and uncertainties which are encountered to some extent on all projects. Management of the expected is easy, effective management of the unexpected draws fully on the collaborative approach inherent in the NEC contracts.

Most people working on projects using the NEC contracts for the first time are hugely impressed by the difference between the confrontational characteristics of traditional contracts and the teamwork engendered by the NEC. The NEC does not include specific provisions for dispute avoidance. They are not necessary. Collaborative management itself is designed to avoid disputes and it really works.

It is common for the final account for the work on a project to be settled at the time when the work is finished. The traditional long period of expensive professional work after completion to settle final payments just is not needed.

The NEC contracts are truly a massive change for the better for the industries in which they are used.

Dr Martin Barnes CBE

Originator of the NEC contracts

ACKNOWLEDGEMENTS

The first edition of the NEC3 Term Service Contract was drafted by the Institution of Civil Engineers NEC Panel through its Term Service Contract Working Group whose members were:

P. A. Baird, BSc, CEng, FICE, M(SA)ICE, MAPM
M. Barnes, BSc(Eng), PhD, FREng, FICE, FCIOB, CCMI, ACIArb, MBCS, FInstCES, FAPM
T. W. Weddell, BSc, CEng, DIC, FICE, FIStructE, ACIArb

The Flow Charts were produced by Ross Hayes with assistance from Tom Nicholson.

The original NEC was designed and drafted by Dr Martin Barnes then of Coopers and Lybrand with the assistance of Professor J. G. Perry then of the University of Birmingham, T. W. Weddell then of Travers Morgan Management, T. H. Nicholson, Consultant to the Institution of Civil Engineers, A. Norman then of the University of Manchester Institute of Science and Technology and P. A. Baird, then Corporate Contracts Consultant, Eskom, South Africa.

The members of the NEC Panel are:

P. Higgins, BSc, CEng, FICE, FCIArb (Chairman)
P. A. Baird, BSc, CEng, FICE, M(SA)ICE, MAPM
M. Barnes, BSc(Eng), PhD, FREng, FICE, FCIOB, CCMI, ACIArb, MBCS, FInstCES, FAPM
A. J. Bates, FRICS, MInstCES
A. J. M. Blackler, BA, LLB(Cantab), MCIArb
P. T. Cousins, BEng(Tech), DipArb, CEng, MICE, MCIArb, MCMI
L. T. Eames, BSc, FRICS, FCIOB
F. Forward, BA(Hons), DipArch, MSc(Const Law), RIBA, FCIArb
Professor J. G. Perry, MEng, PhD, CEng, FICE, MAPM
N. C. Shaw, FCIPS, CEng, MIMechE
T. W. Weddell, BSc, CEng, DIC, FICE, FIStructE, ACIArb

NEC Consultant:

R. A. Gerrard, BSc(Hons), MRICS, FCIArb, FCInstCES

Secretariat:

A. Cole, LLB, LLM, BL
J. M. Hawkins, BA(Hons), MSc
F. N. Vernon (Technical Adviser), BSc, CEng, MICE

AMENDMENTS

Full details of all amendments are available on www.neccontract.com.

Legend

CHART START

HEADINGS
> Headings in caps
> provide guidance

STATEMENTS
> If a clause is
> referenced, text
> is from the NEC

LOGIC LINKS
> Links go to right
> and/or downward
> unless shown

QUESTION
> Answer question
> to determine the
> route to follow

SUBROUTINE
> Include another
> flow chart here

CONTINUATION
> Link to matching
> point(s) on other
> chart sheets

CHART TITLE
> Chart number,
> title and sheet

CONTINUATION

CHART FINISH

CHART TITLE

Start

HELPFUL HEADING

Statement explaining next step → Clause or Statement using part or all of the NEC text in clause

Does this clause apply? — YES / NO

FC or Description

A sheet 2

B sheet 2

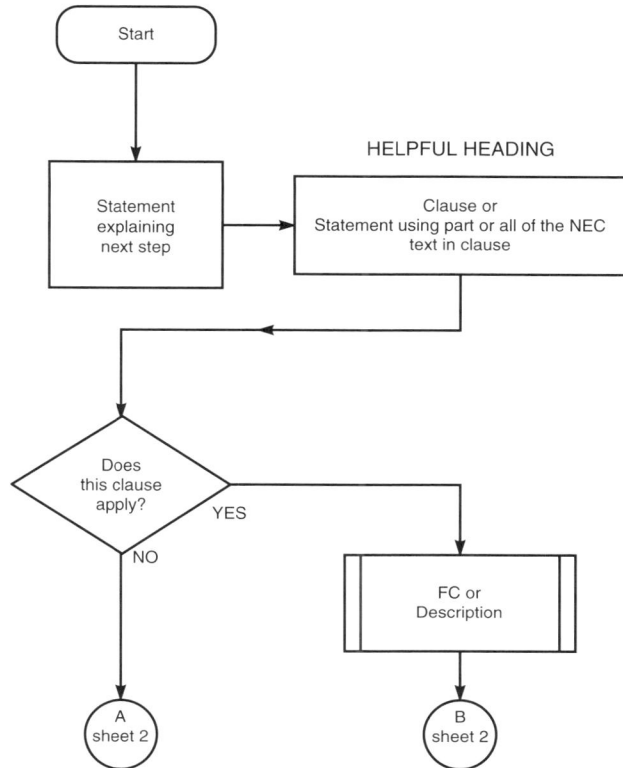

**Flow chart or Sheet 1 of 2
Description**

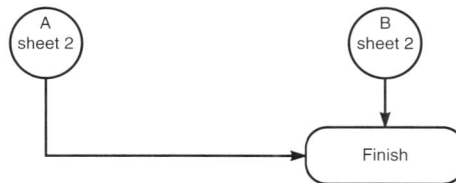

A sheet 2

B sheet 2

Finish

**Flow chart or Sheet 2 of 2
Description**

ABBREVIATIONS USED IN THE FLOW CHART BOXES

FC 61	Flow chart for clause 61
FC X2	Flowchart for secondary Option X2
E	*Employer*
C	*Contractor*
SM	*Service Manager*
SC	Subcontractor
CD	Contract Data
CE	Compensation event
P&M	Plant and Materials
PAF	Price Adjustment Factor
PSPD	Price for Services Provided to Date
SI	Service Information

FORM OF COMMUNICATION

Start

A communication is to be made

COMMUNICATIONS REQUIRED BY THIS CONTRACT

13.1
This contract requires instructions, certificates, submissions, proposals, records, acceptances, notifications, replies and other communications

13.1
A communication is in a form which can be read, copied and recorded

13.1
Writing is in the *language of this contract*

LANGUAGE OF THIS CONTRACT

The *language of this contract* is stated in the CD

RECEIPT OF COMMUNICATIONS

13.2
A communication has effect when it is received at the last address notified by the recipient for receiving communications or, if none is notified, at the address of the recipient stated in the CD

NOTIFICATIONS

13.7
Is this communication a notification?

YES

13.7
A notification which this contract requires is communicated separately from other communications

NO

A
Sheet 2

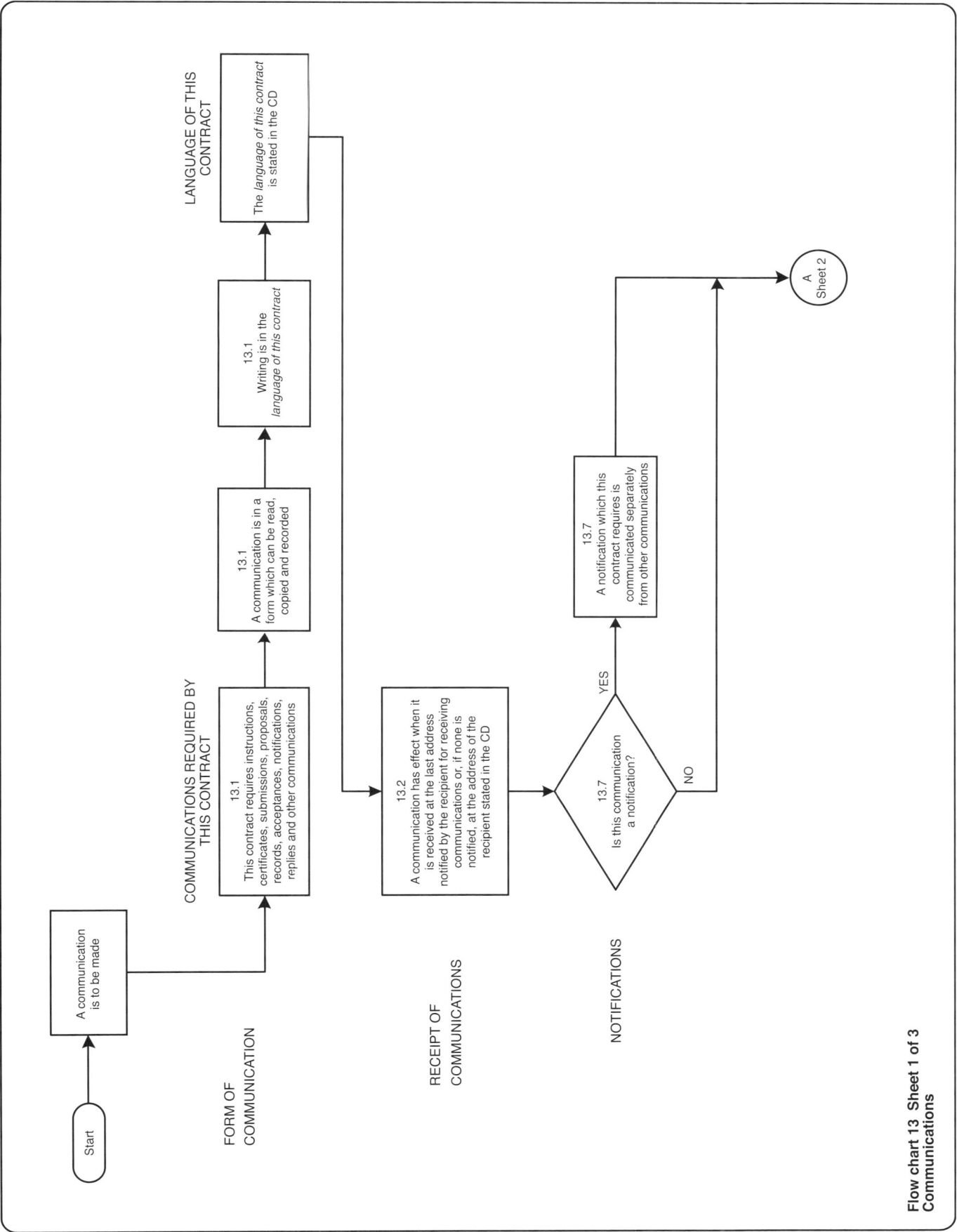

Flow chart 13 Sheet 1 of 3
Communications

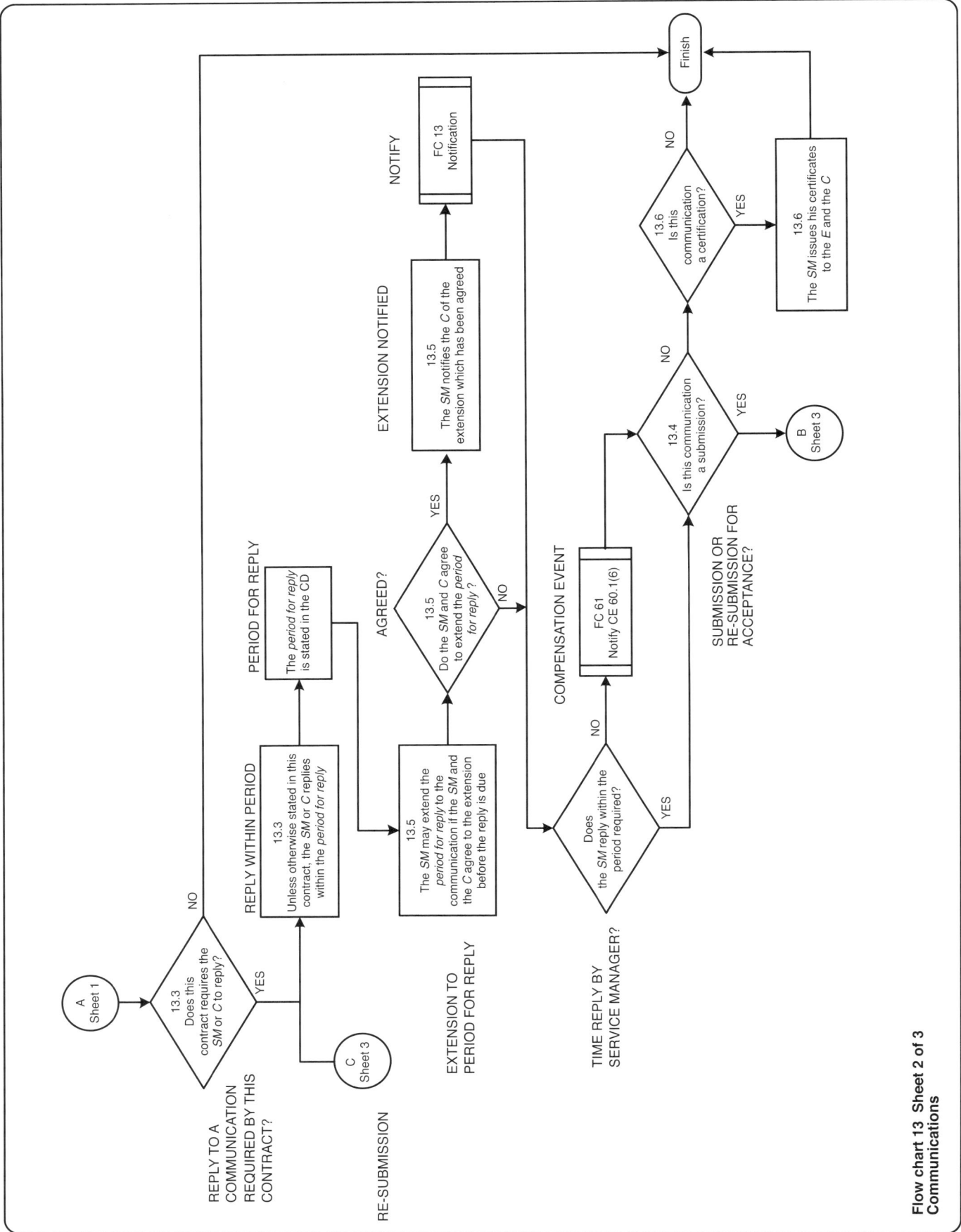

REPLY TO A COMMUNICATION REQUIRED BY THIS CONTRACT?

13.3
Does this contract requires the *SM* or *C* to reply?

RE-SUBMISSION

C
Sheet 3

REPLY WITHIN PERIOD

13.3
Unless otherwise stated in this contract, the *SM* or *C* replies within the *period for reply*

PERIOD FOR REPLY

The *period for reply* is stated in the CD

EXTENSION TO PERIOD FOR REPLY

13.5
The *SM* may extend the *period for reply* to the communication if the *SM* and the *C* agree to the extension before the reply is due

AGREED?

13.5
Do the *SM* and *C* agree to extend the *period for reply*?

EXTENSION NOTIFIED

13.5
The *SM* notifies the *C* of the extension which has been agreed

NOTIFY

FC 13
Notification

TIME REPLY BY SERVICE MANAGER?

Does the *SM* reply within the period required?

COMPENSATION EVENT

FC 61
Notify CE 60.1(6)

13.4
Is this communication a submission?

SUBMISSION OR RE-SUBMISSION FOR ACCEPTANCE?

B
Sheet 3

13.6
Is this communication a certification?

13.6
The *SM* issues his certificates to the *E* and the *C*

Finish

A
Sheet 1

**Flow chart 13 Sheet 2 of 3
Communications**

ACCEPTANCE
WITHHELD

REASON GIVEN

13.4
The *SM* replies to a
communication
submitted or
resubmitted to him by
the *C* for acceptance

13.4
If his reply is not
acceptance, the SM
states his reasons

13.8
The *SM* may withhold
acceptance of a
submission by the *C*

13.4
A reason for withholding
acceptance is that more
information is needed in
order to assess the *C*'s
submission fully

THE COMMUNICATION
IS A SUBMISSION OF
RE-SUBMISSION FOR
ACCEPTANCE

B
Sheet 2

NOT
COMPENSATION
EVENT

13.8
Withholding acceptance
for a reason stated in
this contract is not a CE

RESPONSIBILITIES
UNCHANGED

FC 14
The *C*'s responsibility to
Provide the Service or his
liability for his plan or his
design are not changed
by this acceptance

Finish

SUBMISSION
ACCEPTED?

13.4
Does the *SM*
accept the *C*'s
submission?

YES

NO

CONTRACTOR NOTIFIES

FC 61
The *C* notifies acceptance
withheld as a
CE 60.1(8)

INVALID REASON
FOR WITHHOLDING
ACCEPTANCE?

Does the
C believe that the *SM*
has withheld acceptance
for an invalid
reason

YES

NO

RE-SUBMISSION
REQUIRED

13.4
The *C* re-submits the
communication within
the *period for reply*
taking account of the
SM's reasons

C
Sheet 2

Flow chart 13 Sheet 3 of 3
Communications

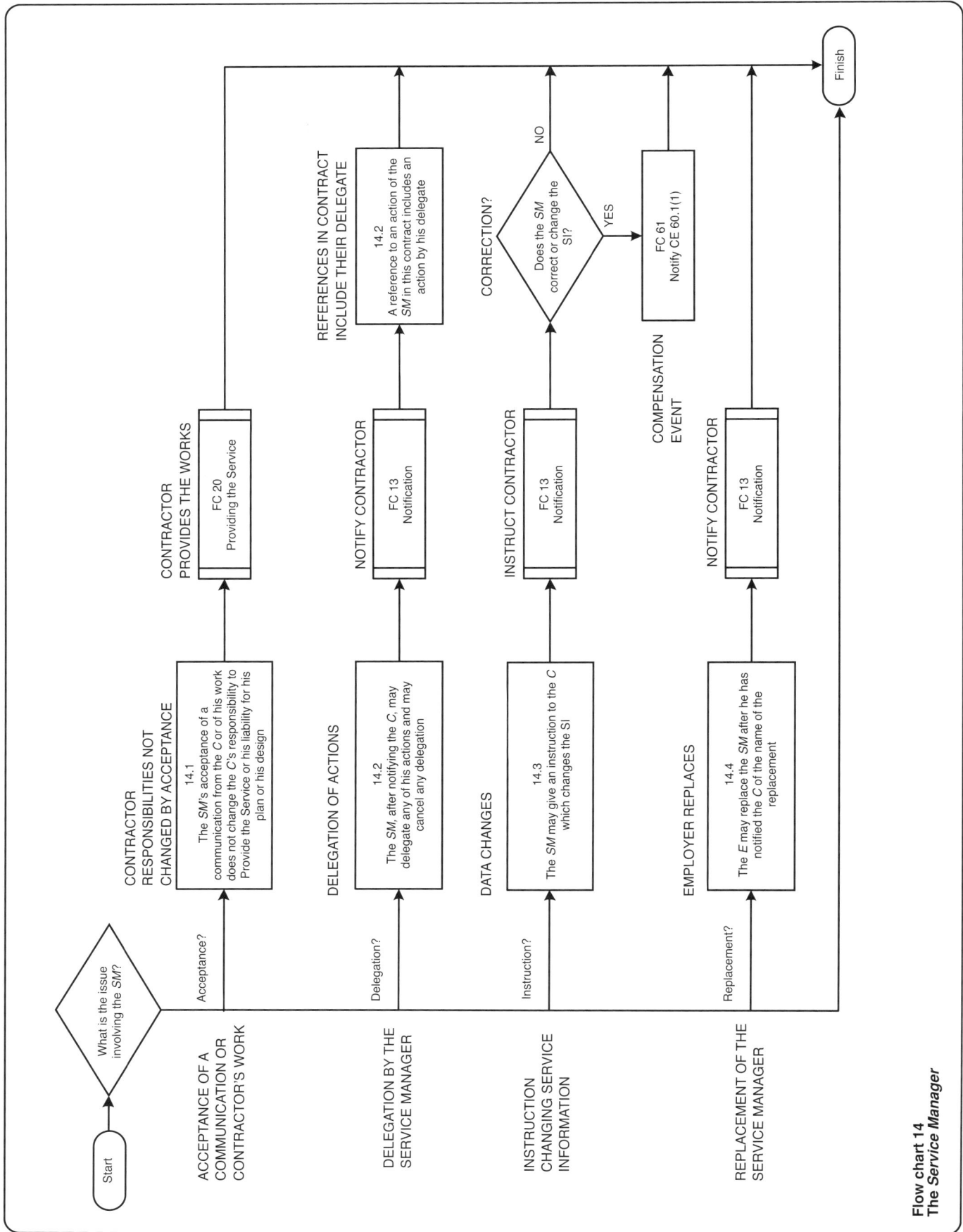

Flow chart 14
The Service Manager

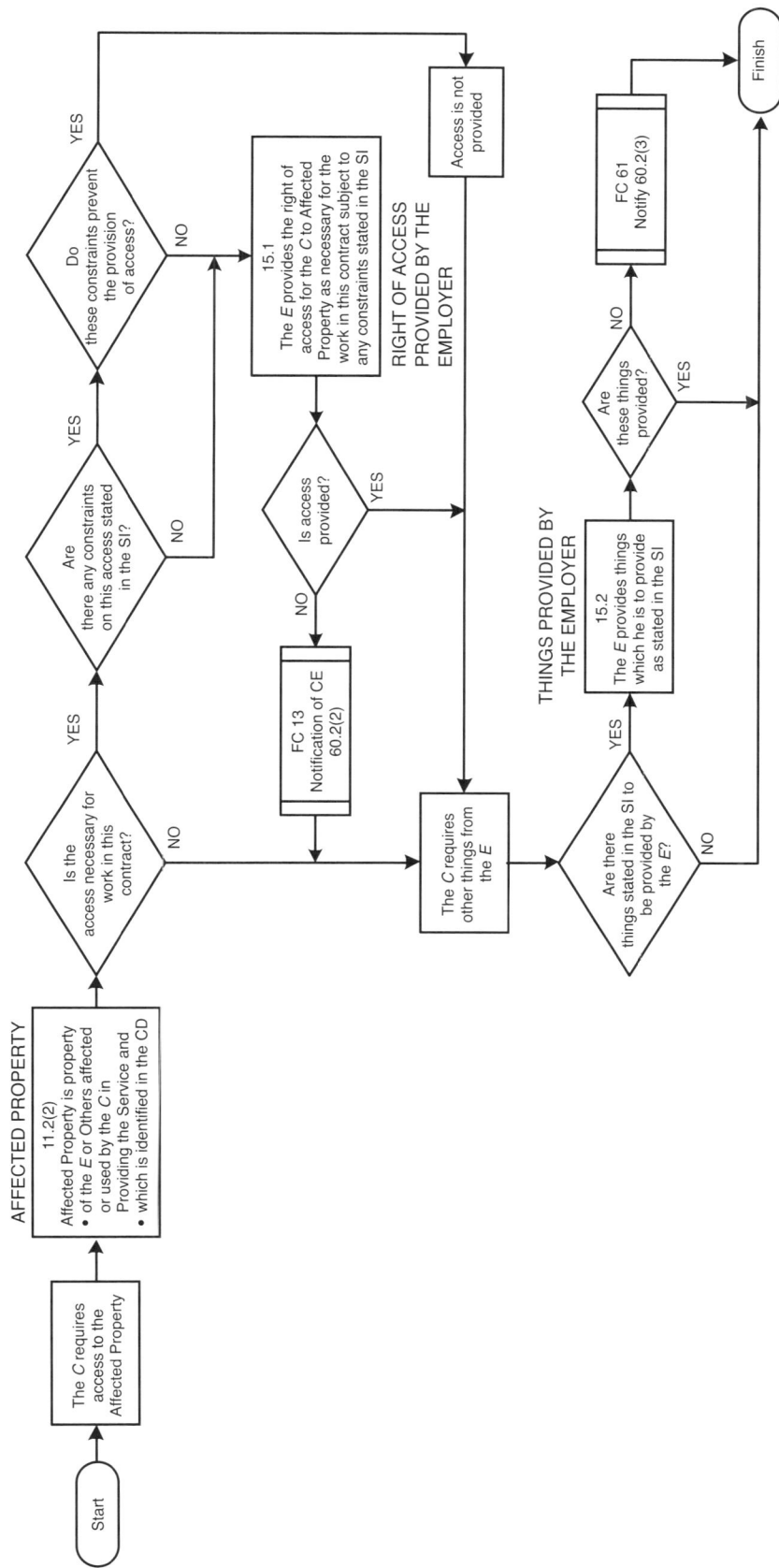

Flow chart 15
Employer provides right of access and things

Start

→

The *C* requires access to the Affected Property

→

AFFECTED PROPERTY
11.2(2)
Affected Property is property
- of the *E* or Others affected or used by the *C* in Providing the Service and
- which is identified in the CD

→

Is the access necessary for work in this contract?

- **YES** →
- **NO** →

(YES path) → **Are there any constraints on this access stated in the SI?**

- **YES** → **Do these constraints prevent the provision of access?**
  - **YES** (loops up)
  - **NO** →
- **NO** →

Do these constraints prevent the provision of access?
- **YES** (top loop)
- **NO** →

RIGHT OF ACCESS PROVIDED BY THE EMPLOYER

15.1
The *E* provides the right of access for the *C* to Affected Property as necessary for the work in this contract subject to any constraints stated in the SI

→

Is access provided?
- **NO** → **FC 13** **Notification of CE** **60.2(2)**
- **YES** →

Access is not provided

The *C* requires other things from the *E*

→

THINGS PROVIDED BY THE EMPLOYER

Are there things stated in the SI to be provided by the *E*?
- **YES** → **15.2** The *E* provides things which he is to provide as stated in the SI
- **NO** →

15.2
The *E* provides things which he is to provide as stated in the SI

→

Are these things provided?
- **NO** → **FC 61** **Notify 60.2(3)** → **Finish**
- **YES** →

Finish

Start

16.1
The *C* and the *SM* give an early warning by notifying the other as soon as either becomes aware of any matter which could
- increase the total of the Prices,
- interfere with the timing of the *service* or
- impair the effectiveness of the *service*

16.1
The *C* may give an early warning by notifying the *SM* of any other matter which could increase his total cost

16.1
Does such a notifiable matter occur? — NO

16.1
Does such a notifiable matter occur? — YES

16.1
Has a CE already been notified — YES

16.1
Has a CE already been notified — NO

16.1
Early warning of a matter for which a CE has previously been notified is not required

COMPENSATION EVENT NOTIFIED

FC 13
Notification

16.2
Either the *SM* or the *C* may instruct the other to attend a risk reduction meeting

16.2
Is a risk reduction meeting instructed? — NO

INSTRUCTED?

16.2
Is a risk reduction meeting instructed? — YES

RISK REDUCTION MEETING

OTHERS MAY BE INSTRUCTED TO ATTEND

27.3
The *C* obeys an instruction which is in accordance with its contract and is given to him by the *SM*

16.2
Does the *SM* wish to instruct other people to attend? — YES

16.2
Does the *SM* wish to instruct other people to attend? — NO

16.2
Does the *C* agree to those other people attending? — YES

16.2
Does the *C* agree to those other people attending? — NO

16.2
The *SM* may instruct those other people to attend

16.2
Does the *C* wish to instruct other people to attend? — YES

16.2
Does the *C* wish to instruct other people to attend? — NO

16.2
Does the *SM* agree to those other people attending? — YES

16.2
Does the *SM* agree to those other people attending? — NO

16.2
The *C* may instruct those other people to attend

16.2
A risk reduction meeting is held

THE PARTIES CO-OPERATE TO RESOLVE THE MATTER

16.3
At a risk reduction meeting those who attend co-operate in
- making and considering proposals for how the effect of the registered risks can be avoided or reduced,
- seeking solutions that will bring advantage to all those who will be affected,
- deciding upon actions which will be taken and who, in accordance with this contract, will take them and
- deciding which risks have now been avoided or have passed and can be removed from the Risk Register

PROPOSALS AND DECISIONS

16.4
The *SM* revises the Risk Register to record the decisions made at each risk reduction meeting and issues the revised Risk Register to the *C*

16.4
If a decision needs a change to the SI, the SM instructs the change at the same time as he issues the revised Risk Register

SM's INSTRUCTION

FC 13
SM's Instruction

Does the decision need a change to the SI? — YES

Does the decision need a change to the SI? — NO

Finish

Flow chart 16
Early warning

Start

17.1
The *SM* or the *C* notifies the other as soon as either becomes aware of an ambiguity or inconsistency in or between the documents which are part of this contract

Does either become aware of such a state? — NO

YES

FC 13
Notification

NOTIFY OTHER PARTY

17.1
The *SM* gives an instruction resolving the ambiguity or inconsistency

INSTRUCTION RESOLVING AMBIGUITY

FC 13
SM's instruction

27.3
The *C* obeys an instruction which is in accordance with this contract and is given to him by the *SM*

CONTRACTOR OBEYS THE INSTRUCTION

Is the instruction a change to the SI? — NO

YES

FC 61
Notify CE 60.1(1) and reference 63.9

COMPENSATION EVENT

CHANGE TO THE SERVICE INFORMATION?

Finish

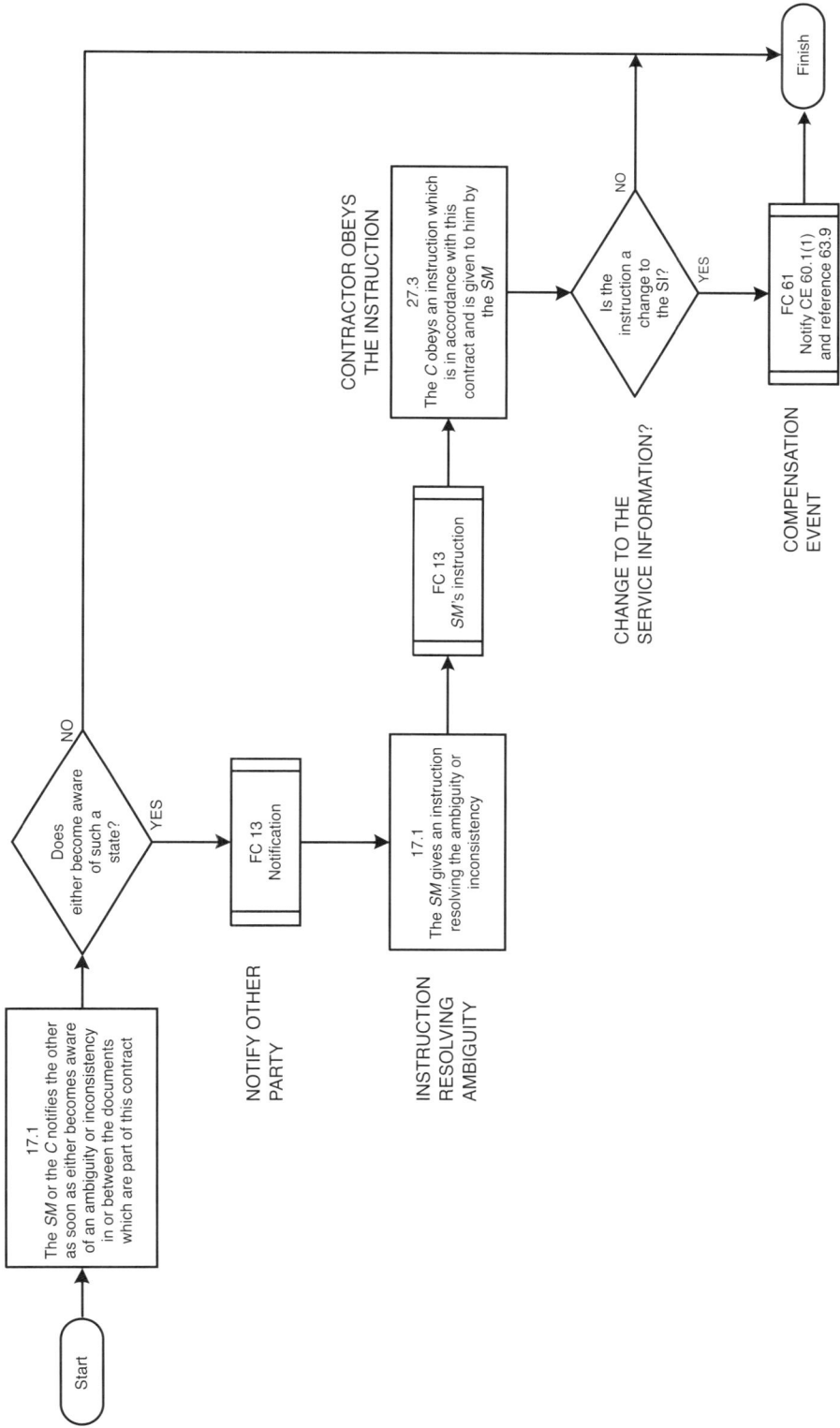

Flow chart 17
Ambiguities and inconsistencies

Start

NOTIFICATION OF ILLEGAL OR IMPOSSIBLE REQUIREMENT

18.1
The *C* notifies the *SM* as soon as he considers that the SI requires him to do anything which is illegal or impossible

Does the *C* consider such a situation has occurred?

NO → (to Finish)

YES ↓

FC 13
C's notification

FC 13
SM's reply

DOES SERVICE MANAGER AGREE?

18.1
Does the *SM* agree?

NO → (to Finish)

YES ↓

INSTRUCTION TO CHANGE SERVICE INFORMATION

18.1
The *SM* gives an instruction to change the SI appropriately

CONTRACTOR OBEYS THE INSTRUCTION

27.3
The *C* obeys an instruction which is in accordance with this contract and is given to him by the *SM*

COMPENSATION EVENT

FC 61
Notify CE 60.1(1)

Finish

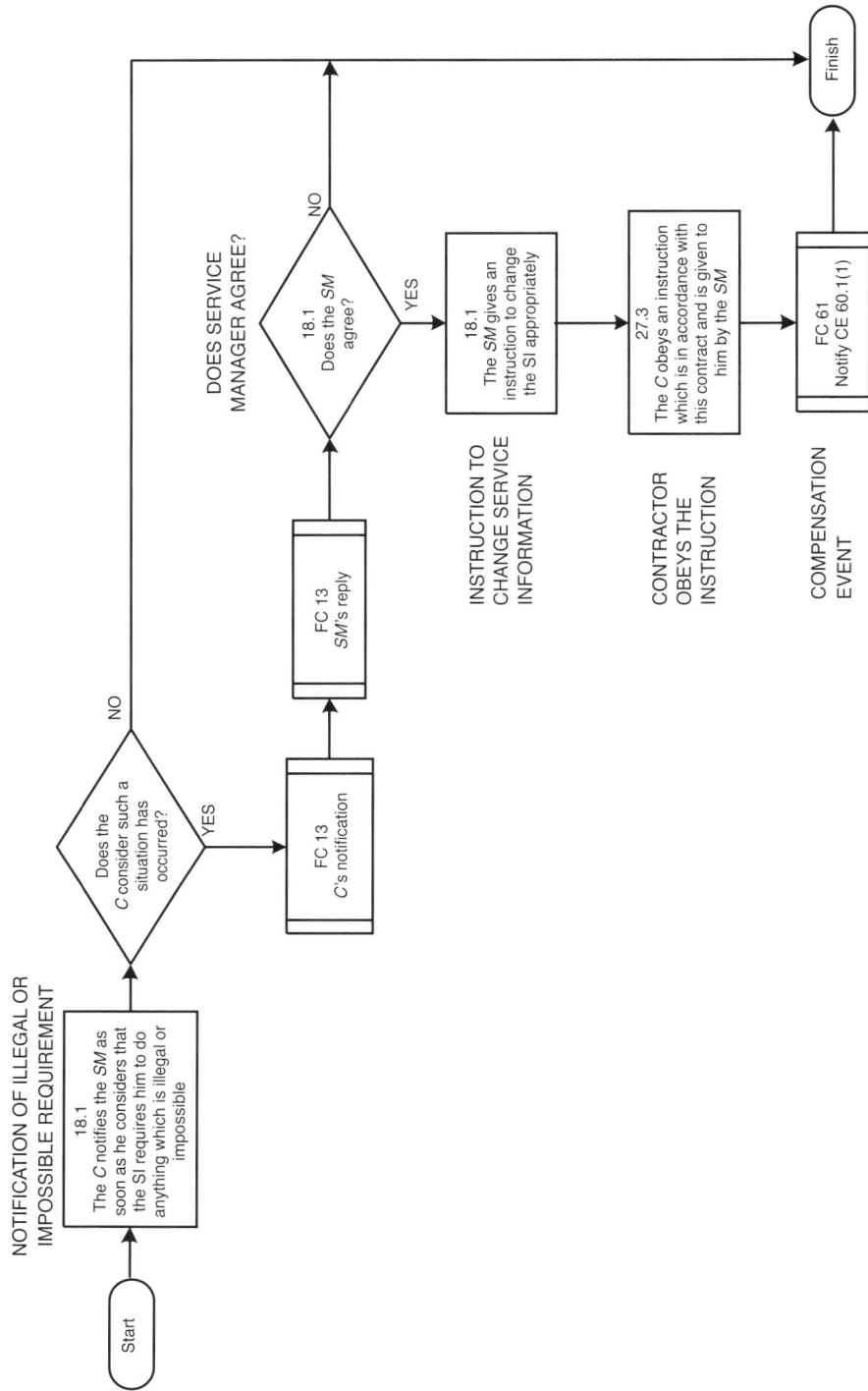

Flow chart 18
Illegal and impossible requirements

TO PROVIDE THE SERVICE

11.2 (13)
To Provide the Service means to do the work necessary to provide the *service* in accordance with this contract and all incidental work, services and actions which this contract requires

THE SERVICE

20.1
The service is identified in the CD

THE CONTRACTOR PROVIDES THE SERVICE

20.1
The *C* Provides the Service in accordance with the SI

SERVICE INFORMATION

11.2 (15)
SI is information which either
- specifies and describes the *service* or
- states any constraints on how the *C* Provides the Service

and is either
- in the documents which the CD states it is in or
- in an instruction given in accordance with this contract

INTERFERENCE

20.2
In Providing the Service, the *C* minimises the interference caused to the Affected Property and the activities taking place in it

11.2 (2)
Affected Property is property of the *E* or Others which is affected by the work of the *C* or used by the *C* in Providing the Service and which is identified in the CD

Which main Option applies?

A

C or E

PRICED CONTRACTS

20.5
The *C* prepares forecasts of the final total of the Prices for the whole of the *service* in consultation with the *SM* and submits them to the *SM*

FORECASTS OF TOTAL DEFINED COST

20.5
Forecasts are prepared at the intervals stated in the CD from the *starting date* until the end of the *service period*

20.5
An explanation of the changes made since the previous forecast is submitted with each forecast

COST REIMBURSABLE CONTRACTS

CONTRACTOR ADVISES ON IMPLICATIONS OF PLAN AND SUBCONTRACTING

20.3
The *C* advises the *SM* on the practical implications of the Accepted Plan and on subcontracting arrangement

20.4
The *C* prepares forecasts of the total Defined Cost for the whole of the *service* in consultation with the *SM* and submits them to the *SM*

TIME INTERVAL BETWEEN FORECASTS

20.4
Forecasts are prepared at the intervals stated in the CD from the *starting date* until the end of the *service period*

EXPLANATION OF CHANGES MADE

20.4
An explanation of the changes made since the previous forecast is submitted with each forecast

Start

Finish

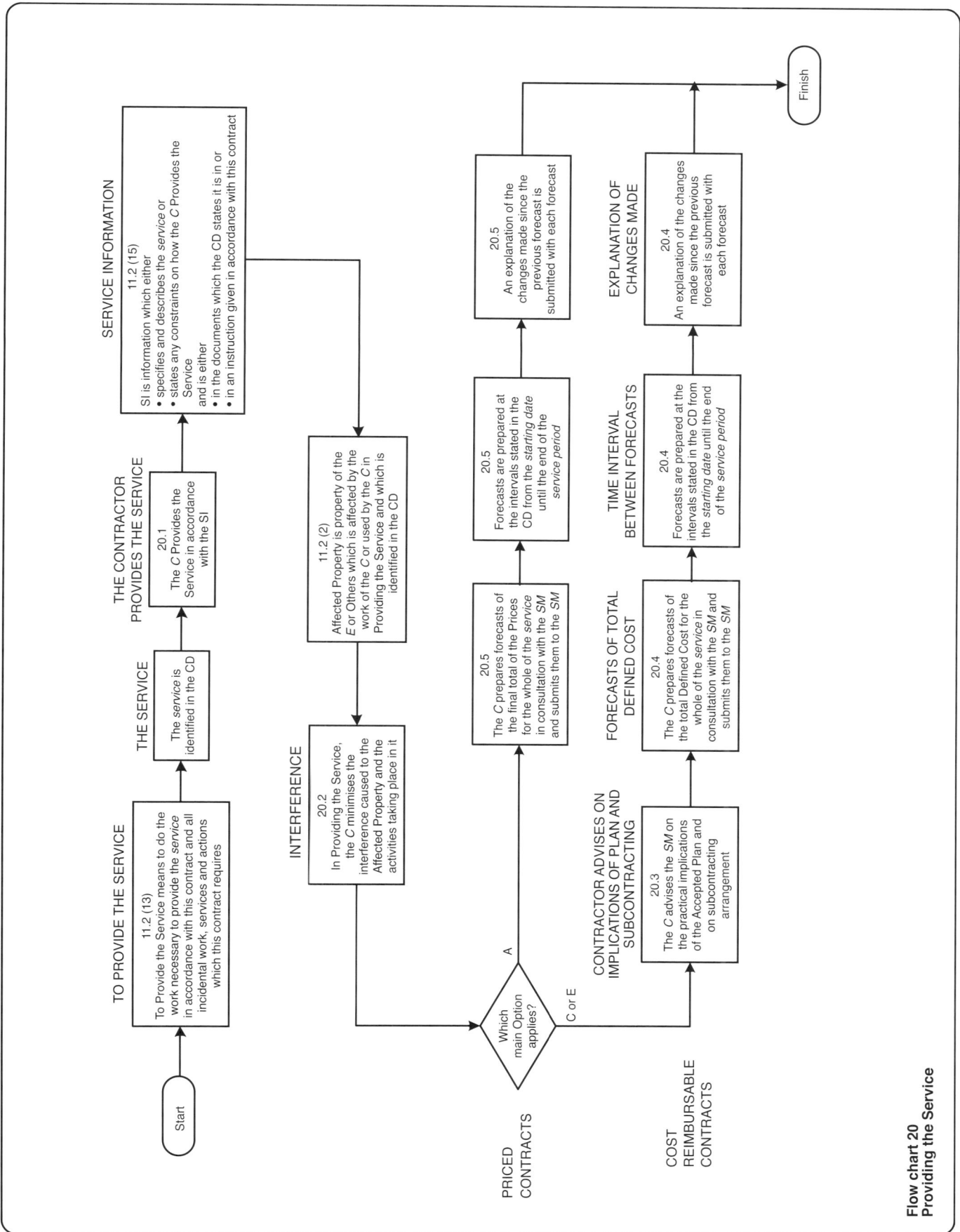

Flow chart 20
Providing the Service

PLAN IN CONTRACT DATA?

Start

Is there an Accepted Plan? — NO / YES

Is a plan identified in the CD? — YES / NO

11.2(1)
The Accepted Plan is the plan identified in the CD

Finish

11.2(1)
The Accepted Plan is the latest plan accepted by the SM

21.1
If a plan is not identified in the CD, the C submits a first plan to the SM for acceptance within the period stated in the CD

PERIOD FOR SUBMISSION FOR FIRST PLAN

FIRST PLAN

Does the C submit a plan within the period stated? — YES / NO

FC 50
Assessing the amount done 50.3

RETAIN ONE QUARTER OF PAYMENT

21.2
The C shows on each plan which he submits for acceptance
• the *starting date* and the end of the *service period*,
• the order and timing of the work of the E and Others as last agreed with them by the C or, if not so agreed, as stated in the SI,
• provisions for
  • time risk allowances,
  • health and safety requirements and
  • the procedures set out in this contract,
• the dates when, in order to Provide the Service in accordance with his plan, the C will need
  • access to the Affected Property as stated in the SI,
  • acceptances,
  • P&M, equipment and other things to be provided by the E and
  • information from Others,
• for each operation, a statement of how the C plans to do the work identifying the principal Equipment and other resources which he plans to use, and
• other information which the SI requires the C to show on a plan submitted for acceptance

INFORMATION ON ACCEPTED PLAN

REVISED PLAN

FC 22
Revising the plan

RELATIONSHIP OF PRICE LIST TO PLAN

21.4
The C provides information which shows how each item description on the Price List relates to the operations on each plan which he submits for acceptance

Which main Option applies? — A or C / E

The *starting date* and *service period* are stated in the CD

PLAN SUBMITTED

FC 53
Price List

FC 13
Submission for Acceptance

A
Sheet 2

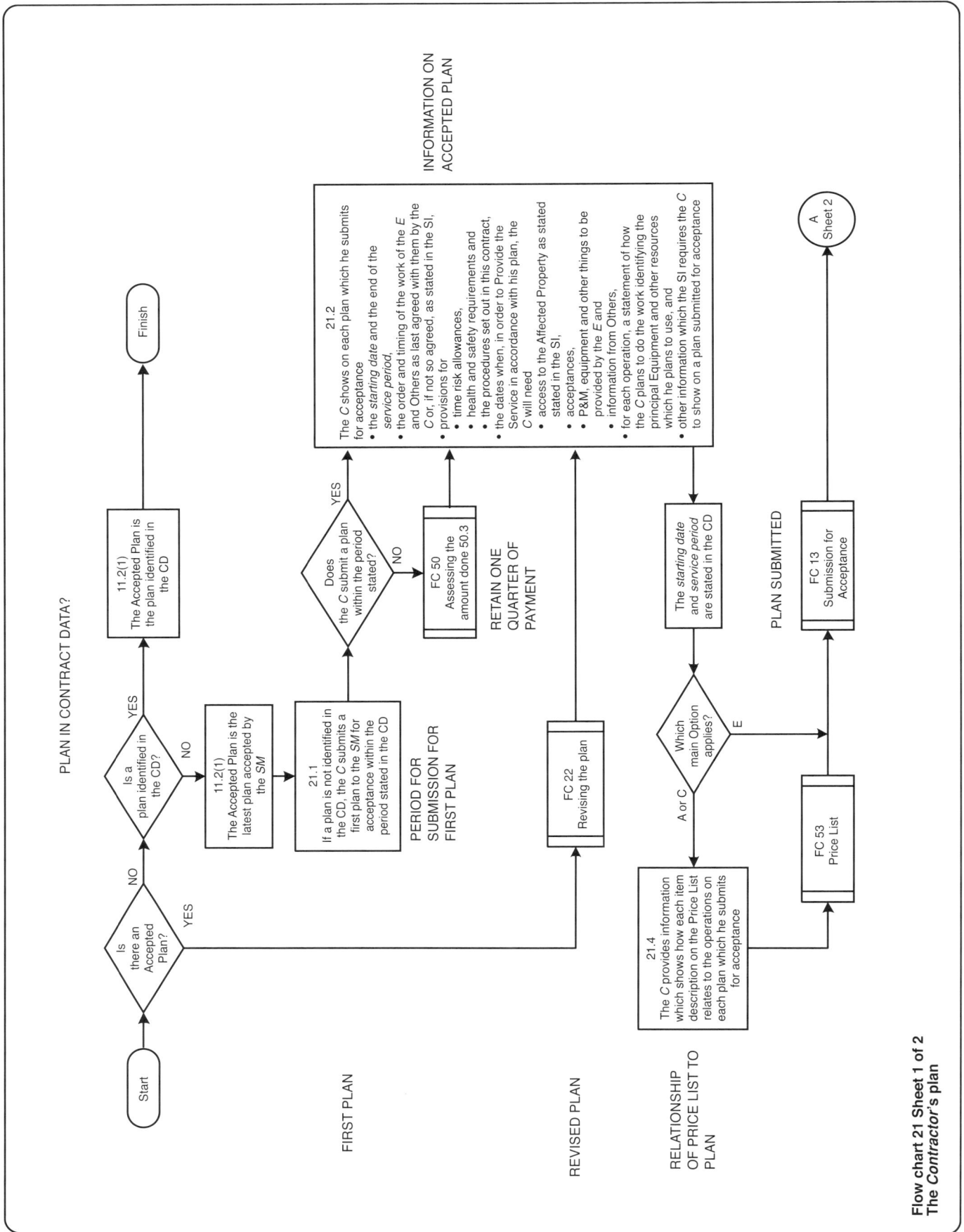

Flow chart 21 Sheet 1 of 2
The *Contractor's* plan

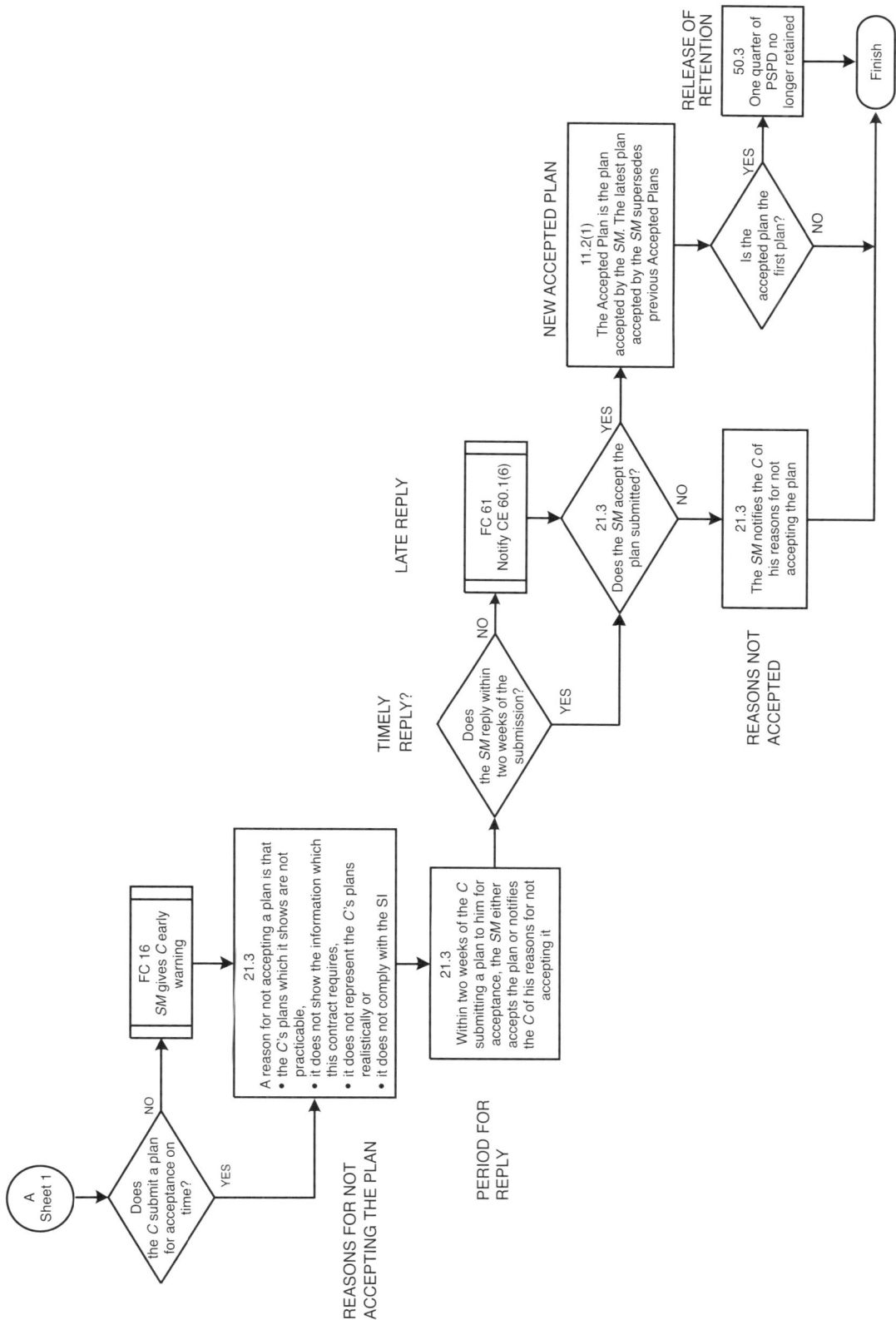

Flow chart 21 Sheet 2 of 2
The *Contractor*'s plan

REVISED PLAN

A revised plan is to be submitted for acceptance

Start

22.1
The C submits a revised plan to the SM for acceptance

SERVICE MANAGER
INSTRUCTS A REVISED
PLAN TO BE
SUBMITTED

Does the SM instruct the C to submit a revised plan?

YES

NO

22.1
The C submits a revised plan to the SM for acceptance within the period for reply after the SM has instructed him to

The period for reply is stated in the CD

CONTRACTOR
CHOOSES TO
SUBMIT A REVISED
PLAN

Does the C choose to submit a revised plan?

YES

NO

PERIOD FOR
SUBMISSION

22.1
The C submits a revised plan when he chooses to

INFORMATION TO
BE SHOWN ON
REVISED PLAN

22.1
The C shows on the revised plan the effects of implemented CEs and other changes

ACCEPTING THE
REVISED PLAN

FC 21
The C's Plan

Finish

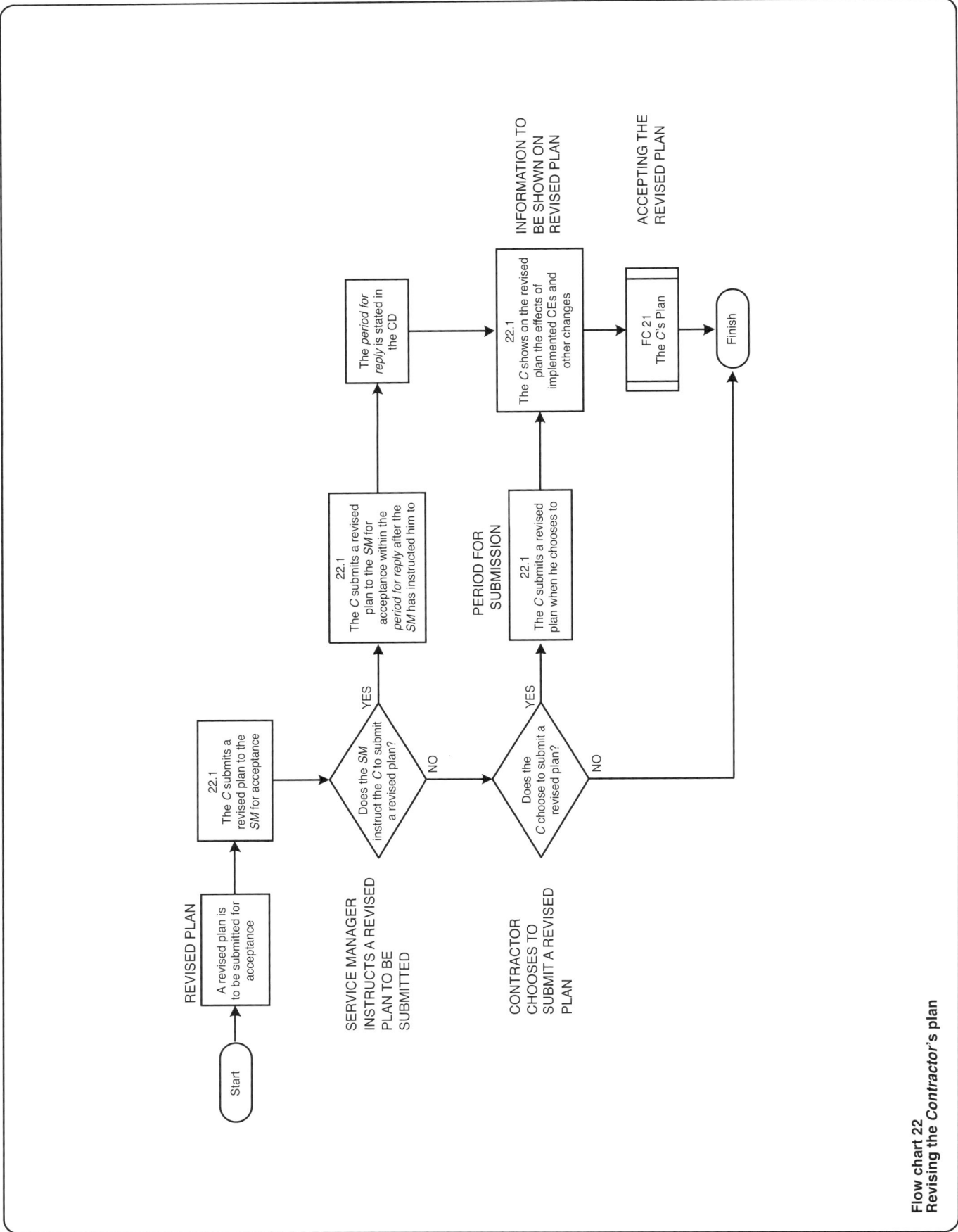

Flow chart 22
Revising the Contractor's plan

EQUIPMENT

DESIGN PARTICULARS

Start

The C proposes to use an item of Equipment

11.2(7)
Equipment is items provided by the C and used by him to Provide the Service and which the SI does not require him to include in the Affected Property

23.1
The C submits particulars of the design of an item of Equipment to the SM for for acceptance if the SM instructs him to

DESIGN TO BE SUBMITTED?

Does the SM instruct the C to submit particulars for acceptance?

YES

NO

REASON FOR NOT ACCEPTING

23.1
A reason for not accepting is that the design of the item will not allow the C to Provide the Service in accordance with
• the SI,
• the Accepted Plan or
• the applicable law

DESIGN SUBMISSION FOR ACCEPTANCE

FC 13
Submission for acceptance

FC 20
Providing the Service

CONTRACTOR PROVIDES THE SERVICE

Finish

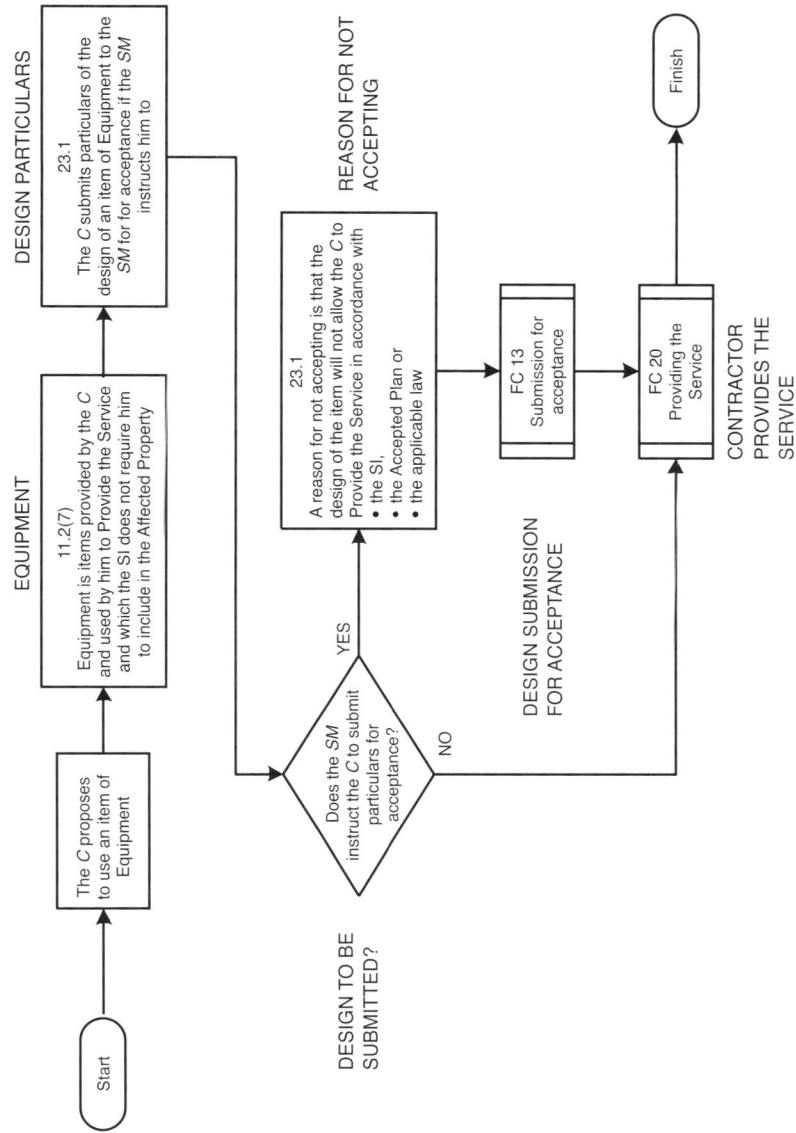

Flow chart 23
Design of Equipment

CO-OPERATION WITH OTHERS

PROVISION OF INFORMATION

Start

11.2(9)
Others are people or organisations who are not the *E*, the *SM*, the Adjudicator, the *C* or any employee, SC or supplier of the *C*

25.1
Do Others need information about the *service*?

YES → **25.1** The *C* co-operates with Others in obtaining and providing information which they need in connection with the *service*

NO →

25.1
Do Others need to share the Affected Property?

YES → **25.1** The *C* co-operates with Others and shares the Affected Property with them as stated in the SI

NO →

25.2
Are facilities and other things to be provided?

NO →

YES → **25.2** The *E* and the *C* provide facilities and other things as stated in the SI

PROVISION OF FACILITIES AND OTHER THINGS

25.2
Are the facilities and other things provided by the *E* or the *C*?

BY *E* → **Does the *E* provide them?**

YES →

NO → FC 60 CE 60.1(3)

BY *C* → **Does the *C* provide them?**

YES →

NO → **25.2** Any cost incurred by the *E* as a result of the *C* not providing the facilities and other things he is to provide is assessed by the *SM* and paid by the *C*

Finish

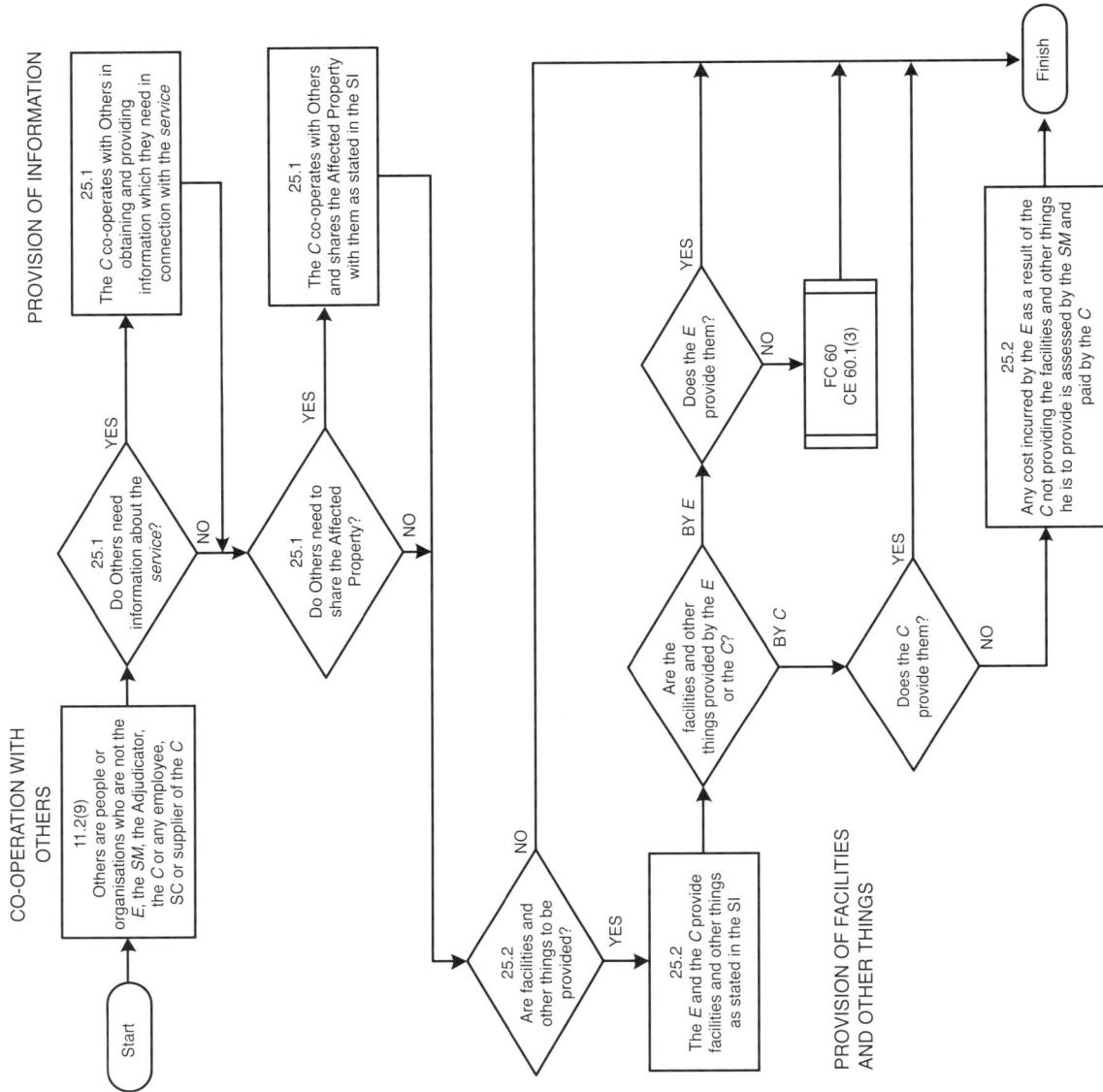

Flow chart 25
Working with the *Employer* and Others

Start

The *C* proposes to subcontract part of the *service*

11.2(16)
A SC is a person or organisation who has a contract with the *C* to
• provide a part of the *service* or
• supply P&M which the person or organisation has wholly or partly designed specifically for the *service*

If the *C* subcontracts work, he is responsible for Providing the Service as if he had not subcontracted

26.1
This contract applies as if a SC's employees and equipment were the *C*'s

OPTION X12?

Is the Partnering Option X12 included?

YES

NO

X12.3(9)
A Partner notifies the Core Group before subcontracting any work

FC 13
Notification

Which main Option applies?

C or E

A

FC 20
Providing the Service

OBLIGATION ON CONTRACTOR TO ADVISE ON SUBCONTRACTING ARRANGEMENTS

26.2
The *C* does not appoint a proposed SC until the *SM* has accepted him

Has the *SM* already accepted the proposed SC?

NO

YES

26.2
The *C* submits the name of each proposed SC to the *SM* for acceptance

26.3
The *C* does not appoint a SC on the proposed subcontract conditions until the *SM* has accepted them

26.2
A reason for not accepting the SC is that his appointment will not allow the *C* to Provide the Service

FC 13
Submission for acceptance

B
Sheet 2

SUBCONTRACTOR ACCEPTED?

Has the *SM* accepted the proposed SC

NO

YES

A
Sheet 2

Flow chart 26 Sheet 1 of 2
Subcontracting

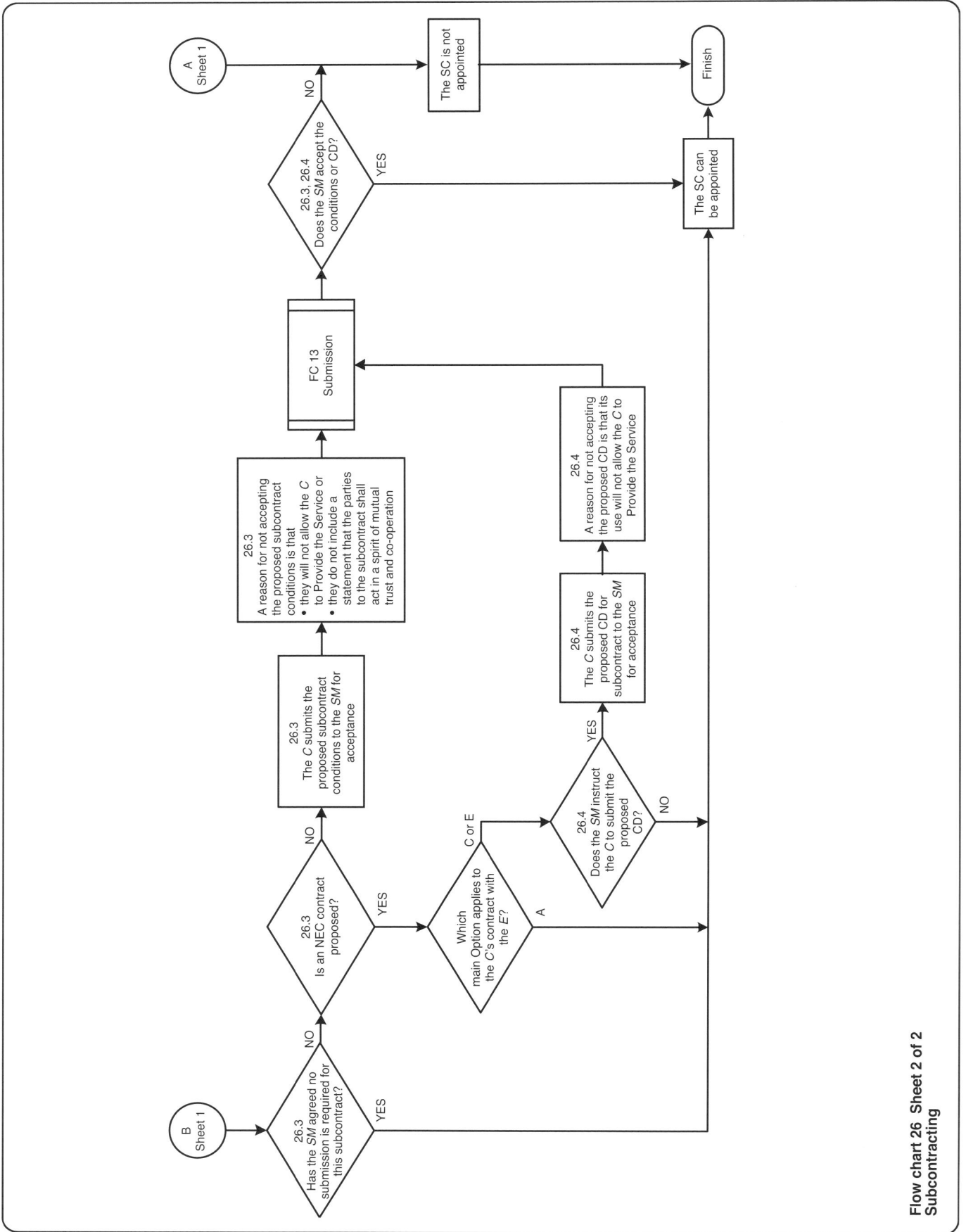

Flow chart 26 Sheet 2 of 2
Subcontracting

Start

CONTRACTOR NEEDS DESIGN APPROVAL

Does the *C* need approval from Others? — YES / NO

APPROVAL NEEDED
Approval is necessary from Others

OTHERS
11.2(9)
Others are people or organisations who are not the *E*, the *SM*, the *Adjudicator*, the *C* or any employee, SC or supplier of the *C*

EARLY WARNING?
16.1
Does failure to get approval warrant early warning? — YES / NO

EARLY WARNING
FC 16
Early warning by the *C* to the *SM*

APPROVAL OBTAINED?
Is the *C* successful in obtaining approval from Others? — YES / NO

REVISE AND RESUBMIT
The *C* revises (with the *SM*'s acceptance) and resubmits

DESIGN APPROVED
27.1
The *C* obtains approval from Others where necessary

CONTRACTOR PROVIDES ACCESS

Is access required from the *C*? — YES / NO

ACCESS REQUIRED
The *SM* and Others require access to work and/or to stored P&M

BY WHOM?
Who requires access? — Others / *SM*

NOTIFICATION OF OTHERS
27.2
The *SM* notifies the *C* of Others who require access

ACCESS PROVIDED
27.2
The *C* provides access to work being done and to P&M being stored for this contract

CONTRACTOR OBEYS INSTRUCTION

OBEY INSTRUCTION
27.3
The *C* obeys an instruction which is in accordance with this contract and is given to him by the *SM*

CONTRACTOR OBSERVES HEALTH AND SAFETY REQUIREMENTS

HEALTH AND SAFETY
27.4
The *C* acts in accordance with the health and safety requirements stated in the SI

Finish

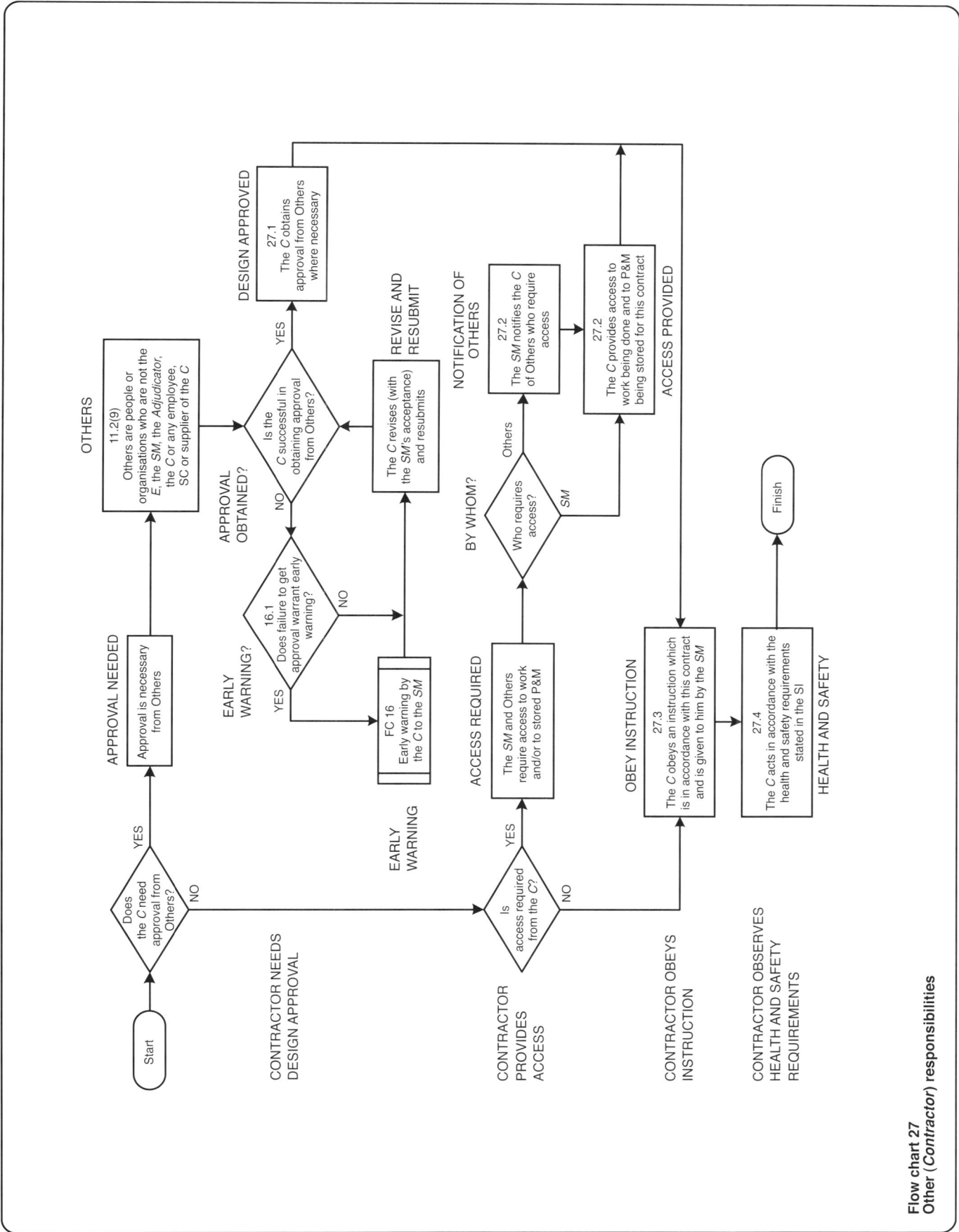

Flow chart 27
Other (*Contractor*) responsibilities

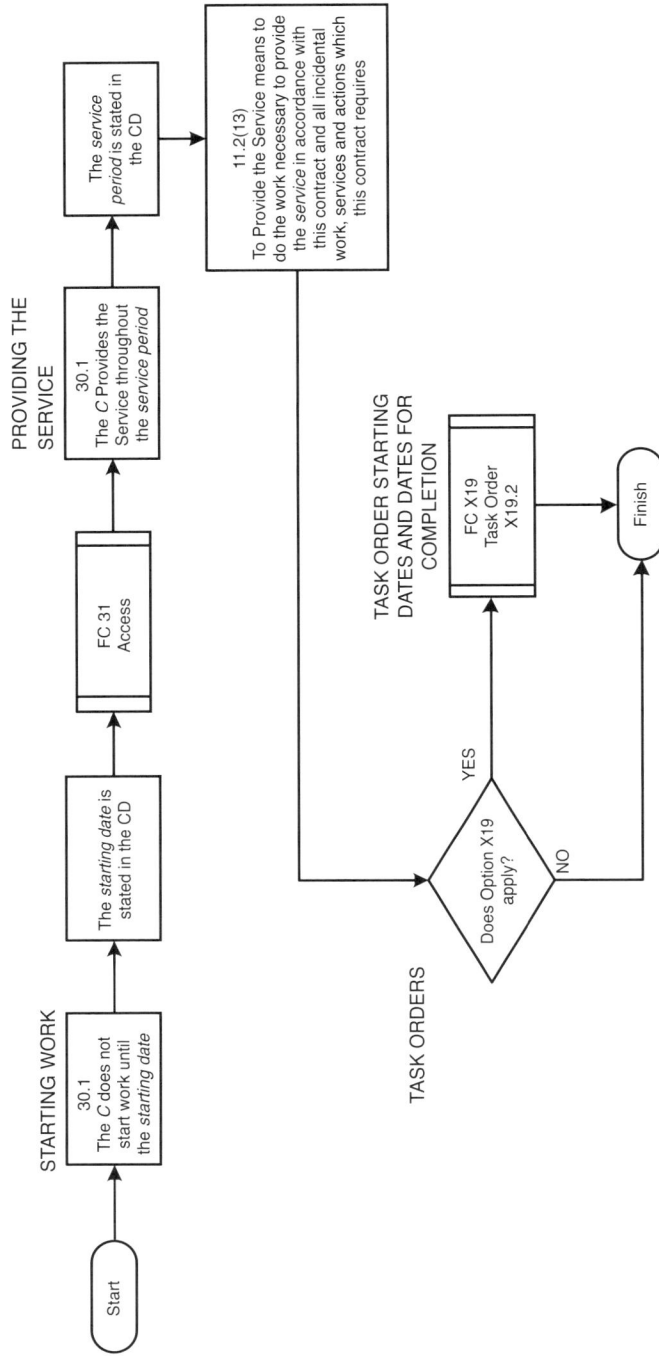

STARTING WORK

Start

30.1
The C does not
start work until
the starting date

The starting date is
stated in the CD

FC 31
Access

PROVIDING THE
SERVICE

30.1
The C Provides the
Service throughout
the service period

The service
period is stated in
the CD

11.2(13)
To Provide the Service means to
do the work necessary to provide
the service in accordance with
this contract and all incidental
work, services and actions which
this contract requires

TASK ORDERS

Does Option X19
apply?

YES

NO

TASK ORDER STARTING
DATES AND DATES FOR
COMPLETION

FC X19
Task Order
X19.2

Finish

ACCESS
REQUIRED

Start

The *C* needs
access to the
Affected Property

AFFECTED PROPERTY

11.2 (2)
Affected Property is property of the *E*
or Others which is affected by the
work of the *C* or used by the *C* in
Providing the Service and which is
identified in the CD

ACCEPTED PLAN

11.2 (1)
The Accepted Plan is the plan
identified in the CD or is the latest
plan accepted by the *SM*. The latest
plan accepted by the *SM* supersedes
previous Accepted Plans

SITE
ACCESS

31.1
The *E* allows the *C* access to
the Affected Property as
shown on the Accepted Plan

TIMELY
ACCESS?

Does the *E*
allow the *C* access
to the Affected
Property?

NO

YES

CONTRACTOR WARNS

FC 16
Early warning and
possible CE 60.1(2)

Finish

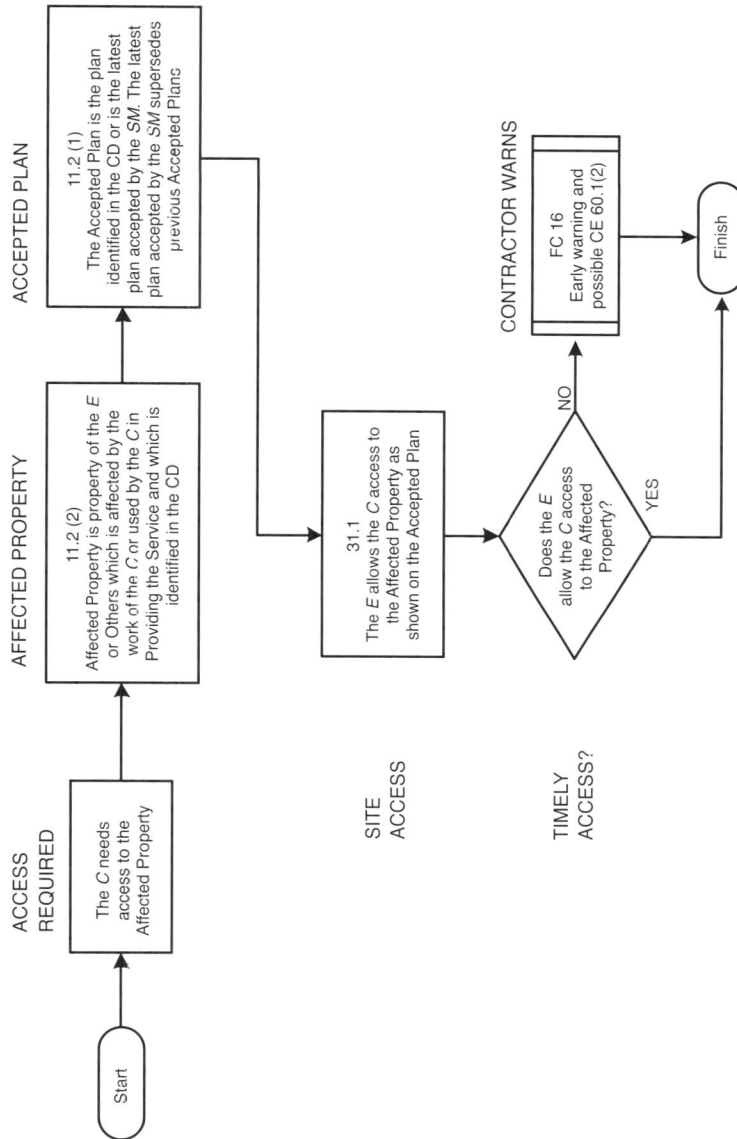

Flow chart 31
Access

Start

32.1
The *SM* may instruct the *C* to stop or not to start any work

32.1
Does the *SM* give such an instruction?

NO

YES

INSTRUCTION TO STOP OR NOT TO START WORK

FC 13
Instruction

COMPENSATION EVENT

FC 61
Notify
CE 60.1(4)

OBEY INSTRUCTION

27.3
The *C* obeys an instruction which is in accordance with this contract and is given to him by the *SM*

RE-START OR START WORK

32.1
The *SM* may later instruct the *C* that he may re-start or start it

Does the *SM* give such an instruction?

YES

NO

INSTRUCTION TO RE-START OR TO START WORK

FC 13
Instruction

OBEY INSTRUCTION

27.3
The *C* obeys an instruction which is in accordance with this contract and is given to him by the *SM*

REASON FOR TERMINATION?

91.6
Is all or substantial service affected?

YES

NO

91.6
Have 13 weeks elapsed since the instruction stopping or not starting work?

YES

NO

FC 91
Termination
(R18 to R20)

Finish

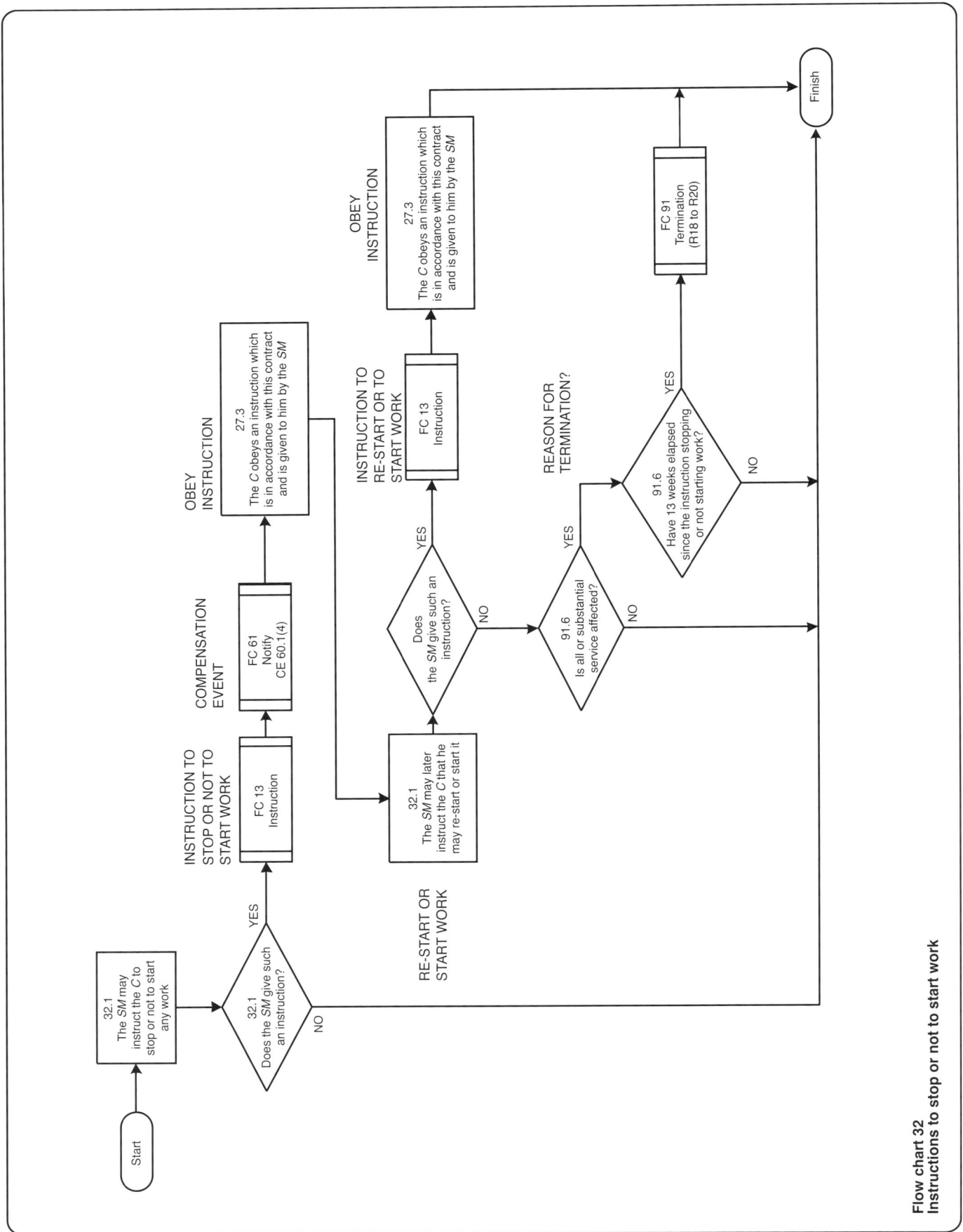

Flow chart 32
Instructions to stop or not to start work

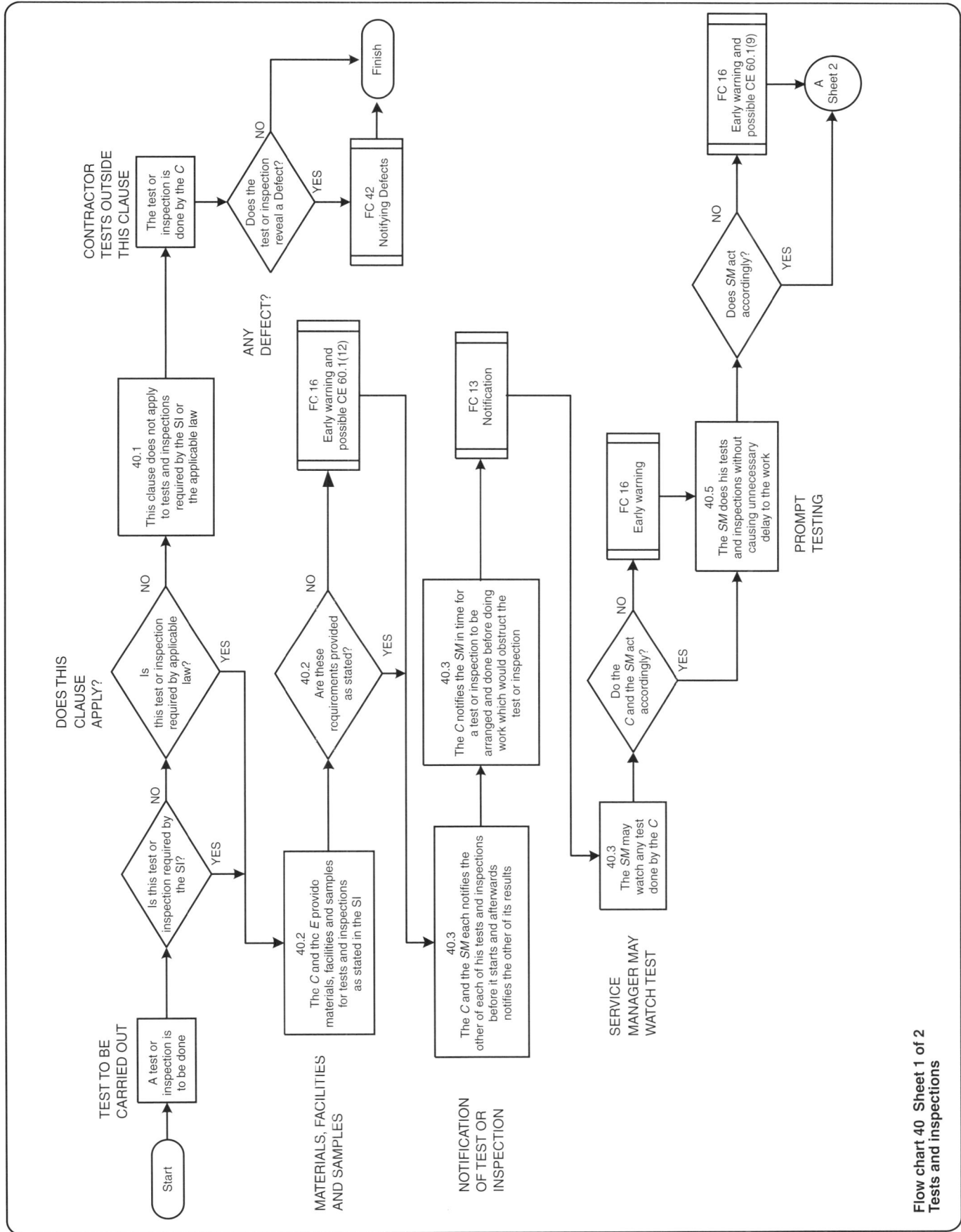

Flow chart 40 Sheet 1 of 2
Tests and inspections

TEST TO BE CARRIED OUT

Start

→ A test or inspection is to be done

IS THIS TEST REQUIRED BY THE SI?

Is this test or inspection required by the SI? — YES → 40.2 The C and the E provide materials, facilities and samples for tests and inspections as stated in the SI

NO ↓

DOES THIS CLAUSE APPLY?

Is this test or inspection required by applicable law? — YES → (loop)

NO ↓

40.1 This clause does not apply to tests and inspections required by the SI or the applicable law

→ The test or inspection is done by the C

CONTRACTOR TESTS OUTSIDE THIS CLAUSE

ANY DEFECT?

Does the test or inspection reveal a Defect? — NO → Finish

YES ↓

FC 42 Notifying Defects

MATERIALS, FACILITIES AND SAMPLES

40.2 Are these requirements provided as stated? — NO → FC 16 Early warning and possible CE 60.1(12)

YES ↓

40.3 The C and the SM each notifies the other of each of his tests and inspections before it starts and afterwards notifies the other of its results

NOTIFICATION OF TEST OR INSPECTION

→ 40.3 The C notifies the SM in time for a test or inspection to be arranged and done before doing work which would obstruct the test or inspection → FC 13 Notification

SERVICE MANAGER MAY WATCH TEST

40.3 The SM may watch any test done by the C

→ Do the C and the SM act accordingly? — NO → FC 16 Early warning

YES ↓

PROMPT TESTING

40.5 The SM does his tests and inspections without causing unnecessary delay to the work

→ Does SM act accordingly? — NO → FC 16 Early warning and possible CE 60.1(9) → A Sheet 2

YES ↓

(A Sheet 2)

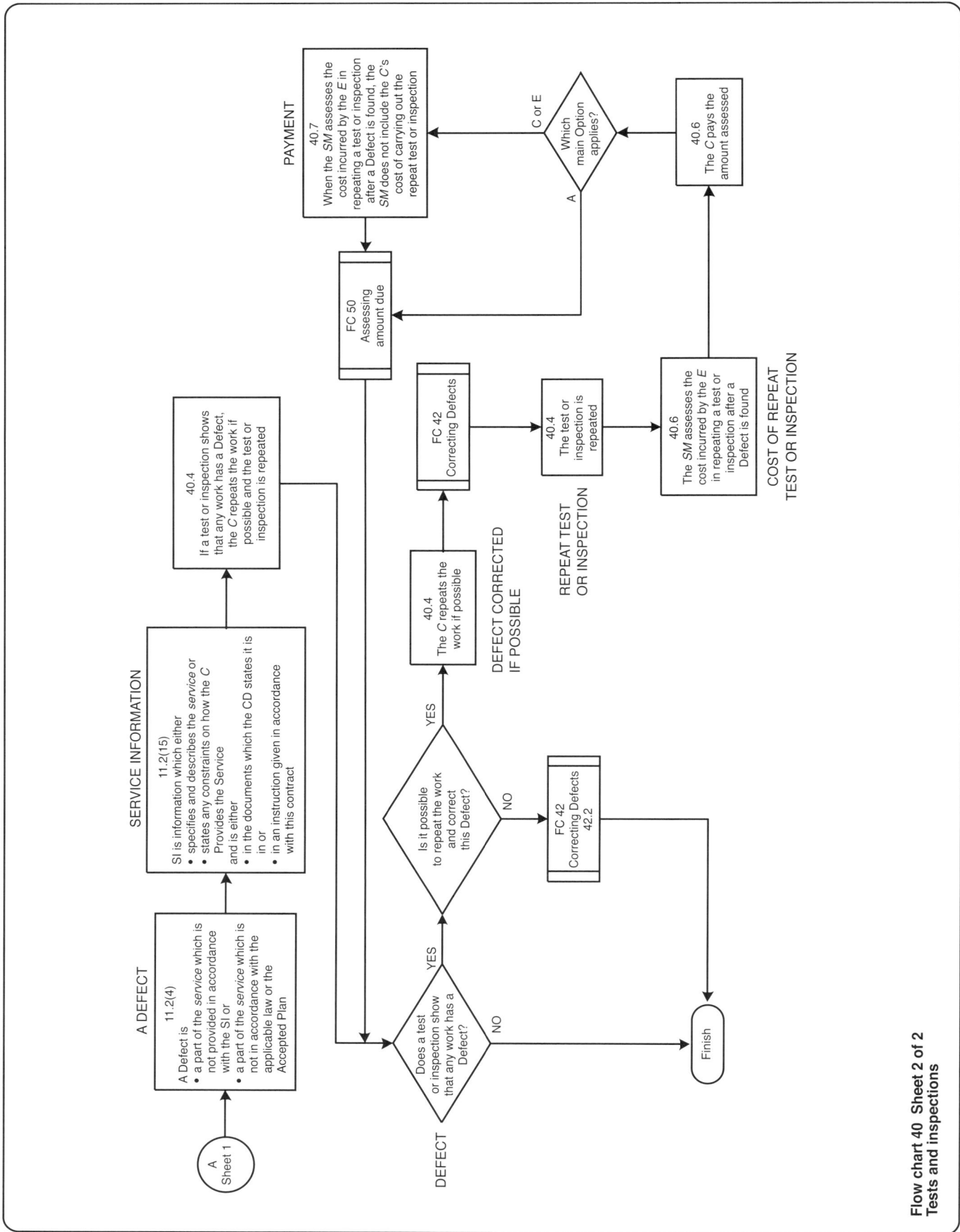

PAYMENT

40.7
When the *SM* assesses the cost incurred by the *E* in repeating a test or inspection after a Defect is found, the *SM* does not include the *C*'s cost of carrying out the repeat test or inspection

FC 50
Assessing amount due

Which main Option applies?

C or E

A

40.6
The *C* pays the amount assessed

SERVICE INFORMATION

11.2(15)
SI is information which either
• specifies and describes the *service* or
• states any constraints on how the *C* Provides the Service
and is either
• in the documents which the CD states it is in or
• in an instruction given in accordance with this contract

40.4
If a test or inspection shows that any work has a Defect, the *C* repeats the work if possible and the test or inspection is repeated

FC 42
Correcting Defects

40.4
The test or inspection is repeated

40.6
The *SM* assesses the cost incurred by the *E* in repeating a test or inspection after a Defect is found

COST OF REPEAT
TEST OR INSPECTION

REPEAT TEST
OR INSPECTION

40.4
The *C* repeats the work if possible

DEFECT CORRECTED
IF POSSIBLE

A DEFECT

11.2(4)
A Defect is
• a part of the *service* which is not provided in accordance with the SI or
• a part of the *service* which is not in accordance with the applicable law or the Accepted Plan

A
Sheet 1

Is it possible to repeat the work and correct this Defect?

YES

NO

FC 42
Correcting Defects
42.2

Does a test or inspection show that any work has a Defect?

DEFECT

YES

NO

Finish

Flow chart 40 Sheet 2 of 2
Tests and inspections

PLANT AND MATERIALS

11.2(11)
P&M are items intended to be included in the Affected Property

AFFECTED PROPERTY

11.2(2)
Affected Property is property of the *E* or Others which is affected by the work of the *C* or used by the *C* in Providing the Service and which is identified in the CD

Affected Property is identified in the CD

Start

TEST OR INSPECTION REQUIRED PRIOR TO DELIVERY?

41.1
Does the *C* wish to deliver an item of P&M which the SI states is to be tested or inspected before delivery?

YES

NO

TEST OR INSPECTION

41.1
The *C* does not deliver those P&M which the SI states are to be tested or inspected before delivery until the *SM* has notified the *C* that they have passed the test or inspection

YES

FC 40
Tests and inspections

SUPERVISOR'S NOTIFICATION

41.1
Does the *SM* notify the *C* that the item of P&M has passed the test or inspection?

NO

YES

Is notification withheld because the *C* or the *SM* notifies the other of a Defect?

YES

NO

FC 16
C's Early Warning and possible CE 60.1(9)

DELIVERY

The *C* may deliver the item of P&M

FC 20
C Provides the Service

Finish

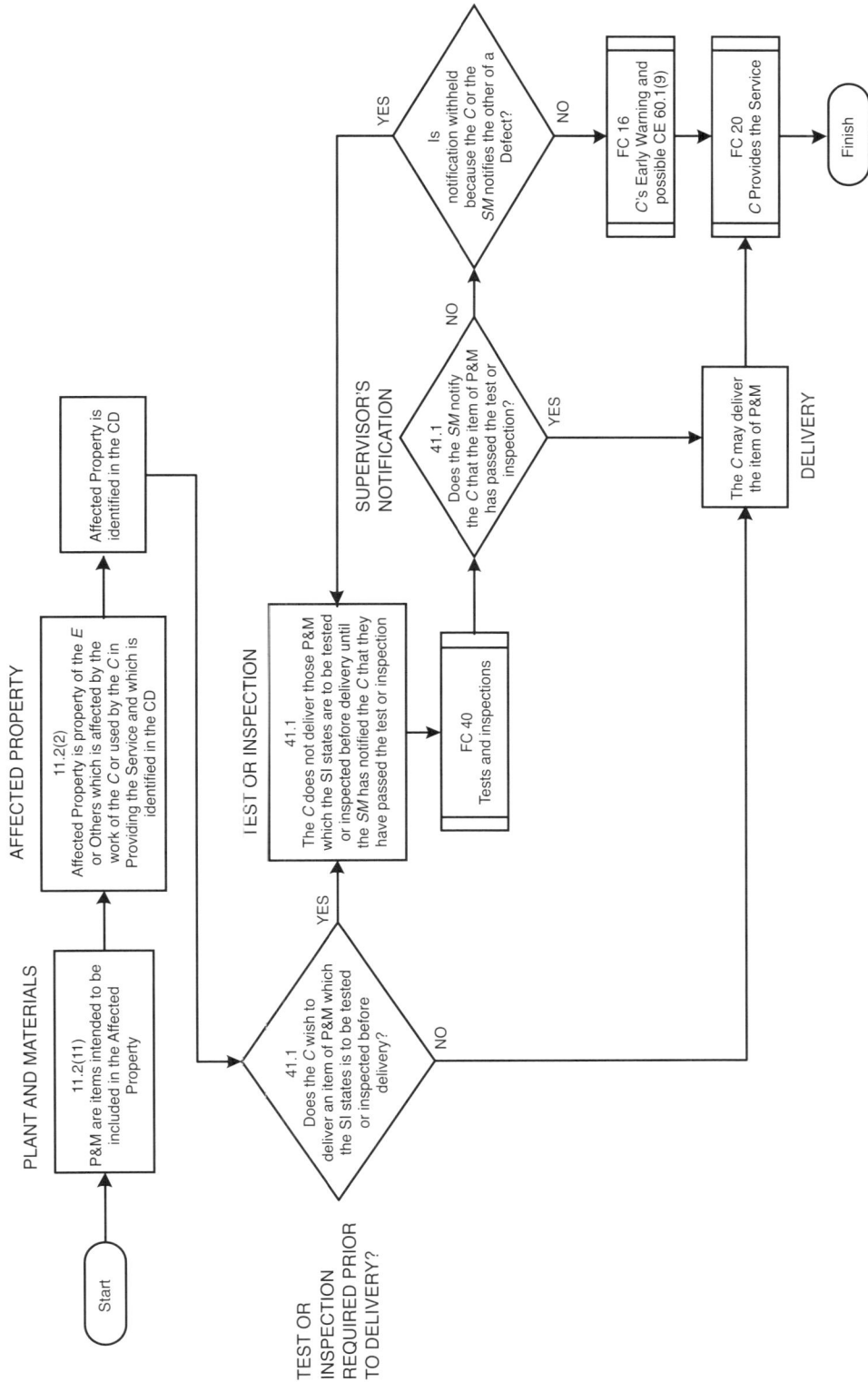

Flow chart 41
Testing and inspection before delivery

Start

DEFECT

11.2(4)

A Defect is
- a part of the *service* which is not provided in accordance with the SI or
- a part of the *service* which is not in accordance with the applicable law or the Accepted Plan

A Defect needs correcting

42.1

Until the end of the *service period*, the *SM* notifies the *C* of each Defect as soon as he finds it and the *C* notifies the *SM* of each Defect as soon as he finds it. The *C* corrects a Defect whether or not the *SM* notifies him of it.

Does the *SM* accept the Defect does not have to be corrected?

YES → **FC 43** Accepting Defects → Finish

NO

42.2

The *C* corrects Defects within a time which minimises the adverse effect on the *E* or Others

11.2(9)

Others are people or organisations who are not the *E*, the *SM*, the *Adjudicator*, the *C* or any employee, SC or supplier of the *C*

CORRECT AT CONVENIENT TIME

42.3

The *SM* arranges for the *E* to allow the *C* access if it is needed for correcting a Defect

SERVICE MANAGER ARRANGES ACCESS

42.2

Does the *C* correct the Defect within the time required by this contract?

YES → Finish

NO

42.2

If the *C* does not correct a Defect within the time required by this contract, the *SM* assesses the cost to the *E* of having the Defect corrected by other people and the *C* pays this amount

CONTRACTOR PAYS COST OF HAVING DEFECT CORRECTED

Finish

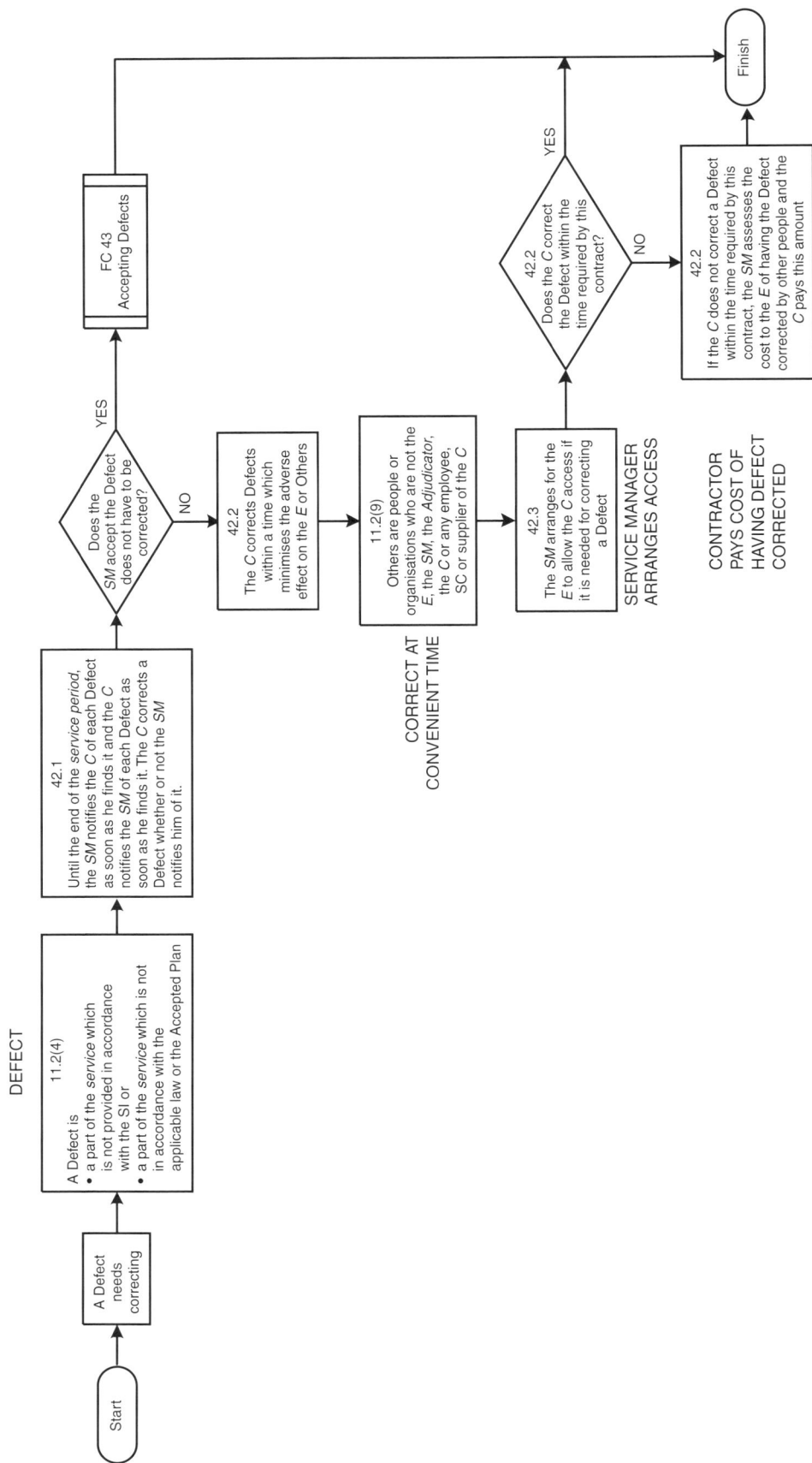

Flow chart 42
Notifying and correcting Defects

```
Start
  │
  ▼
A Defect may
not have to be
corrected
  │
  ▼
43.1
The C and the SM may each
propose to the other that the
SI should be changed so that
a Defect does not have to be
corrected
  │
  ▼
Does            NO
either the C or ────────► FC 42
the SM so                 Correcting Defects ──────────────────────────┐
propose?                                                               │
  │ YES                                                                │
  ▼                                                                    │
Are             NO                                                     │
both the C and  ─────────────────────────────────────────────┐        │
the SM prepared to consider the change?                       │       │
  │ YES                                                        │       ▼
  ▼                                                            │     Finish
43.1                                                           │       ▲
If the C and the SM are                                        │       │
prepared to consider the                                       │       │
change, the C submits a                                        │       │
quotation for reduced Prices                                   │       │
to the SM for acceptance                                       │       │
  │                                                            │       │
  ▼                                                            │       │
FC 13                                                          │       │
C's submission                                                 │       │
  │                                                            │       │
  ▼                                                            │       │
Does the        NO                                             │       │
SM accept the C's ──────► FC 42                                │       │
quotation?                Correcting Defects ─────────────────┘       │
  │ YES                                                                │
  ▼                                                                    │
43.1                                                                   │
If the SM accepts the                                                  │
quotation, he gives an                                                 │
instruction to change the                                             │
SI and the Prices accordingly                                          │
  │                                                                    │
  ▼                                                                    │
FC 60                                                                  │
Not a CE ──────────────────────────────────────────────────────────┘
60.1(8)
```

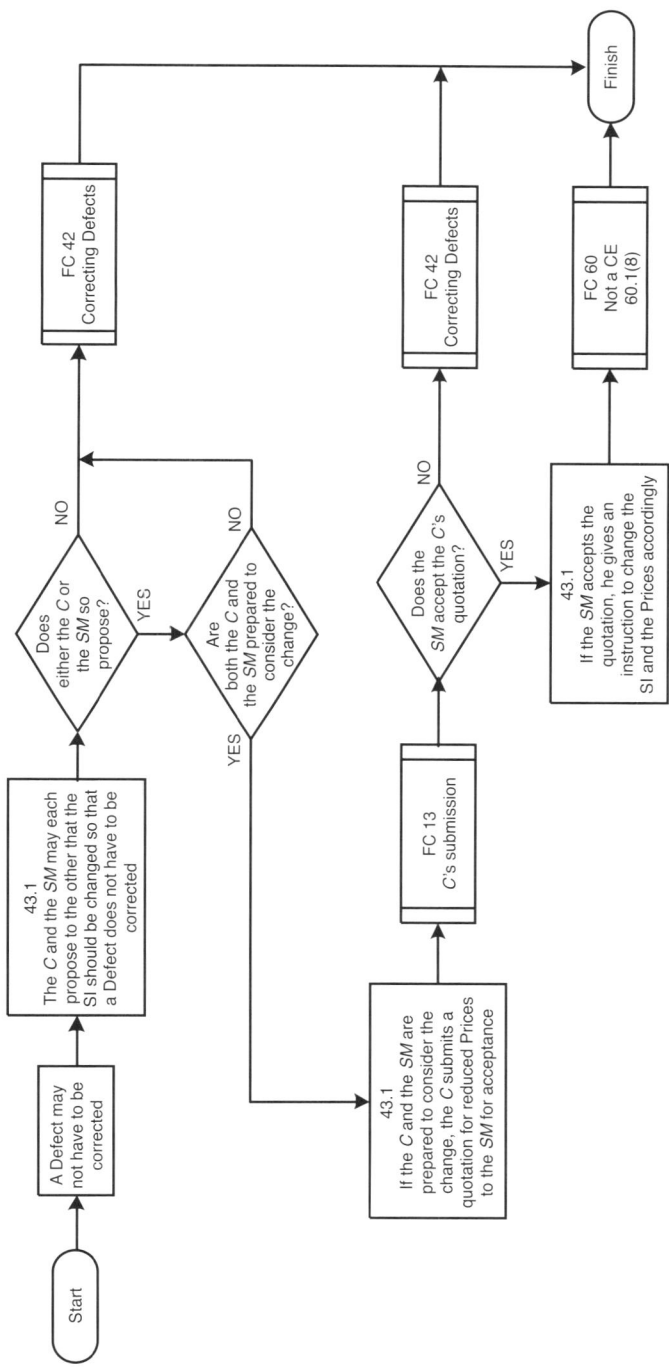

Flow chart 43
Accepting Defects

Start

ASSESSMENT

50.1
The SM assesses the amount due at each assessment date

ASSESSMENT DATE

Assessment date
(see procedure on sheet 2)

ASSESSMENT DATE?

Is it an assessment date?

NO

YES

Finish

CALCULATIONS

PSPD
(see procedure on sheets 3–4)

OTHER AMOUNTS

Retentions, inflation, interest, bonuses, damages, currency and other amounts (see procedure on sheets 5–6)

AMOUNT DUE

50.2
The amount due is
• the PSPD,
• plus other amounts to be paid to the C,
• less amounts to be paid by or retained from the C

TAXES

50.2
Any tax which the law requires the E to pay to the C is included in the amount due

EXPLANATION

50.4
The SM gives the C details of how the amount due has been assessed

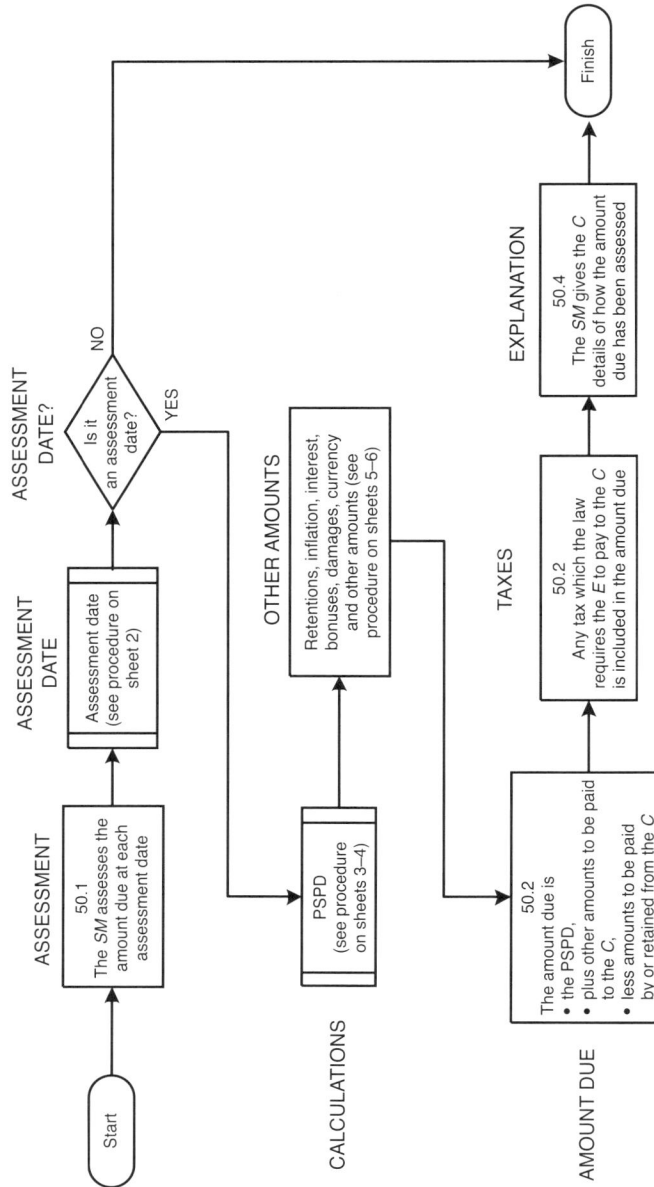

Flow chart 50 Sheet 1 of 6
Assessing the amount due

Called from sheet 1

```
┌─────────┐
│  Begin  │
└─────────┘
```

```
┌──────────────────────┐
│ The assessment,      │
│ interval, starting date │
│ and service period   │
│ are stated in the CD │
└──────────────────────┘
```

```
┌──────────────────────────┐
│ 50.1                     │
│ The first assessment date is │
│ decided by the SM to suit the │
│ procedures of the Parties and is │
│ not later than the assessment │
│ interval after the starting date │
└──────────────────────────┘
```

Is it after the starting date?

NO → Not assessment date

YES

```
┌──────────────────────────┐
│ 50.1                     │
│ Later assessment dates occur at │
│ the end of each assessment │
│ interval until four weeks after the │
│ end of the service period │
└──────────────────────────┘
```

Is it more than four weeks after end of service period?

YES → Not assessment date

NO

Is it one of the assessments dates for this contract?

NO → Not assessment date → Return

YES → Assessment date → Return

Return to sheet 1

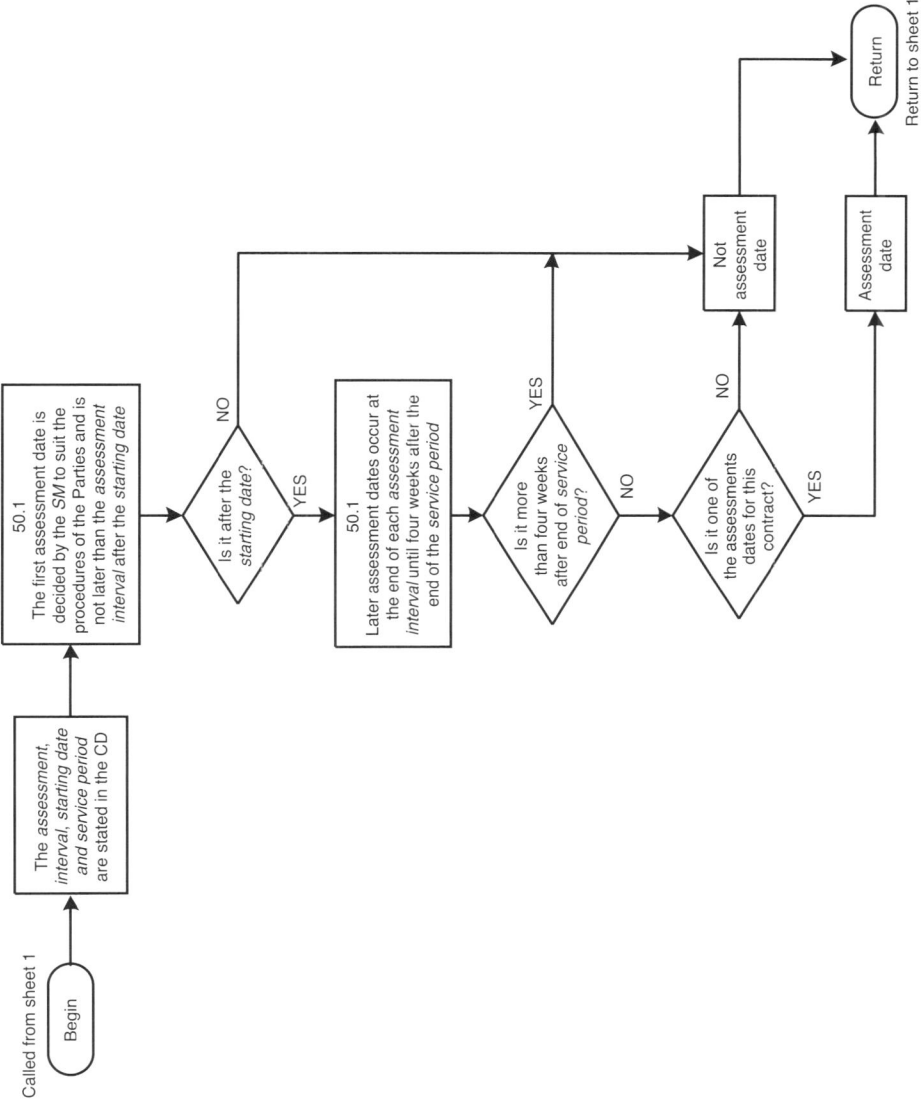

Flow chart 50 Sheet 2 of 6
Assessing the amount due

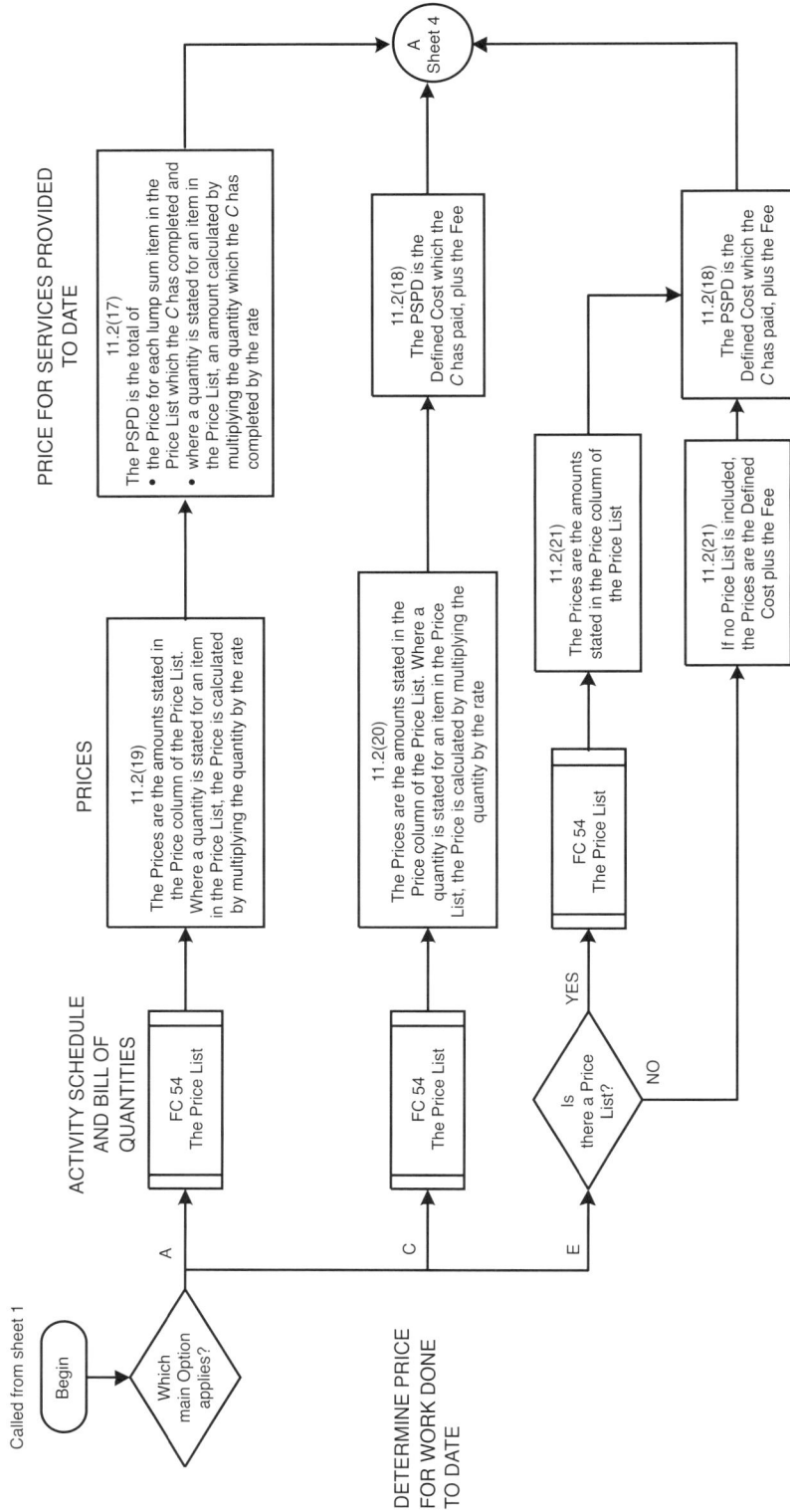

Flow chart 50 Sheet 3 of 6
Assessing the amount due

DEFINED COST

11.2(5)

Defined Cost is payments by the *C* in Providing the Service for
• people who are employed by the *C*,
• P&M,
• work subcontracted by the *C* and
• Equipment
less Disallowed Cost

The amount for Equipment includes amounts paid for hired Equipment and an amount for the use of Equipment owned by the *C* which is the amount the *C* would have paid if the Equipment had been hired

DISALLOWED COST

11.2(6)

Disallowed Cost is cost which the *SM* decides
• is not justified by the *C*'s accounts and records,
• should not have been paid to a SC or supplier in accordance with his contract,
• was incurred only because the *C* did not
  • follow an acceptance or procurement procedure stated in the SI or
  • give an early warning which this contract required him to give
and the cost of
• P&M not used to Provide the Service (after allowing for reasonable wastage) unless resulting from a change to the SI,
• resources not used to Provide the Service (after allowing for reasonable availability and utilisation) or not taken away when the *SM* requested,
• events for which this contract requires the *C* to insure and
• preparation for and conduct of an adjudication or proceedings of the *tribunal*
and other amounts paid to the *C* by insurers

SUBCONTRACTOR

11.2(16)

A SC is a person or organisation who has a contract with the *C* to
• provide a part of the *service* or
• supply P&M which the person or organisation has wholly or partly designed specifically for the *service*

THE FEE

11.2(8)

The Fee is the sum of the amounts calculated by applying the *subcontracted fee percentage* to the Defined Cost of subcontracted work and the *direct fee percentage* to the Defined Cost of other work

The *subcontracted fee percentage* and the *direct fee percentage* are stated in the CD

(Return)

Return to sheet 1

A
Sheet 3

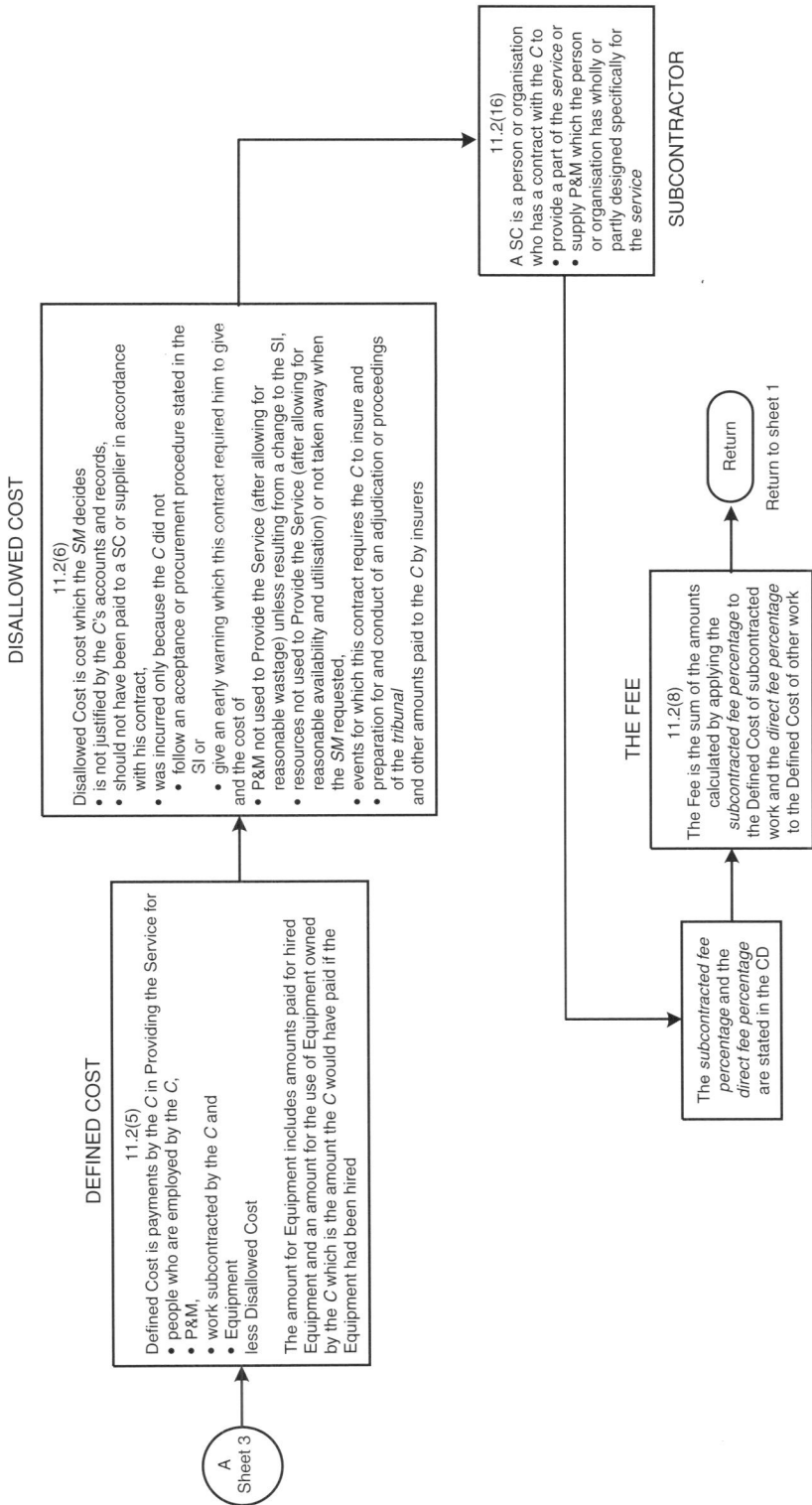

Flow chart 50 Sheet 4 of 6
Assessing the amount due

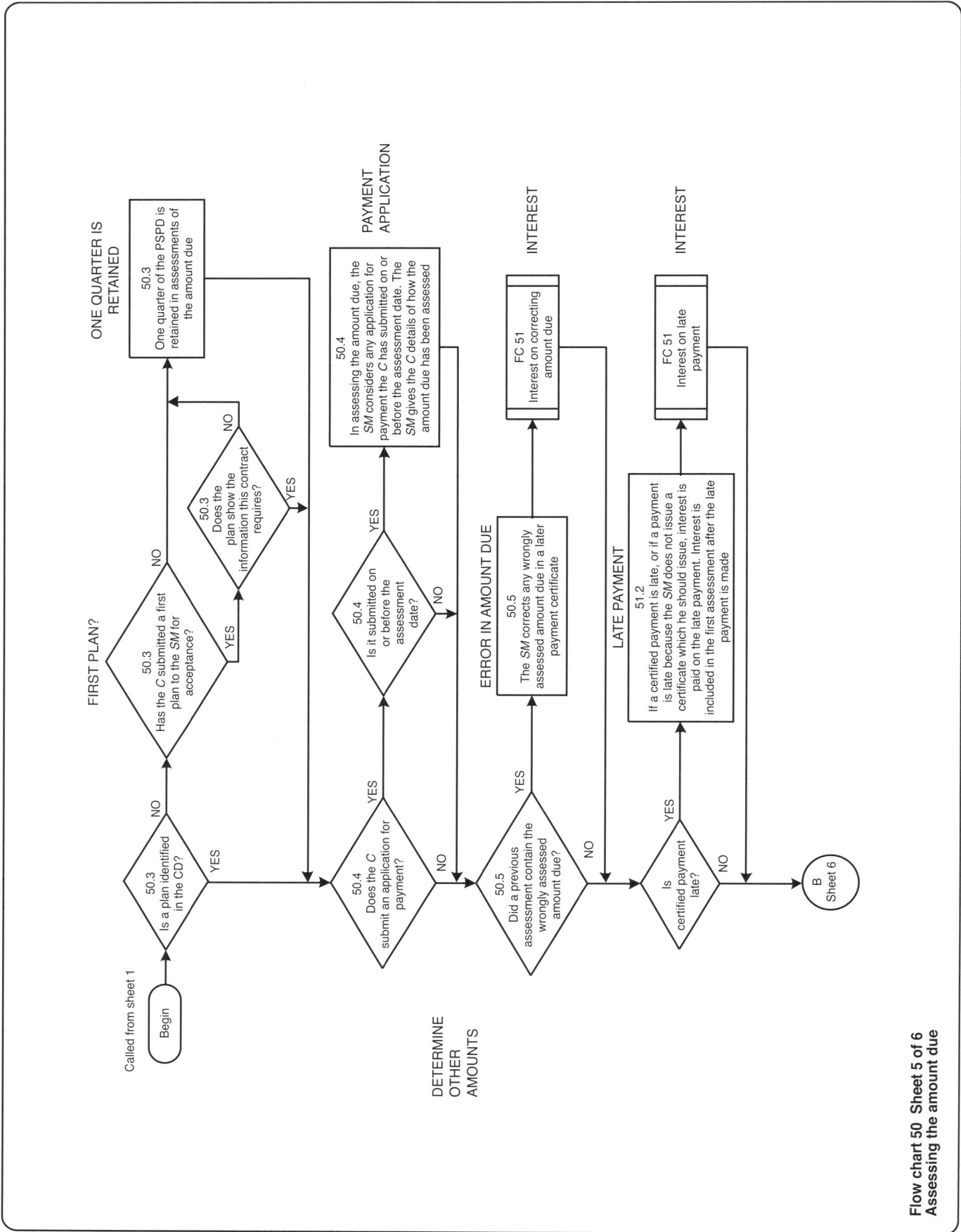

Called from sheet 1

Begin

50.3
Is a plan identified in the CD?

— NO →

FIRST PLAN?

50.3
Has the C submitted a first plan to the SM for acceptance?

— NO →

— YES → (up to)

50.3
Does the plan show the information this contract requires?

— NO →

— YES →

ONE QUARTER IS RETAINED

50.3
One quarter of the PSPD is retained in assessments of the amount due

— YES (from 50.3 first decision, down) →

50.4
Does the C submit an application for payment?

— YES →

50.4
Is it submitted on or before the assessment date?

— YES →

PAYMENT APPLICATION

50.4
In assessing the amount due, the SM considers any application for payment the C has submitted on or before the assessment date. The SM gives the C details of how the amount due has been assessed

— NO →

DETERMINE OTHER AMOUNTS

50.5
Did a previous assessment contain the wrongly assessed amount due?

— YES →

ERROR IN AMOUNT DUE

50.5
The SM corrects any wrongly assessed amount due in a later payment certificate

INTEREST

FC 51
Interest on correcting amount due

— NO →

51.2
Is certified payment late?

— YES →

LATE PAYMENT

51.2
If a certified payment is late, or if a payment is late because the SM does not issue a certificate which he should issue, interest is paid on the late payment. Interest is included in the first assessment after the late payment is made

INTEREST

FC 51
Interest on late payment

— NO →

B
Sheet 6

PRICE ADJUSTMENT

FC X1
Price adjustment for inflation

Does Option X1 apply? — YES → FC X1
NO

A or C

Which main Option applies? — A or C → Does Option X1 apply?
E

Does Option A or C apply?
A
C

B
Sheet 5

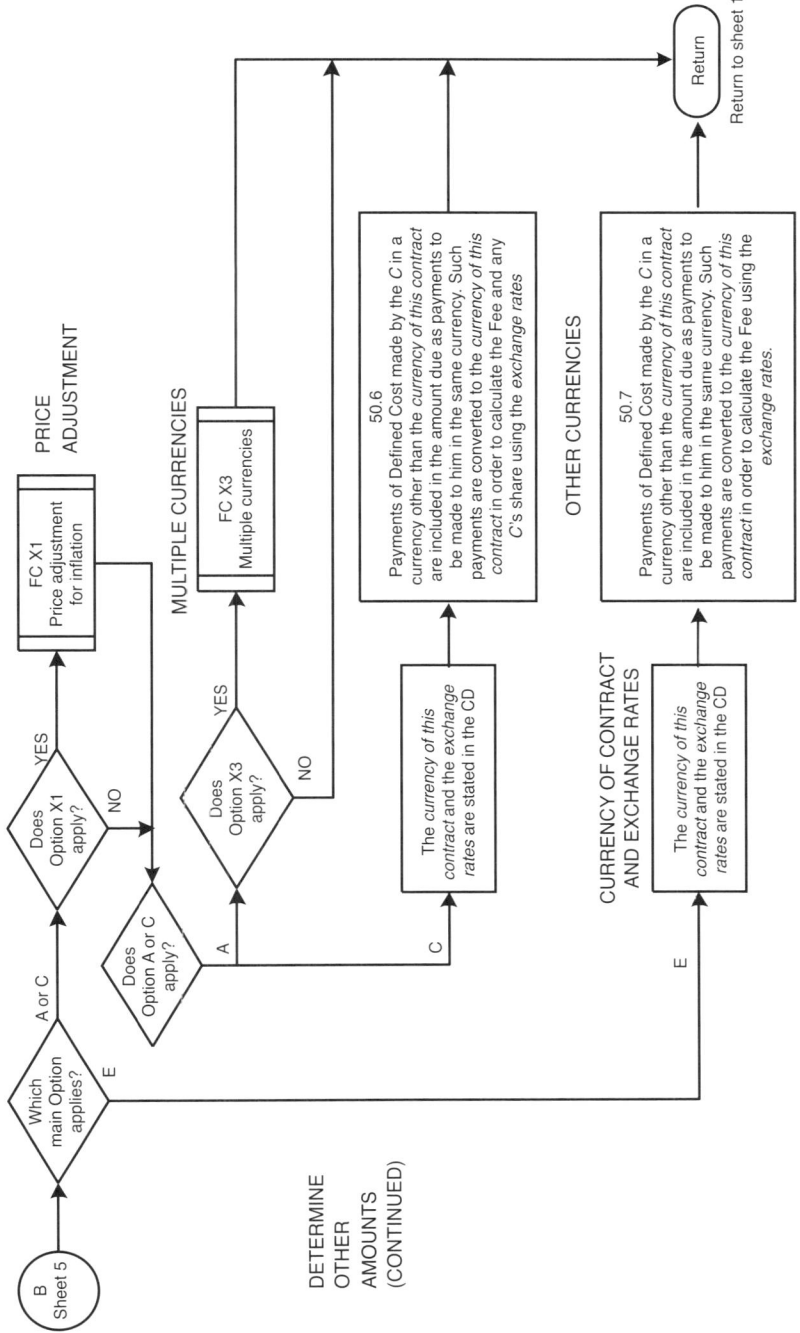

DETERMINE OTHER AMOUNTS (CONTINUED)

MULTIPLE CURRENCIES

FC X3
Multiple currencies

Does Option X3 apply? — YES → FC X3
NO

The currency of this contract and the exchange rates are stated in the CD

50.6
Payments of Defined Cost made by the C in a currency other than the currency of this contract are included in the amount due as payments to be made to him in the same currency. Such payments are converted to the currency of this contract in order to calculate the Fee and any C's share using the exchange rates

OTHER CURRENCIES

CURRENCY OF CONTRACT AND EXCHANGE RATES

E

The currency of this contract and the exchange rates are stated in the CD

50.7
Payments of Defined Cost made by the C in a currency other than the currency of this contract are included in the amount due as payments to be made to him in the same currency. Such payments are converted to the currency of this contract in order to calculate the Fee using the exchange rates.

Return

Return to sheet 1

Flow chart 50 Sheet 6 of 6
Assessing the amount due

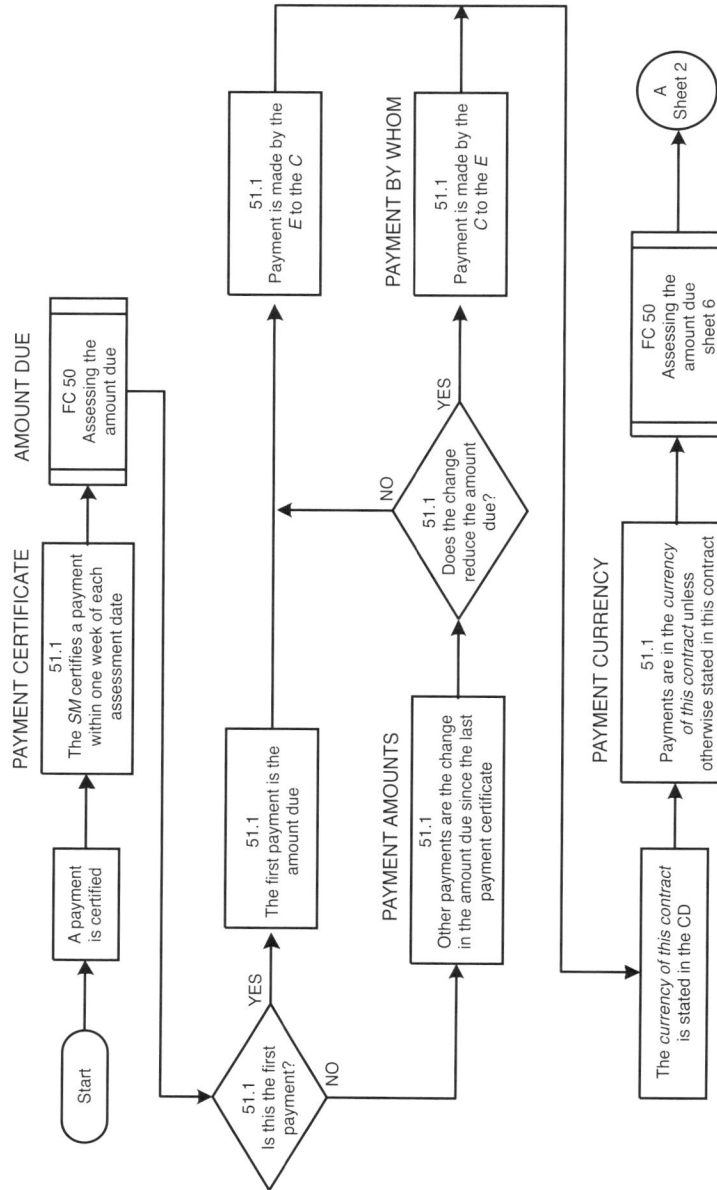

PAYMENT CERTIFICATE

AMOUNT DUE

51.1
The *SM* certifies a payment within one week of each assessment date

FC 50
Assessing the amount due

51.1
Is this the first payment?

51.1
The first payment is the amount due

51.1
Other payments are the change in the amount due since the last payment certificate

PAYMENT AMOUNTS

51.1
Payment is made by the *E* to the *C*

51.1
Does the change reduce the amount due?

PAYMENT BY WHOM

51.1
Payment is made by the *C* to the *E*

The *currency of this contract* is stated in the CD

51.1
Payments are in the *currency of this contract* unless otherwise stated in this contract

PAYMENT CURRENCY

FC 50
Assessing the amount due sheet 6

A
Sheet 2

A payment is certified

Start

**Flow chart 51 sheet 1 of 2
Payment**

www.neccontract.com

MAKING A PAYMENT

A Sheet 1 → Making a payment →

Does Option Y(UK)2 apply?
- NO → **CERTIFIED PAYMENT** — 51.2 Each certified payment is made within three weeks of the assessment date or, if a different period is stated in the CD, within the period stated.
- YES → FC Y(UK)2.2 Dates for payment

CERTIFIED PAYMENT

51.2 Each certified payment is made within three weeks of the assessment date or, if a different period is stated in the CD, within the period stated.

CALCULATING INTEREST ON A LATE PAYMENT

Calculating interest on a late payment?
- YES → **Is a certified payment late?**
  - YES → 51.2 Interest is paid on the late payment → **INTEREST RATE** — The *interest rate* is stated in the CD → **INTEREST CALCULATION** — 51.4 Interest is calculated on a daily basis at the *interest rate* and is compounded annually → **PERIOD FOR INTEREST** — 51.2 Interest is assessed from the date by which the late payment should have been made until the date when late payment is made, and is included in the first assessment after the late payment is made
  - NO → **51.2 Is a payment late because the SM does not issue a certificate which he should issue?**
    - YES → 51.2 Interest is paid on the late payment
    - NO →
- NO →

CORRECTING AN AMOUNT DUE

Correcting an amount due?
- YES → **CORRECTING AMOUNT** — 51.3 If an amount due is corrected in a later certificate either
  - by the SM, in relation to a mistake or a CE or
  - following a decision of the *Adjudicator* or the *tribunal*
  interest on the correcting amount is paid → **CORRECTION?** — Does the amount due include a correcting amount?
    - YES → **INTEREST RATE** — The *interest rate* is stated in the CD → **INTEREST CALCULATION** — 51.4 Interest is calculated on a daily basis at the *interest rate* and is compounded annually → **PERIOD FOR INTEREST** — 51.3 Interest is assessed from the date when the incorrect amount was certified until the date when the correcting amount is certified and is included in the assessment which includes the correcting amount → Finish
    - NO →
- NO → Finish

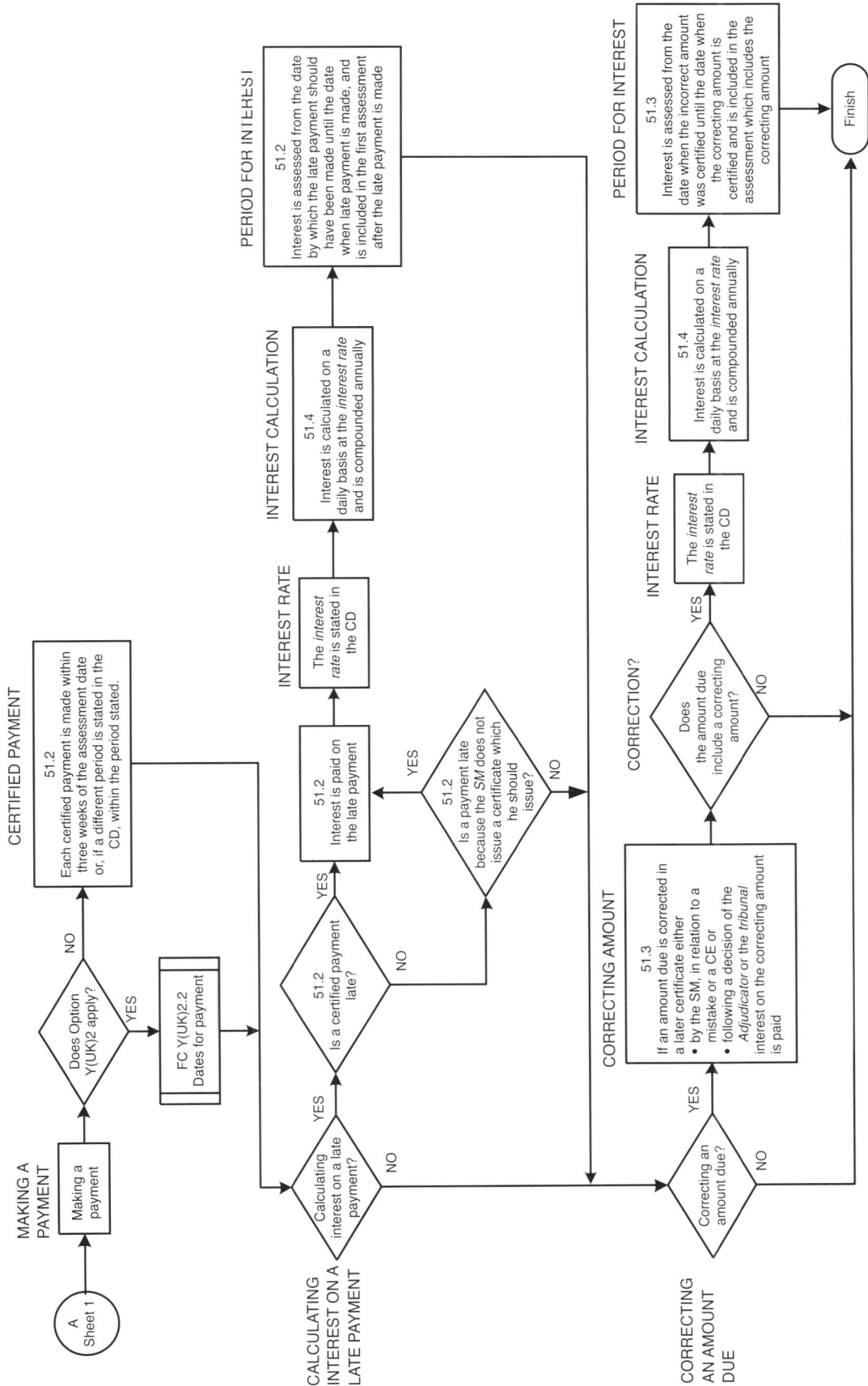

Flow chart 51 sheet 2 of 2
Payment

DEFINED COST

11.2(5)

Defined Cost is payments by the *C* in Providing the Service for
- people who are employed by the *C*,
- P&M,
- work subcontracted by the *C* and
- Equipment
less Disallowed Cost

Start

COSTS NOT INCLUDED IN DEFINED COST ARE IN FEE

11.2(5)

The amount for Equipment includes amounts paid for hired Equipment and an amount for the use of Equipment owned by the *C* which is the amount the *C* would have paid if the Equipment had been hired

DEFINED COSTS AT OPEN MARKET PRICES

52.1

All the *C*'s costs which are not included in the Defined Cost are treated as included in the Fee

52.1

Amounts included in Defined Cost are at open market or competitively tendered prices with deductions for all discounts, rebates and taxes which can be recovered

WHICH MAIN OPTION?

Which main Option applies?

A

C or E

CONTRACTOR'S ACCOUNTS AND RECORDS

52.2

The C keeps these records
- accounts of payments of Defined Cost,
- proof that the payments have been made,
- communications about and assessments of CEs for SCs and
- other records as stated in the SI

INSPECTION OF RECORDS

52.3

The *C* allows the *SM* to inspect at any time within working hours the accounts and records which he is required to keep

Finish

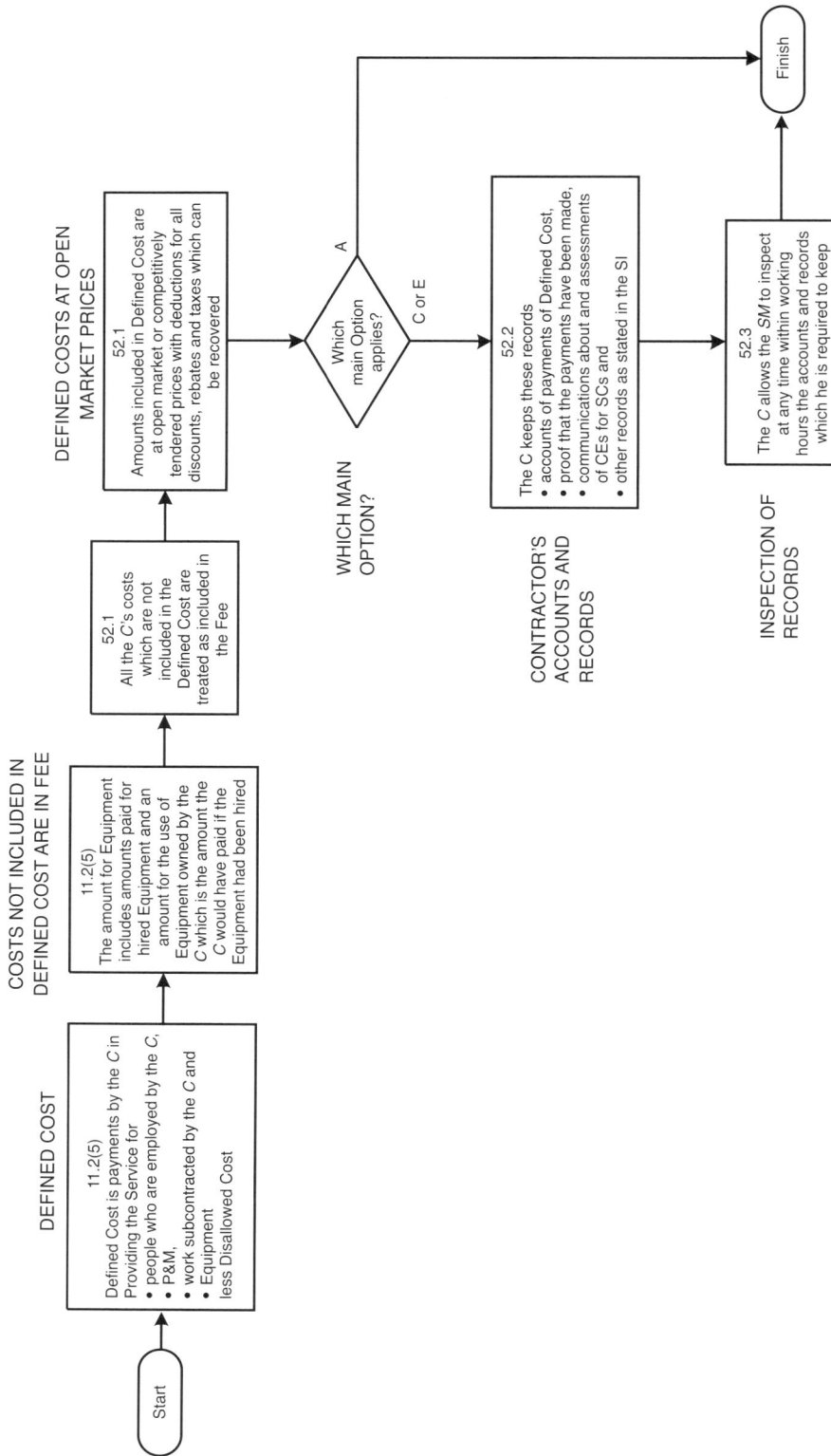

Flow chart 52
Defined Cost

www.neccontract.com

THE PRICES

11.2(20)
The Prices are the amounts stated in the Price column of the Price List. Where a quantity is stated for an item in the Price List, the Price is calculated by multiplying the quantity by the rate

The *share ranges* and *C's share percentage* are stated in the CD

Start

Which main Option applies?

C

A or E

CONTRACTOR'S SHARE

ASSESS SAVING

53.1
The *SM* assesses the *C*'s share of the difference between the total of the Prices and the PSPD.

53.1
The difference is divided into increments falling within each of the *share ranges*. The limits of a *share range* are the PSPD divided by the total of the Prices, expressed as a percentage

53.1
The *C*'s share equals the sum of the products of the increment within each *share range* and the corresponding *C's share percentage*

SHARE ASSESSMENT

53.3
At the dates stated in the CD the *SM* assesses the *C*'s share

53.3
The *SM* uses in his assessment the PSPD at the date of the assessment and the total of the Prices for the work done at the date of the assessment

53.2
Is the PSPD less than the total of the Prices?

YES

NO

53.2
The *C* is paid his share of the saving

53.2
The *C* pays his share of the excess

SAVING OR EXCESS?

INCLUDED IN AMOUNT DUE

53.3
This share is included in the next amount due following each assessment

Finish

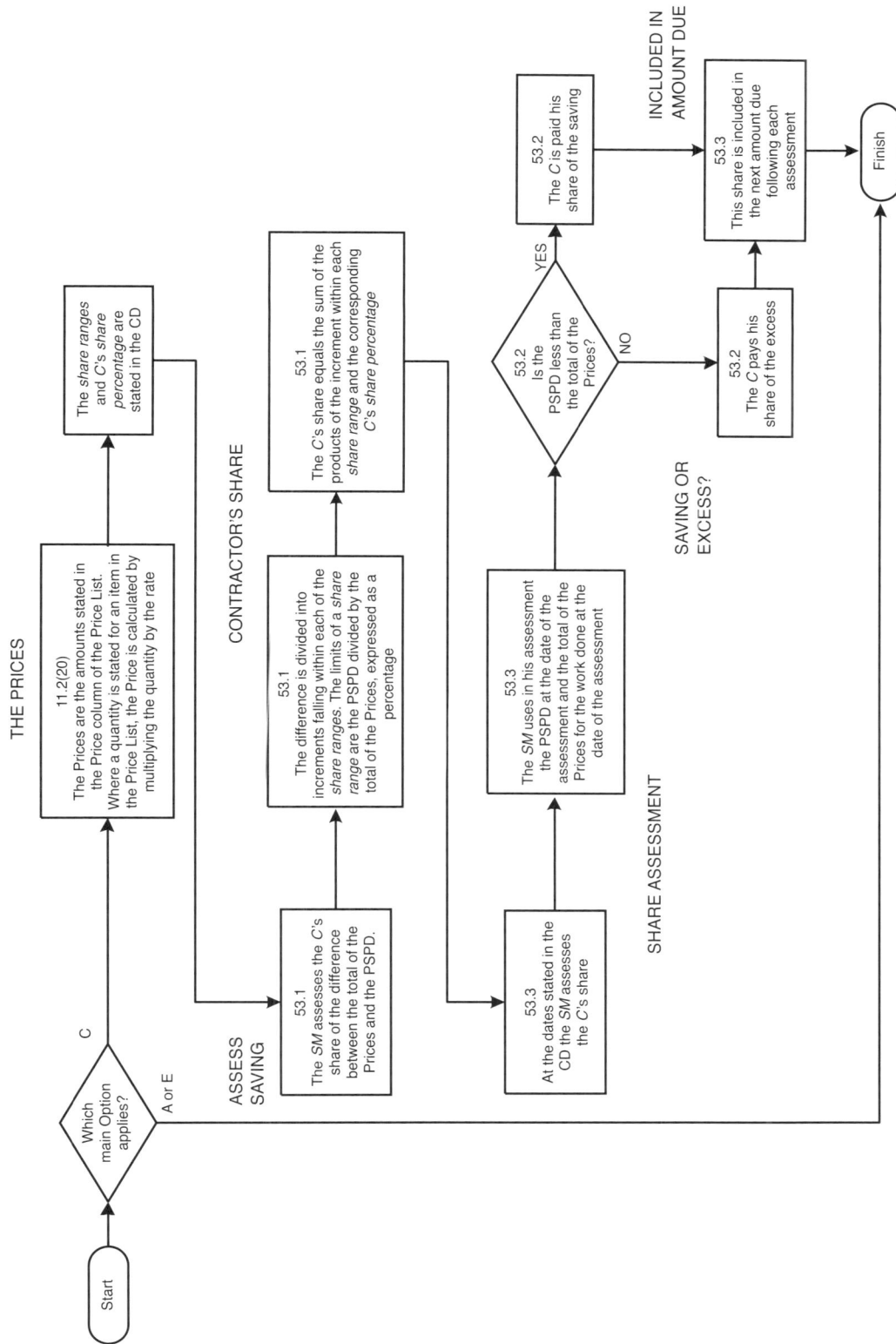

Flow chart 53
The *Contractor*'s share (Option C)

Start

11.2(12)
The Price List is the *price list* unless later changed in accordance with this contract

INFORMATION ON PRICE LIST

54.1
Information in the Price List is not SI

Does the *C* change a planned method of working?

NO → Finish

YES → Is the change at his discretion?

NO → **FC 60** CEs

YES → Do the item descriptions on the Price List relate to the operations on the Accepted Plan?

YES → **FC 22** Revising the *C*'s Plan

NO →

54.2
If the *C* changes a planned method of working at his discretion so that the item descriptions on the Price List do not relate to the operations on the Accepted Plan, he submits a revision of the Price List to the *SM* for acceptance

CONTRACTOR'S REVISION OF PRICE LIST

FC 13 *C*'s submission

54.3
A reason for not accepting a revision of the Price List is that
• it does not comply with the Accepted Plan,
• any changed Prices are not reasonably distributed between the items in the Price List or
• the total of the Prices is changed.

REASON FOR NOT ACCEPTING REVISION

Does the SM accept the submission?

YES → Finish

NO → Is it for a reason stated in the contract?

YES → **FC 13** *C*'s submission

NO → **FC 60** CE 60.1(8)

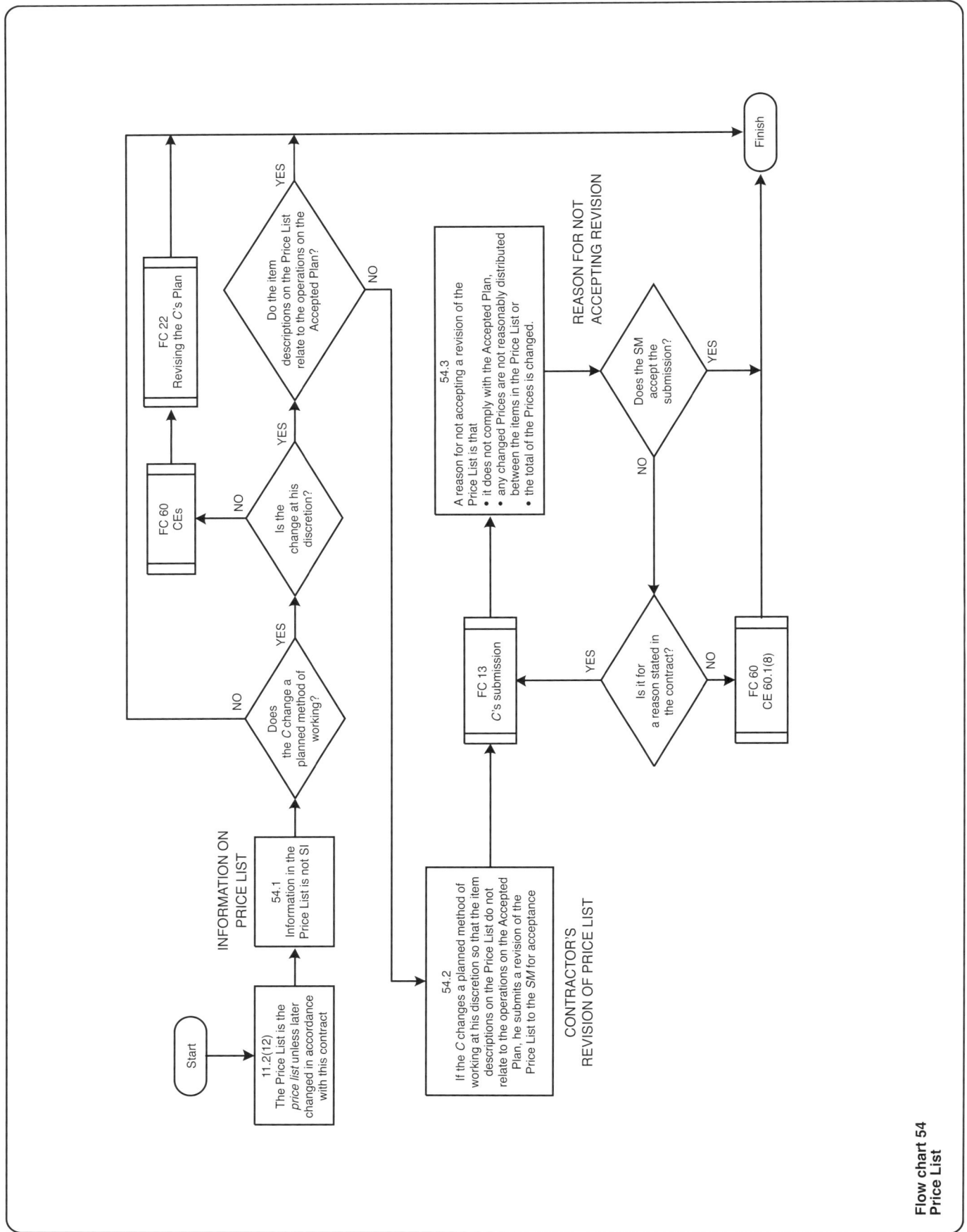

Flow chart 54
Price List

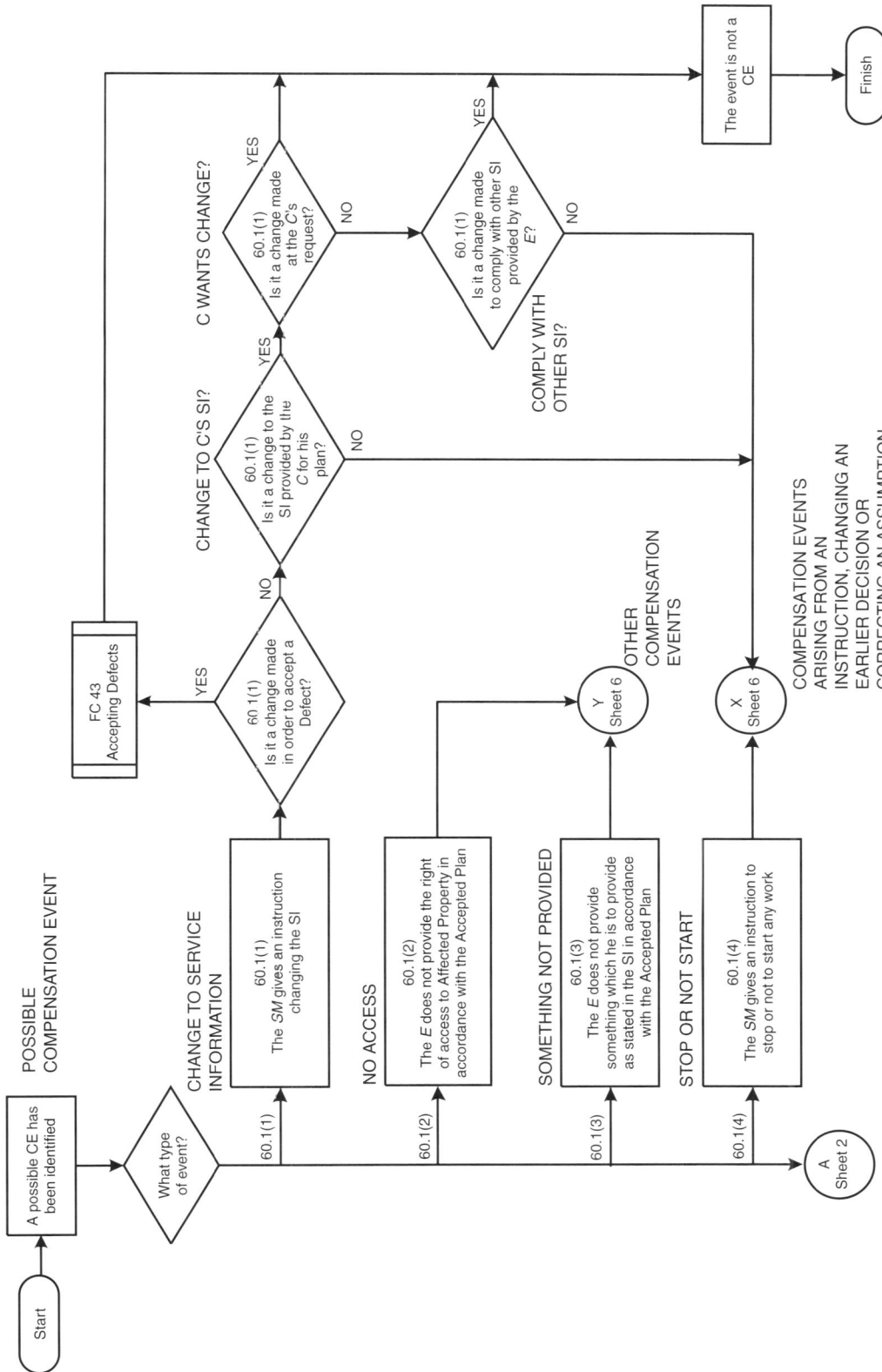

POSSIBLE COMPENSATION EVENT

Start → A possible CE has been identified → What type of event?

CHANGE TO SERVICE INFORMATION
60.1(1) — The *SM* gives an instruction changing the SI

NO ACCESS
60.1(2) — The *E* does not provide the right of access to Affected Property in accordance with the Accepted Plan

SOMETHING NOT PROVIDED
60.1(3) — The *E* does not provide something which he is to provide as stated in the SI in accordance with the Accepted Plan

STOP OR NOT START
60.1(4) — The *SM* gives an instruction to stop or not to start any work

A Sheet 2

FC 43 Accepting Defects

60.1(1) Is it a change made in order to accept a Defect? — YES / NO

CHANGE TO C'S SI?
60.1(1) Is it a change to the SI provided by the *C* for his plan? — YES / NO

C WANTS CHANGE?
60.1(1) Is it a change made at the *C's* request? — YES / NO

COMPLY WITH OTHER SI?
60.1(1) Is it a change made to comply with other SI provided by the *E*? — YES / NO

The event is not a CE → Finish

Y Sheet 6 — **OTHER COMPENSATION EVENTS**

X Sheet 6 — **COMPENSATION EVENTS ARISING FROM AN INSTRUCTION, CHANGING AN EARLIER DECISION OR CORRECTING AN ASSUMPTION**

**Flow chart 60 Sheet 1 of 6
Compensation events**

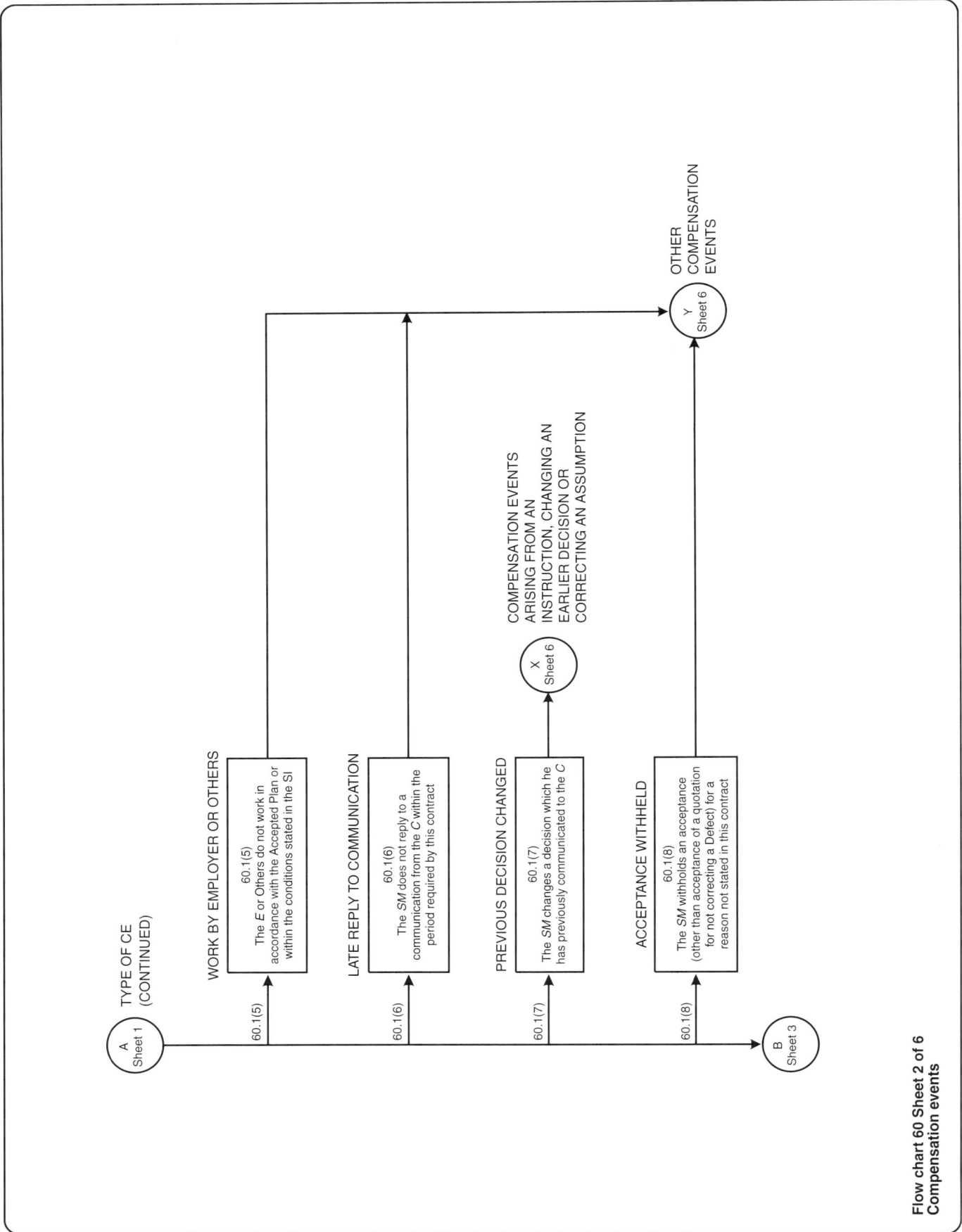

TYPE OF CE (CONTINUED)

A
Sheet 1

WORK BY EMPLOYER OR OTHERS

60.1(5)

The *E* or Others do not work in accordance with the Accepted Plan or within the conditions stated in the SI

LATE REPLY TO COMMUNICATION

60.1(6)

The *SM* does not reply to a communication from the *C* within the period required by this contract

PREVIOUS DECISION CHANGED

60.1(7)

The *SM* changes a decision which he has previously communicated to the *C*

X
Sheet 6

COMPENSATION EVENTS ARISING FROM AN INSTRUCTION, CHANGING AN EARLIER DECISION OR CORRECTING AN ASSUMPTION

ACCEPTANCE WITHHELD

60.1(8)

The *SM* withholds an acceptance (other than acceptance of a quotation for not correcting a Defect) for a reason not stated in this contract

Y
Sheet 6

OTHER COMPENSATION EVENTS

B
Sheet 3

Flow chart 60 Sheet 2 of 6
Compensation events

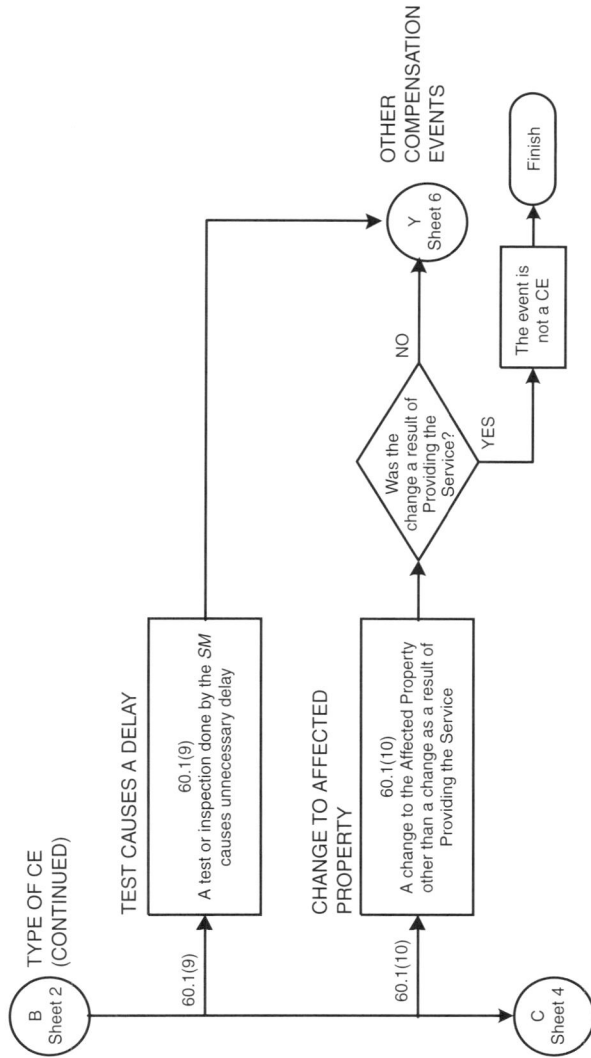

B Sheet 2

TYPE OF CE
(CONTINUED)

TEST CAUSES A DELAY

60.1(9)

60.1(9)
A test or inspection done by the *SM* causes unnecessary delay

CHANGE TO AFFECTED PROPERTY

60.1(10)

60.1(10)
A change to the Affected Property other than a change as a result of Providing the Service

C Sheet 4

Was the change a result of Providing the Service?

NO

YES

The event is not a CE

Y Sheet 6

OTHER COMPENSATION EVENTS

Finish

Flow chart 60 Sheet 3 of 6
Compensation events

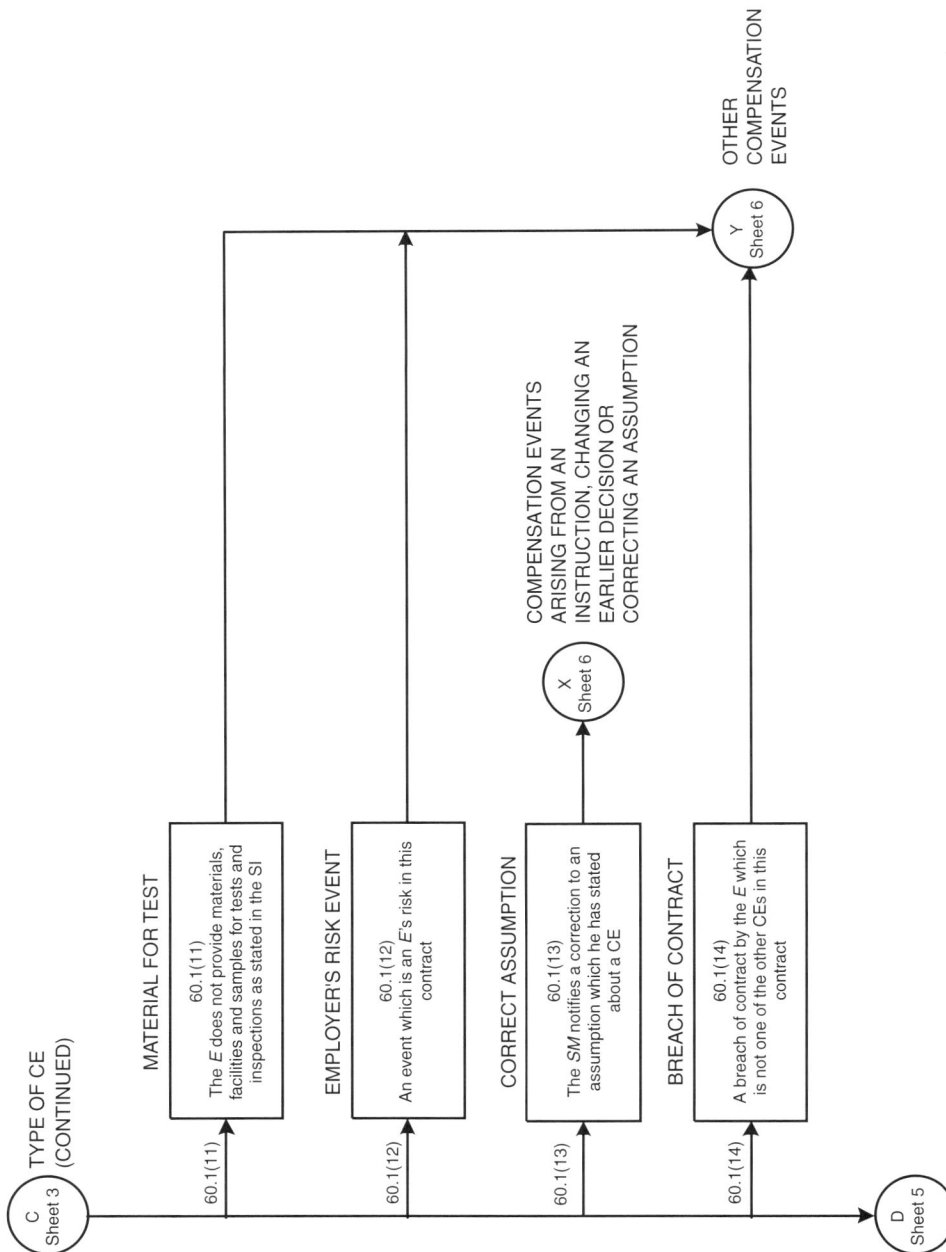

TYPE OF CE (CONTINUED)

C Sheet 3

MATERIAL FOR TEST

60.1(11)

The E does not provide materials, facilities and samples for tests and inspections as stated in the SI

EMPLOYER'S RISK EVENT

60.1(12)

An event which is an E's risk in this contract

CORRECT ASSUMPTION

60.1(13)

The SM notifies a correction to an assumption which he has stated about a CE

BREACH OF CONTRACT

60.1(14)

A breach of contract by the E which is not one of the other CEs in this contract

X Sheet 6

COMPENSATION EVENTS ARISING FROM AN INSTRUCTION, CHANGING AN EARLIER DECISION OR CORRECTING AN ASSUMPTION

Y Sheet 6

OTHER COMPENSATION EVENTS

D Sheet 5

Flow chart 60 Sheet 4 of 6
Compensation events

TYPE OF CE (CONTINUED)

X2 CHANGES IN THE LAW

CHANGE IN LAW OF COUNTRY

Does Option X2 apply?

YES → FC X2 Changes in the law → **X2.1** A change in the law of the country in which the Affected Property is located is a CE if it occurs after the Contract Date → **11.2(3)** The Contract Date is the date when this contract came into existence → **Y** Sheet 6 **OTHER COMPENSATION EVENTS**

NO →

CHANGE TO PARTNERING INFORMATION

Does Option X12 apply?

YES → FC X12 Partnering → Is there a change to the Partnering Information?

YES → **X12.3(6)** Each such change to the Partnering Information is a CE which may lead to reduced Prices → **X** Sheet 6

NO → Is there a change to the Partners' timetable?

YES → **X12.3(7)** The C changes his plan if it is necessary to do so in order to comply with the revised timetable. Each such change is a CE which may lead to reduced Prices → **X** Sheet 6 **COMPENSATION EVENTS ARISING FROM AN INSTRUCTION, CHANGING AN EARLIER DECISION OR CORRECTING AN ASSUMPTION**

NO →

Does Option X19 apply?

YES → FC X19 Providing the Service by Task Order X19.10 → **Z** Sheet 6

NO →

D Sheet 4

E Sheet 6

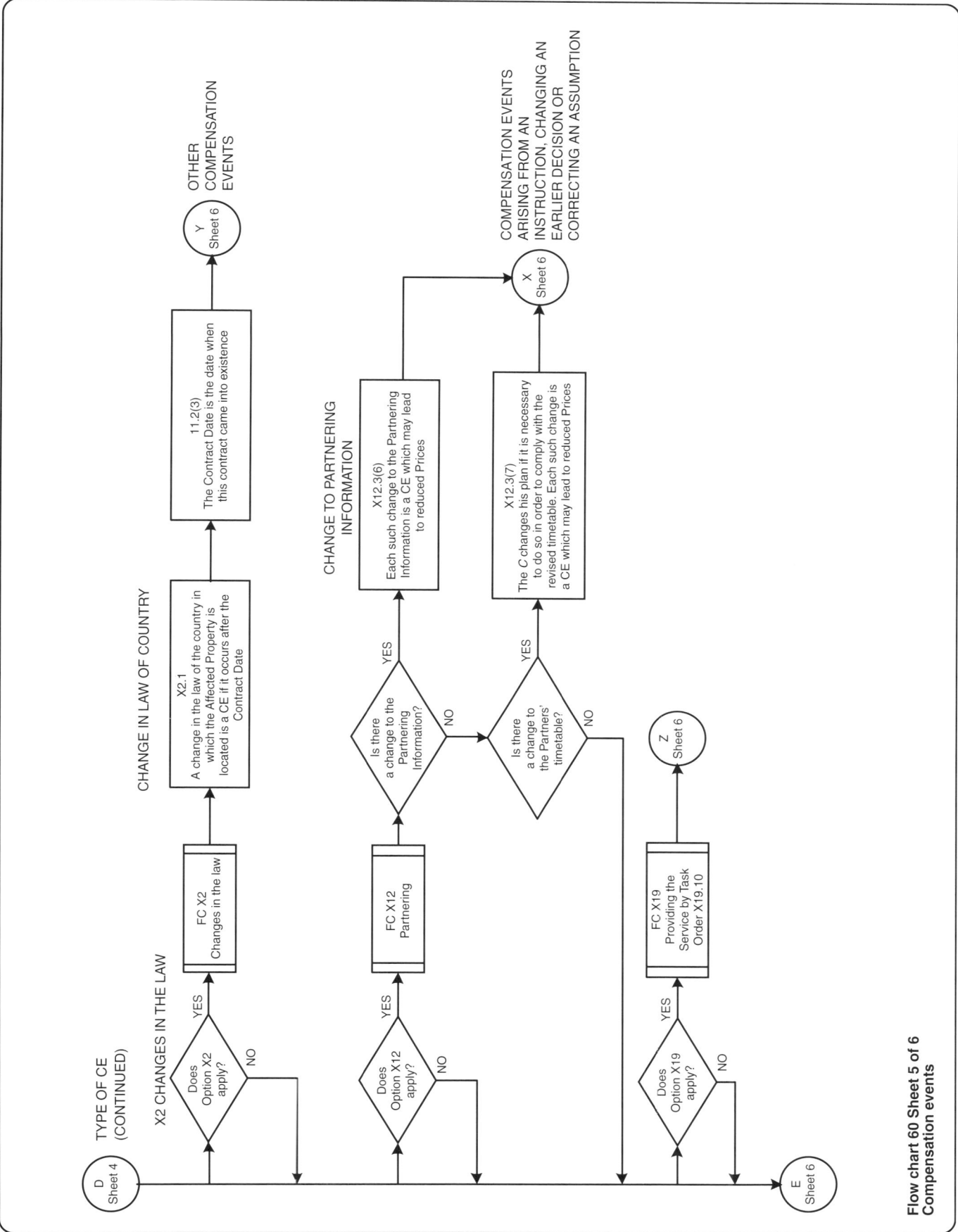

**Flow chart 60 Sheet 5 of 6
Compensation events**

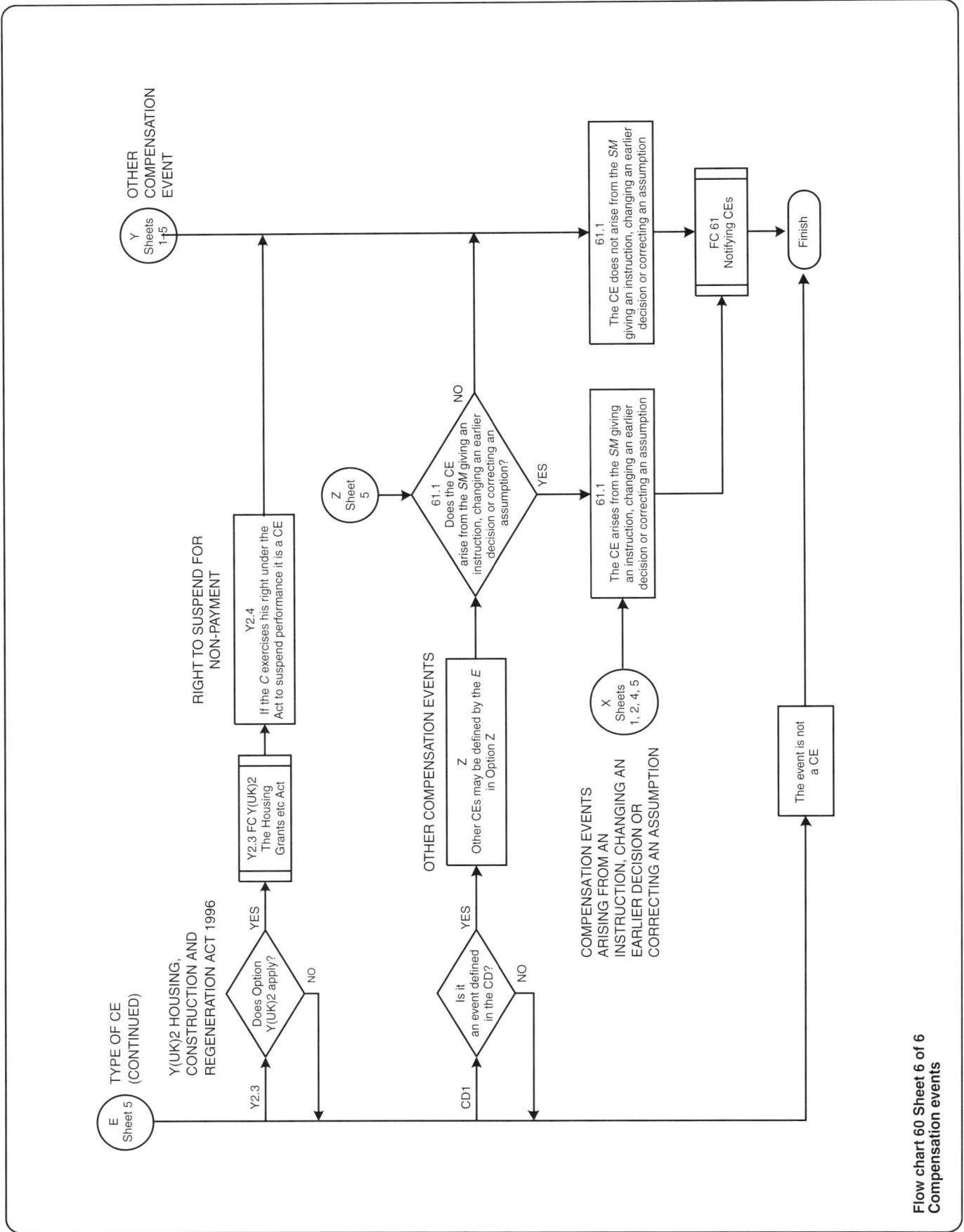

TYPE OF CE (CONTINUED)

E Sheet 5

Y(UK)2 HOUSING, CONSTRUCTION AND REGENERATION ACT 1996

Y2.3 — Does Option Y(UK)2 apply?
- YES → Y2.3 FC Y(UK)2 The Housing Grants etc Act → Y2.4 If the C exercises his right under the Act to suspend performance it is a CE
- NO

RIGHT TO SUSPEND FOR NON-PAYMENT

Y — Sheets 1–5 — OTHER COMPENSATION EVENT

OTHER COMPENSATION EVENTS

CD1 — Is it an event defined in the CD?
- YES → Z Other CEs may be defined by the E in Option Z
- NO

Z Sheet 5

61.1 Does the CE arise from the SM giving an instruction, changing an earlier decision or correcting an assumption?
- NO → 61.1 The CE does not arise from the SM giving an instruction, changing an earlier decision or correcting an assumption
- YES → 61.1 The CE arises from the SM giving an instruction, changing an earlier decision or correcting an assumption

X Sheets 1, 2, 4, 5

COMPENSATION EVENTS ARISING FROM AN INSTRUCTION, CHANGING AN EARLIER DECISION OR CORRECTING AN ASSUMPTION

FC 61 Notifying CEs → Finish

The event is not a CE → Finish

Flow chart 60 Sheet 6 of 6
Compensation events

COMPENSATION EVENT IDENTIFICATION

COMPENSATION EVENT TO BE NOTIFIED?

Start

A CE is to be notified

FC 60 Identifying CE

Has the event been identified as a CE? NO → ; YES →

The *service period* is stated in the CD

COMPENSATION EVENT IS NOT NOTIFIED

Is it after the end of the *service period*? YES → ; NO →

61.7 A CE is not notified after the end of the *service period*

Finish

SERVICE MANAGER MAY STATE ASSUMPTIONS

61.6 If the *SM* decides that the effects of a CE are too uncertain to be forecast reasonably, he states assumptions about the event in his instruction to the *C* to submit quotations. Assessment of the event is based on these assumptions.

PREVIOUS ASSUMPTIONS WRONG?
Does this event concern a correction to the *SM*'s stated assumptions for a CE? YES → ; NO →

61.6 Is any of the *SM*'s stated assumptions later found to be wrong? NO → ; YES →

NO COMPENSATION EVENT
No CE is notified

CORRECTION IS A COMPENSATION EVENT
61.6 The *SM* notifies a correction

FC 13 Notification of CE 60.1(13)

B Sheet 2

FORECAST EFFECT OF CE REASONABLY?
61.6 Does the *SM* decide the effects of the CE cannot be forecast reasonably? YES → ; NO →

SERVICE MANAGER STATES ASSUMPTIONS
61.6 The *SM* states assumptions about the event in his instructions to the *C* to submit quotations. Assessment of the event is based on these assumptions.

A Sheet 2

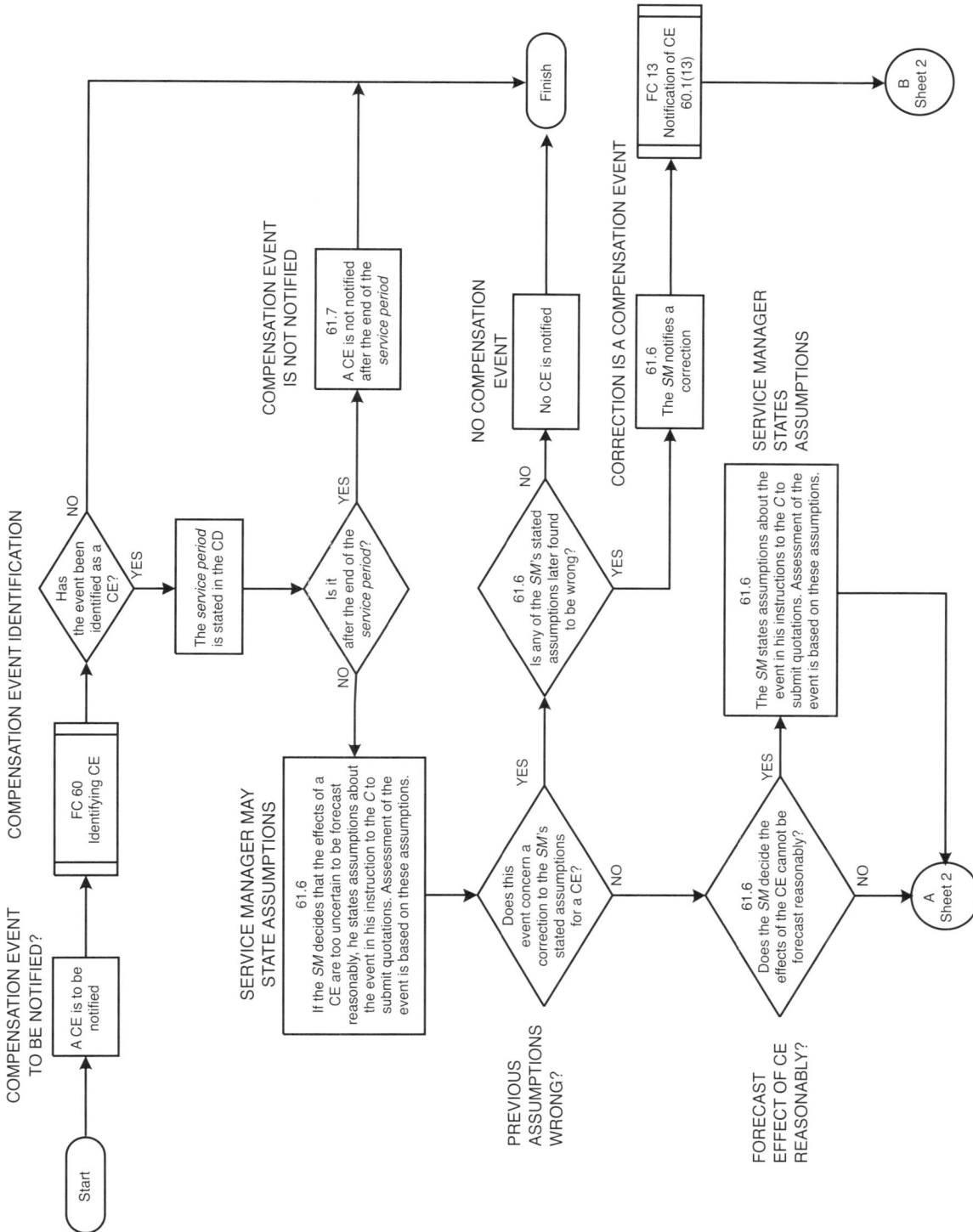

Flow chart 61 Sheet 1 of 3
Notifying compensation events

QUOTATION FOR COMPENSATION EVENT

B Sheet 1

C Sheet 3

QUOTATION FOR PROPOSED INSTRUCTION ETC

PROPOSALS NOT PUT INTO EFFECT

PUTTING INSTRUCTIONS ETC INTO EFFECT

SERVICE MANAGER'S INSTRUCTION AND NOTIFICATION

INSTRUCTION TO SUBMIT QUOTATION

EARLY WARNING

CONTRACTOR NOT ENTITLED TO CHANGES TO PRICES ETC

A Sheet 1

INSTRUCTION, CHANGING AN EARLIER DECISION OR CORRECTING AN ASSUMPTION?

61.2 The *SM* may instruct the *C* to submit quotations for a proposed instruction or a proposed changed decision

61.2 Does the *SM* issue such an instruction or changed decision? — YES / NO

61.2 The *C* does not put a proposed instruction or a proposed changed decision into effect

61.1 Does the CE arise from the *SM* giving an instruction or changing an earlier decision? — YES / NO

61.1 The *SM* notifies the *C* of the CE at the time of that communication

FC 13 Instruction or changed decision and notification of CE

61.1 The *C* puts the instruction or changed decision into effect

FC 13 Instruction to quote

FC 62 Quotations for CEs

Finish

CONTRACTOR'S FAULT?

61.1 Does the event arise from a fault of the *C*? — YES / NO

61.1 Have quotations already been submitted? — NO / YES

61.1 The *SM* also instructs the *C* to submit quotations

61.5 If the *SM* decides that the *C* did not give an early warning of the event which an experienced contractor could have given, he notifies this decision to the *C* when he instructs him to submit quotations

QUOTATION ALREADY SUBMITTED?

INSTRUCTION ALREADY GIVEN?

61.3 Has the *SM* already notified the event to the *C*? — YES / NO

NOT A COMPENSATION EVENT

No CE is notified

CONTRACTOR BELIEVES EVENT IS COMPENSATION EVENT

61.3 Does the *C* believe the event is a CE? — NO / YES

61.3 The *C* notifies the *SM* of an event which has happened or which he expects to happen as a CE

CONTRACTOR NOTIFIES WITHIN EIGHT WEEKS?

61.3 Did the *C* notify a CE within eight weeks of becoming aware of the event? — NO / YES

DOES THE EVENT ARISE FROM THE SERVICE MANAGER GIVING AN INSTRUCTION, CHANGING AN EARLIER DECISION OR CORRECTING AN ASSUMPTION

61.3 Does the event arise from the *SM* giving an instruction, changing an earlier decision or correcting an assumption? — NO / YES

61.3 The *C* is not entitled to a change in the Prices

Does Option X19 apply? — NO / YES

FC X19 Providing the Service by Task Order X19.11

X19.11 The *C* is not entitled to a change in the Task Completion Date if he does not notify the event within eight weeks of becoming aware of it

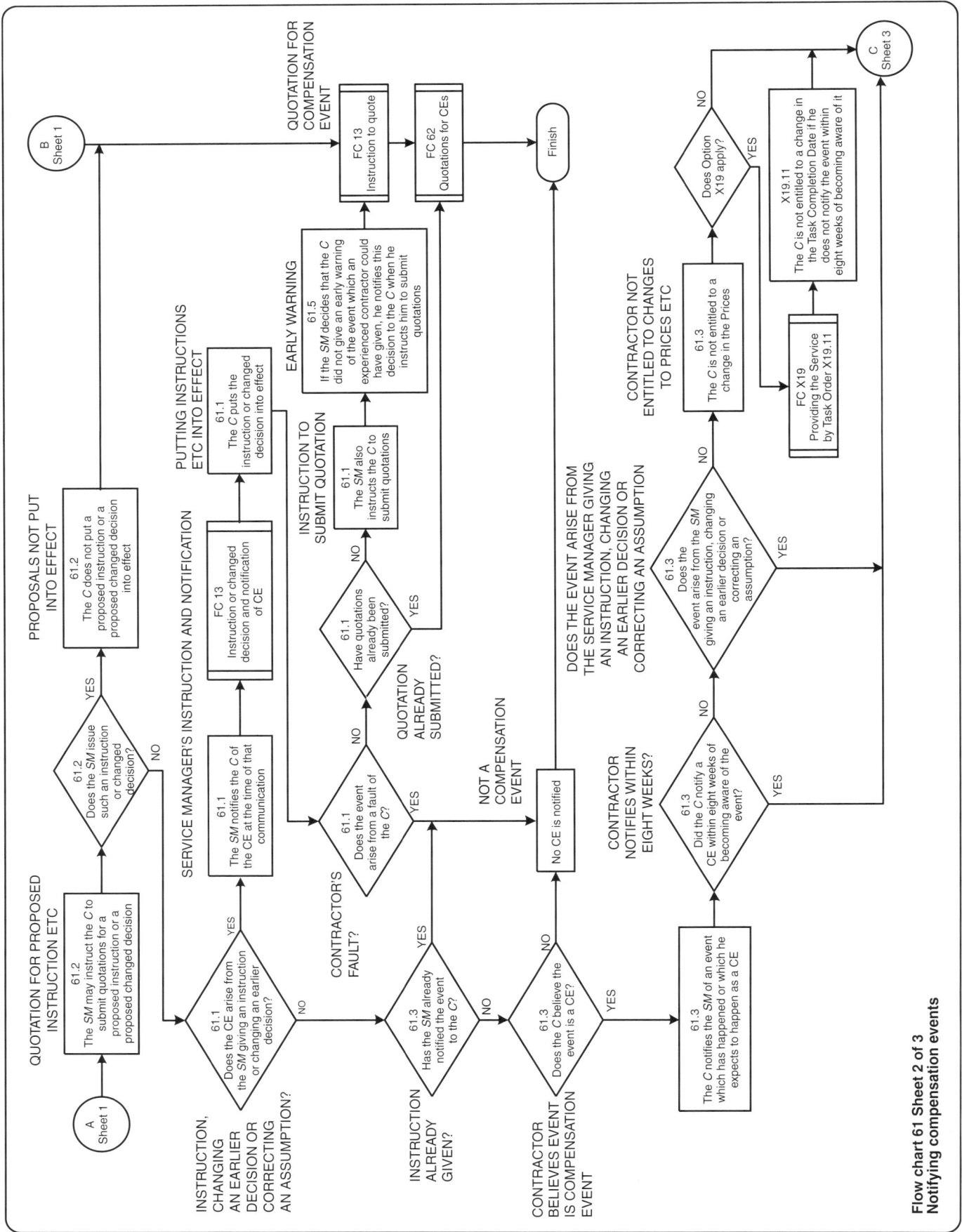

Flow chart 61 Sheet 2 of 3
Notifying compensation events

TIMELY RESPONSE

61.4
Does the *SM* respond within the allowed period?
— NO —

61.4
The *C* may notify the *SM* to this effect

— YES —

PERIOD FOR REPLY

61.4
The *SM* notifies his decision to the *C* and if his decision is that the Prices are to be changed, instructs him to submit quotations before the end of either
• one week after the *C*'s notification or
• a longer period to which the *C* has agreed

FC 60
Late reply CE
60.1(6)

Does the *C* notify?
— NO —
— YES —

FC 13
Notification

61.4
If the *SM* does not notify his decision, the *C* may notify the *SM* of his failure. A failure by the *SM* to reply within two weeks of this notification is treated as acceptance by the *SM* that the event is a CE and an instruction to submit quotations

SERVICE MANAGER'S DECISION

61.4
The *SM* should notify the *C* of his decision that for the event notified by the *C* either
• the Prices are not to be changed or
• the Prices are to be changed

FC 13
Notification of CE

C
Sheet 2

INSTRUCTION
TO SUBMIT
QUOTATIONS

61.4
Does the *SM* decide the event is not one of the CEs stated in this contract?
— NO —
— YES —

61.4
Does the *SM* decide the event has no effect upon Defined Cost?
— NO —
— YES —

61.4
Does the *SM* decide the event has not happened and is not expected to happen?
— NO —
— YES —

61.4
Does the *SM* decide the event arises from a fault of the *C*?
— NO —
— YES —

61.4
The *SM* notifies the *C* accordingly and instructs him to submit quotations

EARLY
WARNING

61.5
If the *SM* decides that the *C* did not give an early warning of the event which an experienced contractor could have given, he notifies this decision to the *C* when he instructs him to submit quotations

EARLY
WARNING
DECISION

61.5
The *SM* notifies this decision to the *C* when he instructs him to submit quotations

FC 13
Notification of decision

61.5
Does the *SM* decide the *C* did not give such an early warning?
— YES —
— NO —

FC 13
Instruction to submit quotations

FC 62
Quotations for CE

NOTIFICATION OF
SERVICE
MANAGER'S
DECISION

61.4
The *SM* notifies the *C* of his decision that Prices are not to be changed

FC 13
Notification by *C*

QUOTATIONS FOR
COMPENSATION EVENT

Finish

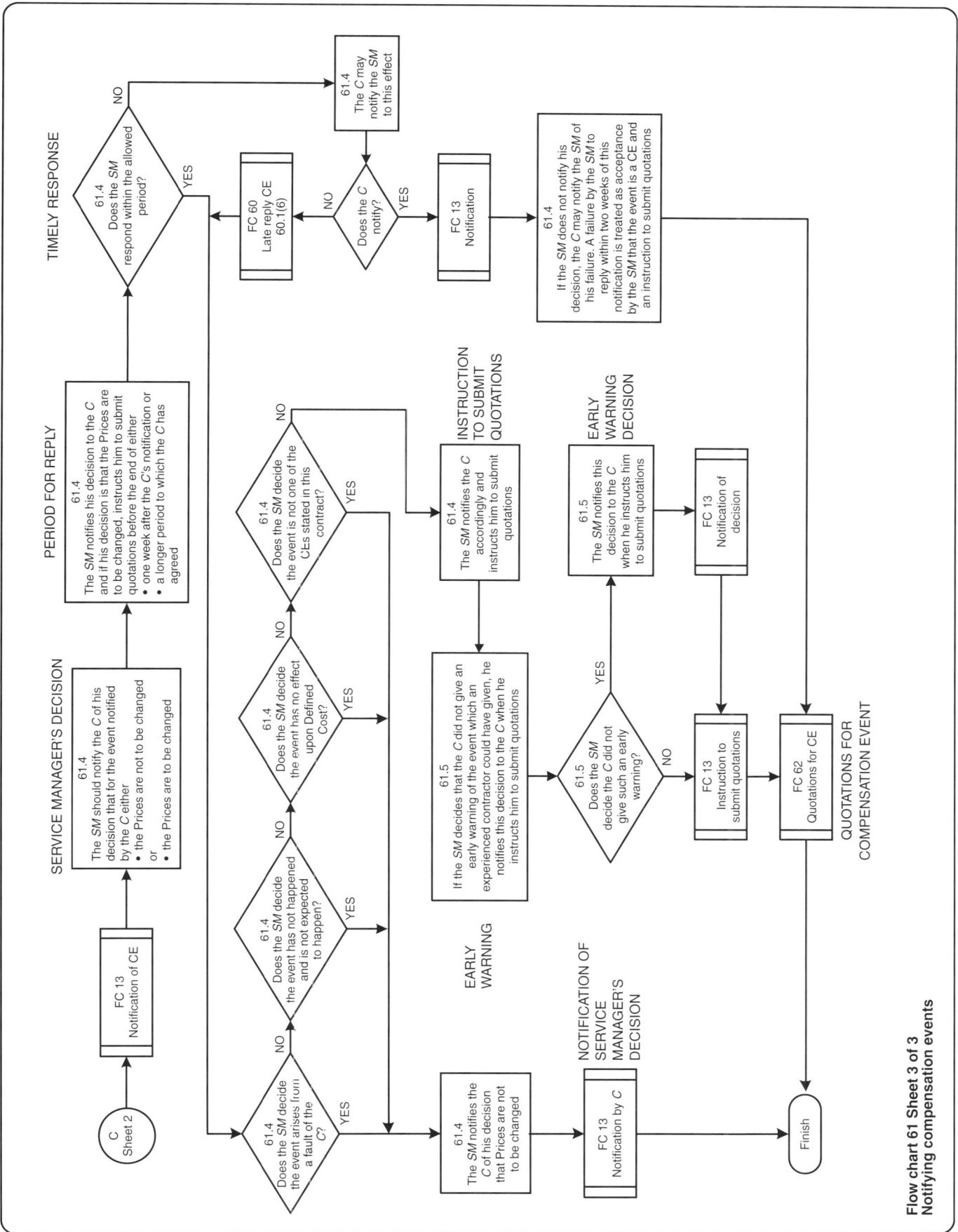

Flow chart 61 Sheet 3 of 3
Notifying compensation events

NEW QUOTATION?

Start

Has the *SM* instructed the *C* to submit quotations for a CE?
— YES / NO

EMPLOYER'S ALTERNATIVES

62.1
After discussing with the *C* different ways of dealing with the CE which are practicable, the *SM* may instruct the *C* to submit alternative quotations

CONTRACTOR'S ALTERNATIVES

62.1
The *C* submits the required quotations to the *SM* and may submit quotations for other methods of dealing with the CE which he considers practicable

FORM OF QUOTATION

62.2
Quotations for CE's comprise proposed changes to the Prices assessed by the *C*

Does Option X19 apply?
— YES / NO

FC X19
Providing the service by Task Order X19.11

CONTRACTOR'S SUBMISSION

62.2
The *C* submits details of his assessment with each quotation

PROGRAMME ALTERATIONS

62.2
Is the plan for remaining work altered by the CE?
— YES / NO

62.2
The *C* includes the alterations to the Accepted Plan in his quotation

CONTRACTOR'S ASSESSMENT

FC 63
Assessment of CE by *C*

PERIOD FOR SUBMISSION

62.3
The *C* submits quotations within three weeks of being instructed to do so by the *SM*

EXTENSION OF PERIOD

62.5
The *SM* extends the time allowed for
• the *C* to submit quotations for a CE and
• the *SM* to reply to a quotation

62.5
Does the *SM* and the *C* agree to extend the time allowed?
— YES / NO

62.5
The *SM* notifies the extension that has been agreed to *C*

FC 13
Notification

QUOTATION SUBMITTED

Has the *C* submitted a quotation to the *SM?*
— YES / NO

Finish

REVISED QUOTATION

FC 63
SM reviews *C's* assessment of CE

FC 13
C's submission

C
Sheet 2

REVIEW QUOTATION

62.3
Does the *C* submit quotations within the period for submission?
— NO / YES

B
Sheet 2

SERVICE MANAGER ASSESSES

SERVICE MANAGER'S REPLY

62.3
The *SM* replies within two weeks of the submission

EXTENSION OF PERIOD

62.5
The *SM* extends the time allowed for
• the *C* to submit quotations for a CE and
• the *SM* to reply to a quotation

62.5
Does the *SM* and the *C* agree to extend the time allowed?
— YES / NO

A
Sheet 2

SERVICE MANAGER REPLIES

62.5
The *SM* notifies the extension that has been agreed to the *C*

FC 13
Notification

Flow chart 62 Sheet 1 of 2
Quotations for compensation events

www.neccontract.com

TIMELY REPLY?

Does the *SM* reply within two weeks of this notification?

Is the quotation for a proposed CE?

NO

YES

NO

YES

WHICH QUOTATION APPLIES

62.6
If the *C* submitted more than one quotation for the CE, he states in his notification which quotation he proposes is to be accepted

IMPLEMENT COMPENSATION EVENT

FC 65
Implementing CEs

LATE OR NO REPLY GIVEN

62.6
If the *SM* does not reply to a quotation within the time allowed, the *C* may notify the *SM* of his failure

FC 13
C notifies to this effect

ACCEPTANCE DEFAULTS TO CONTRACTOR'S QUOTATION

62.6
If the *SM* does not reply to the notification within two weeks, and unless the quotation is for a proposed instruction or a proposed changed decision, the *C*'s notification is treated as acceptance of the quotation by the *SM*

SERVICE MANAGER ASSESSES

FC 64
SM assesses CE

B
Sheet 1

Finish

RE-SUBMISSION PERIOD

62.4
The *C* submits the revised quotation within three weeks of being instructed to do so

C
Sheet 1

RE-SUBMIT

FC 13
SM's instruction

REVISE QUOTATION

The *C* revises his quotation

FC 13
SM's instruction

TIMELY REPLY?

62.3
Does the *SM* reply within the period for his reply to the *C*'s submission?

How does the *SM* reply?

NO

YES

SERVICE MANAGER'S REPLY

ACCEPTANCE OF QUOTATION

62.3
The *SM*'s reply is an acceptance of a quotation

SERVICE MANAGER'S ASSESSMENT

62.3
The *SM*'s reply is a notification that he will be making his own assessment

FC 13
SM's Notification

PROPOSAL NOT ACCEPTABLE

62.3
The *SM*'s reply is a notification that a proposed instruction will not be given or a proposed changed decision will not be made

FC 13
SM's Notification

REVISED QUOTATION

62.3
The *SM*'s reply is an instruction to submit a revised quotation

REASON GIVEN

62.4
The *SM* instructs the *C* to submit a revised quotation only after explaining his reason for doing so to the *C*

62.5
Does the *SM* and the *C* agree to extend the time allowed?

YES

NO

62.5
The *SM* notifies the extension that has been agreed to the *C*

EXTENSION OF PERIOD FOR RE-SUBMISSION

62.5
The *SM* extends the time allowed for
• the *C* to submit quotations for a CE and
• the *SM* to reply to a quotation

A
Sheet 1

SERVICE MANAGER REPLIES

Flow chart 62 Sheet 2 of 2
Quotations for compensation events

Flow chart 63 Sheet 1 of 3
Assessing compensation events

COMPENSATION EVENT IS TO BE ASSESSED

Start → A CE is to be assessed

PRICE REDUCTIONS

63.4
If the effect of a CE is to reduce the total Defined Cost, the Prices are not reduced except as stated in this contract

RIGHTS TO CHANGE PRICE ETC

63.5
The rights of the E and the C to changes to the Prices are their only rights in respect of a CE

RISK ALLOWANCES

63.7
Assessment of the effect of a CE includes risk allowances for cost for matters which have a significant chance of occurring and are at the C's risk under this contract

EARLY WARNING

61.5 and 63.6
The SM notifies the C of his decision that the C did not give an early warning of the CE which an experienced contractor could have given

WARNING GIVEN?

63.6
Has the SM notified the C that the C did not give such early warning?

- NO →
- YES → 63.6 The CE is assessed as if the C had given early warning

What main Option applies?

- A or C → FC 54 Price List
- E → Is there a Price List?
  - YES → FC 54 Price List
  - NO →

CHANGES TO THE PRICES

63.2
For other CEs, the changes to the Prices are assessed as the effect of the CE upon
- the actual Defined Cost of the work already done,
- the forecast Defined Cost of the work not yet done and
- the resulting Fee

WORK DONE DEFINED

63.2
If the CE arose from the SM giving an instruction, changing an earlier decision or correcting an assumption, the date which divides the work already done from the work not yet done is the date of that communication

63.2
In all other cases, the date is the date of the notification of the CE

COMPETENT REACTION

63.8
Assessments are based upon the assumptions that the C reacts competently and promptly to the CE, that any Defined Cost due to the event is reasonably incurred and that the Accepted Plan can be changed

CHANGES TO THE PRICES

63.1
Does the CE only affect the quantities of work shown in the Price List?

- YES → 63.1 For a CE which only affects the quantities of work shown in the Price List, the change to the Prices is assessed by multiplying the changed quantities of work by the appropriate rates in the Price List
- NO → 63.3 If the SM and the C agree, rates and Prices in the Price List may be used as a basis for assessment instead of Defined Cost and the resulting Fee

Do the SM and the C agree?

- YES → 63.3 Rates and Prices in the Price List are used

CHANGES TO THE PRICES

- NO →

CALCULATION FOR QUOTATION

63.2
Effects on Defined Cost are assessed separately for
- people who are employed by the C,
- P&M
- work subcontracted by the C and
- Equipment

63.2
The C shows how each of these effects is built up in each quotation for a CE

FC 62 Quotation for CE

A Sheet 2

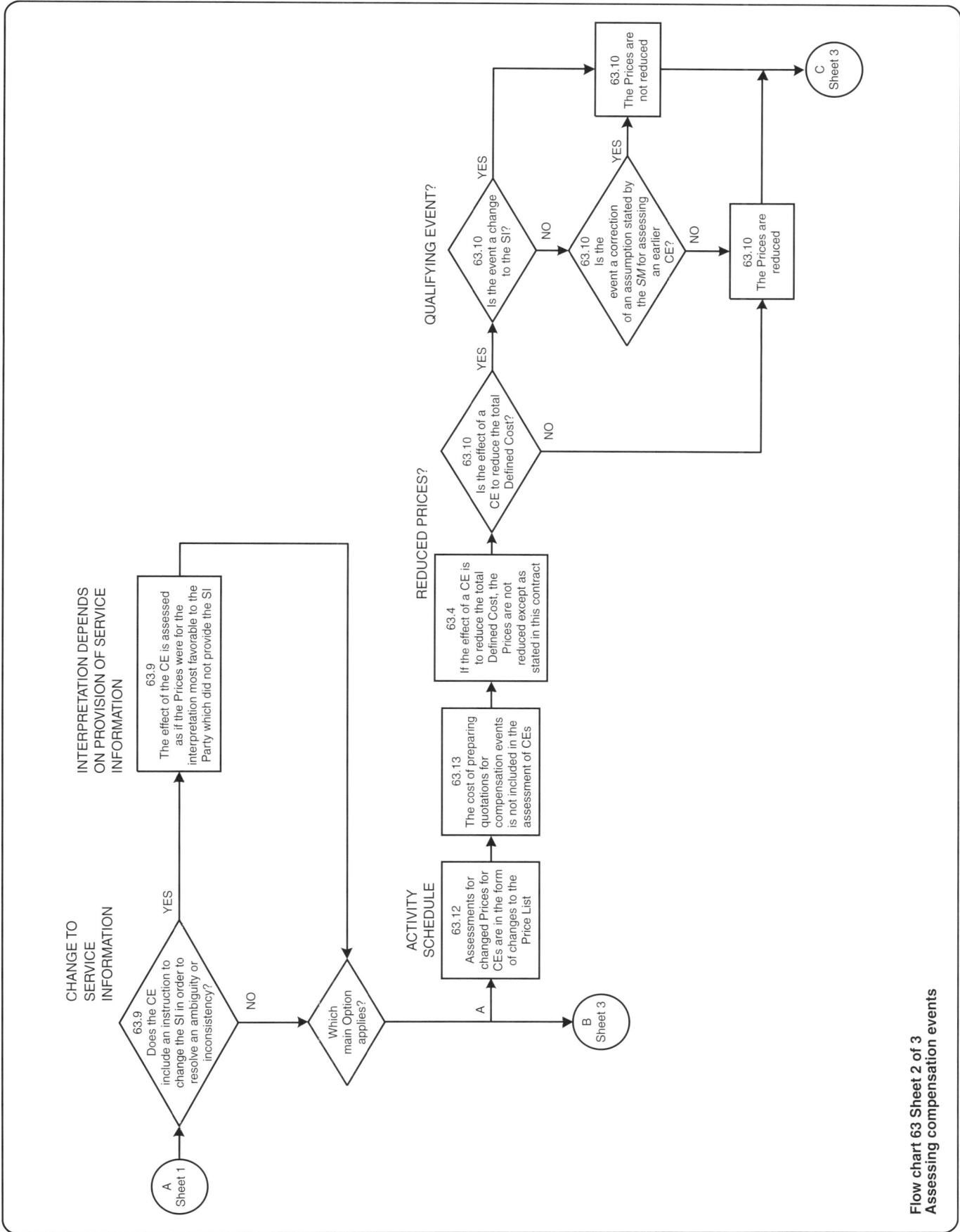

CHANGE TO
SERVICE
INFORMATION

63.9
Does the CE
include an instruction to
change the SI in order to
resolve an ambiguity or
inconsistency?

YES

INTERPRETATION DEPENDS
ON PROVISION OF SERVICE
INFORMATION

63.9
The effect of the CE is assessed
as if the Prices were for the
interpretation most favorable to the
Party which did not provide the SI

NO

Which
main Option
applies?

QUALIFYING EVENT?

63.10
Is the event a change
to the SI?

YES

63.10
The Prices are
not reduced

NO

63.10
Is the
event a correction
of an assumption stated by
the SM for assessing
an earlier
CE?

YES

NO

63.10
The Prices are
reduced

REDUCED PRICES?

63.10
Is the effect of a
CE to reduce the total
Defined Cost?

YES

NO

ACTIVITY
SCHEDULE

63.4
If the effect of a CE is
to reduce the total
Defined Cost, the
Prices are not
reduced except as
stated in this contract

63.13
The cost of preparing
quotations for
compensation events
is not included in the
assessment of CEs

63.12
Assessments for
changed Prices for
CEs are in the form
of changes to the
Price List

A

B
Sheet 3

A
Sheet 1

C
Sheet 3

**Flow chart 63 Sheet 2 of 3
Assessing compensation events**

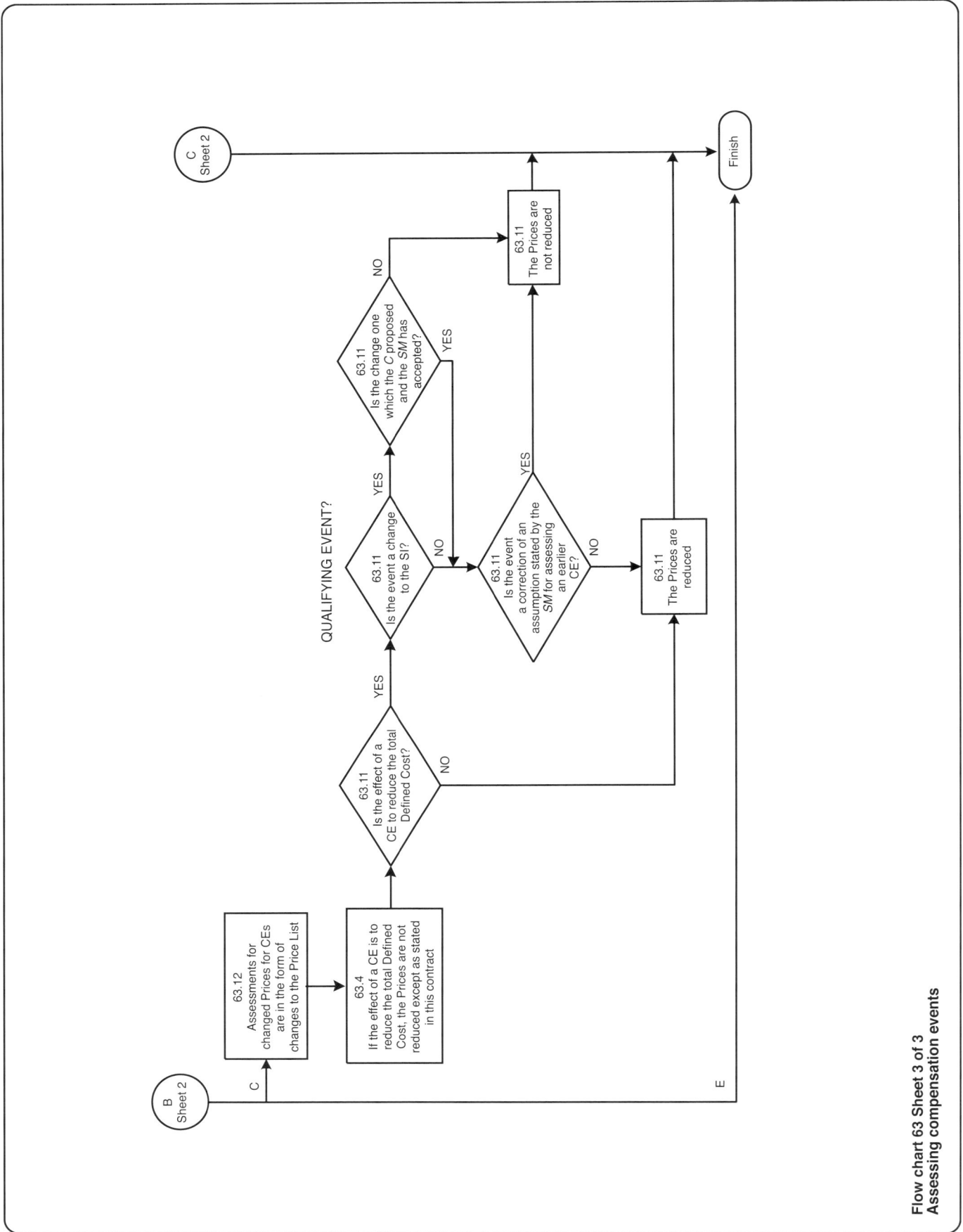

Flow chart 63 Sheet 3 of 3
Assessing compensation events

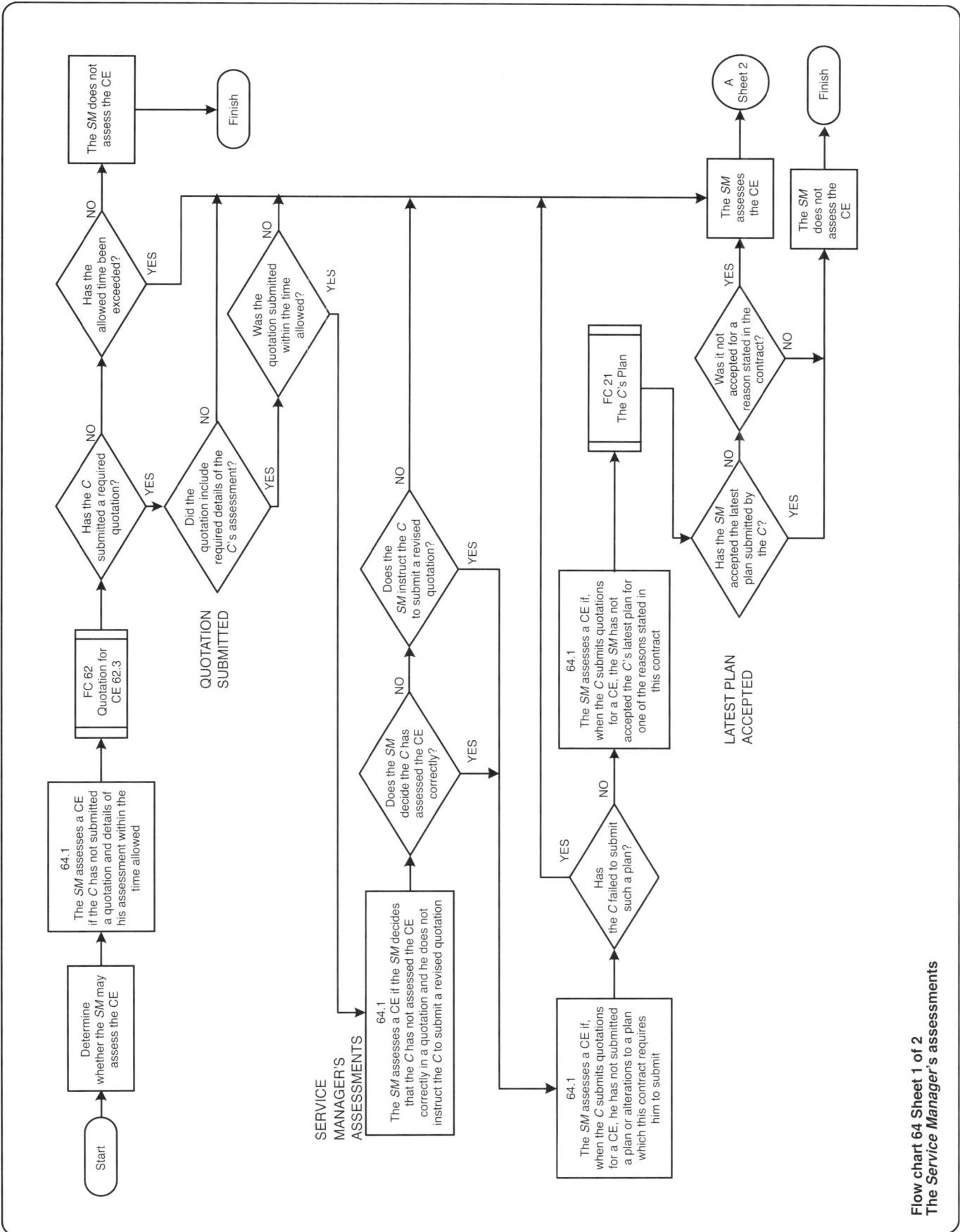

Flow chart 64 Sheet 1 of 2
The *Service Manager*'s assessments

SERVICE
MANAGER'S
ASSESSMENTS

QUOTATION
SUBMITTED

LATEST PLAN
ACCEPTED

ASSESSMENT

A
Sheet 1

FC 63
Assessing CEs

SERVICE MANAGER'S NOTIFICATION

64.2
The *SM* notifies the *C* of his assessment of a CE and gives him details of it within the period allowed for the *C*'s submission of his quotation for the same event

64.2
The period starts when the need for *SM*'s assessment becomes apparent

64.3
If the *SM* does not assess the a CE within the time allowed, the *C* may notify the *SM* of his failure

TIMELY ASSESSMENT?

64.3
Does the *SM* assess the CE within the time allowed?

NO

YES

WHICH QUOTATION TO BE ACCEPTED

FC 13
C notifies to this effect

64.3
If the *C* submitted more than one quotation for the CE, he states in his notification which quotation he proposes to be accepted

TIMELY REPLY?

64.3
Does the *SM* reply within two weeks of this notification?

NO

YES

SERVICE MANAGER NOTIFIES

FC 13
Notification

ACCEPTANCE DEFAULTS TO CONTRACTOR'S QUOTATION

64.3
The *C*'s notification is treated as an acceptance of the *C*'s quotation by the *SM*

Finish

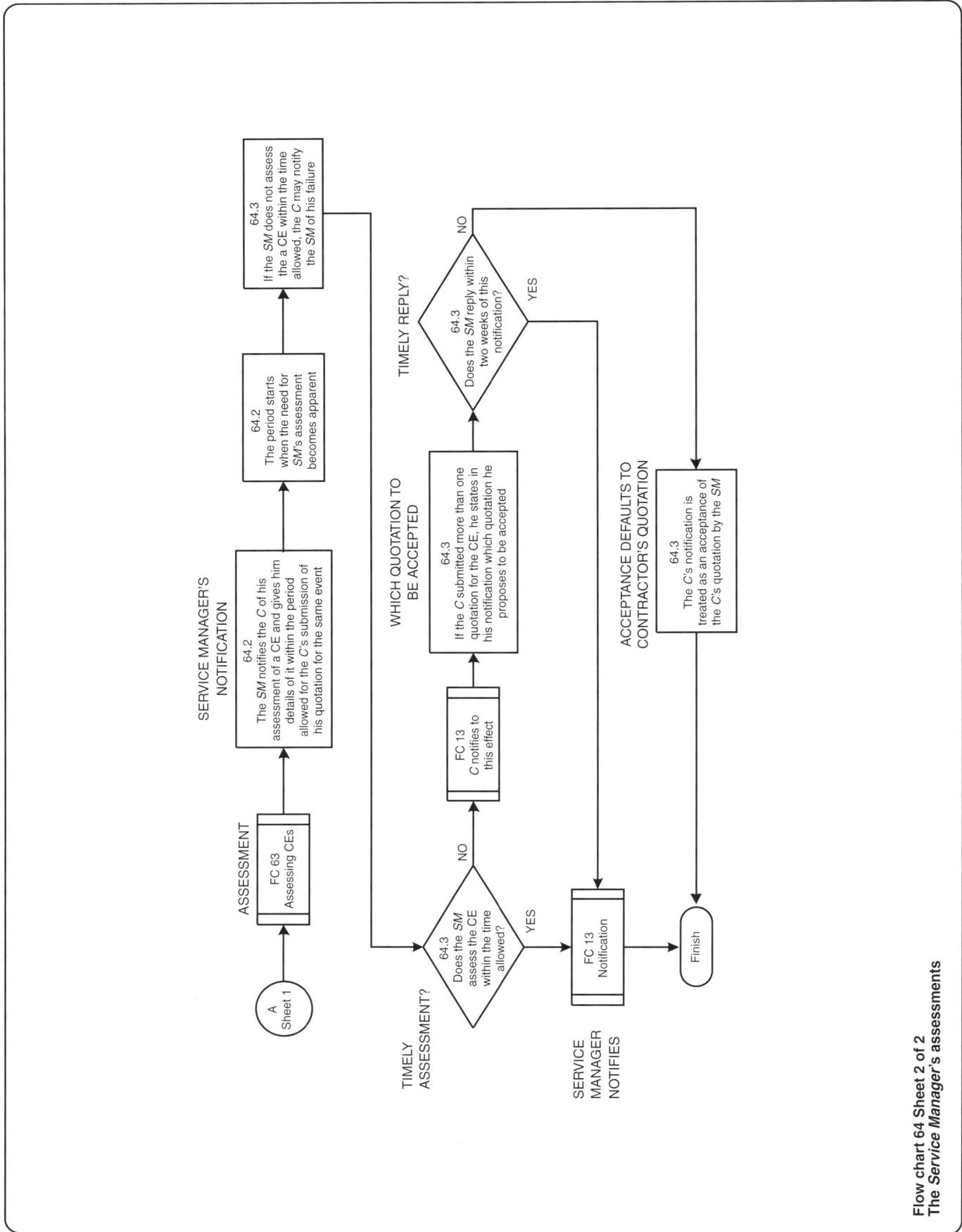

Flow chart 64 Sheet 2 of 2
The *Service Manager*'s assessments

TIMING OF IMPLEMENTATION

Start

A CE is to be implemented

65.1
Has the *SM* notified the *C* of the quotation which he has accepted?

NO →

YES ↓

NOTIFICATION OF CONTRACTOR'S QUOTATION ACCEPTED

65.1
The *SM* implements the CE by notifying the *C* of the quotation which has been accepted

65.1
A compensation event is implemented when
- the *SM* notifies his acceptance of the *C*'s quotation,
- the *SM* notifies the *C* of his own assessment or
- a *C*'s quotation is treated as having been accepted by the *SM*

65.2
The assessment of a CE is not revised if a forecast upon which it is based is shown by later recorded information to have been wrong

ASSESSMENT NOT REVISED

65.1
Has the *SM* notified the *C* of his own assessment of the CE?

NO →

YES ↓

NOTICE OF SERVICE MANAGER'S OWN ASSESSMENT

65.1
The *SM* implements the CE by notifying the *C* of his own assessment

65.1
Has the *C*'s quotation been treated as having been accepted by the *SM*?

NO →

YES ↓

CONTRACTOR'S QUOTATION TREATED AS ACCEPTED

FC 62
Quotation for CE
62.6

Which main Option applies?

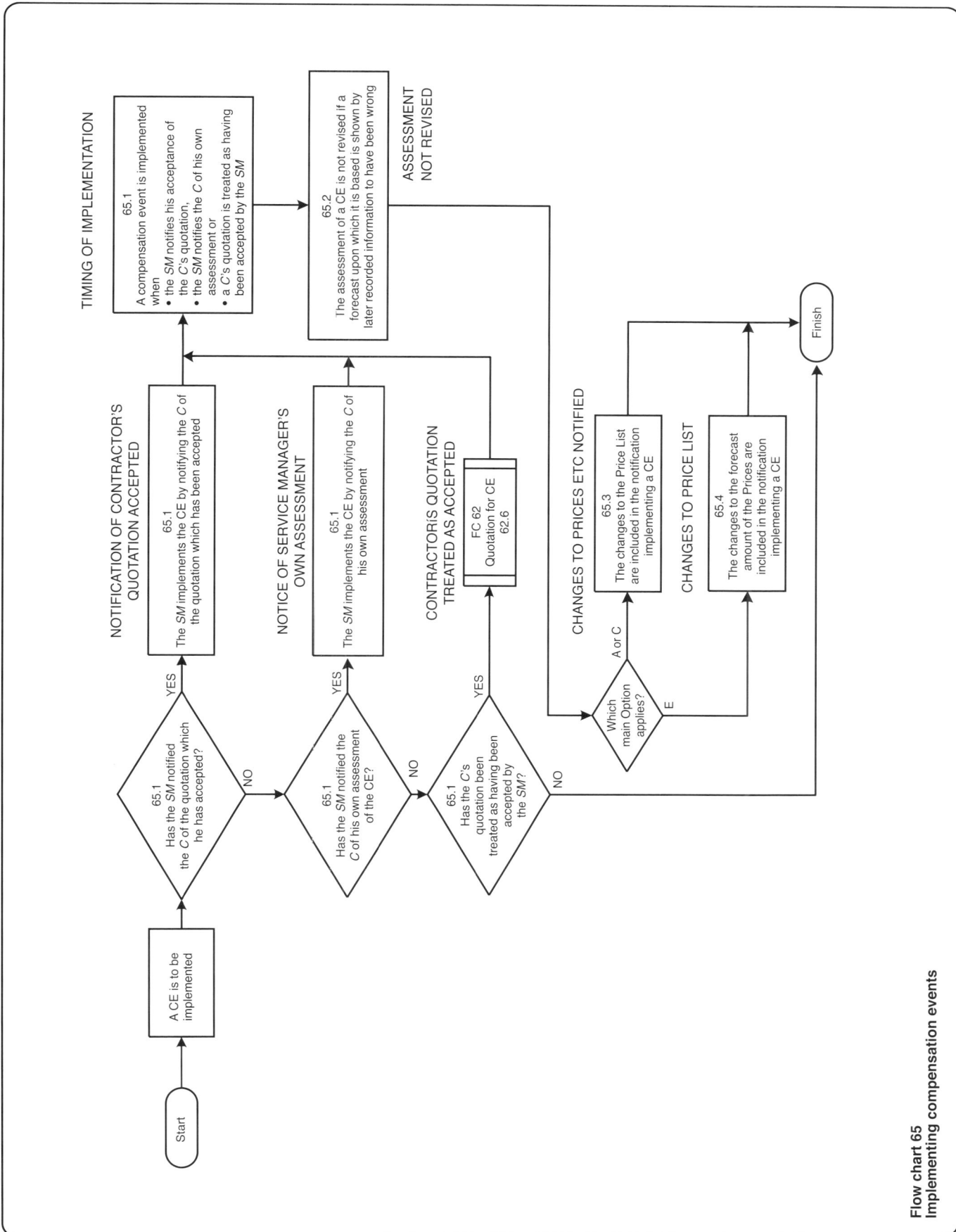

A or C →

E ↓

CHANGES TO PRICES ETC NOTIFIED

65.3
The changes to the Price List are included in the notification implementing a CE

CHANGES TO PRICE LIST

65.4
The changes to the forecast amount of the Prices are included in the notification implementing a CE

Finish

Flow chart 65
Implementing compensation events

THE CONTRACTOR'S RIGHT TO USE THE EMPLOYER'S EQUIPMENT PLANT AND MATERIALS

Start

The E provides equipment, P&M

11.2(11)
P&M are items intended to be included in the Affected Property

Does the C want to use this to Provide the Service?

YES

70.1
The C has the right to use the equipment, P&M provided by the E only to Provide the Service

NO

70.1
The C does not have the right to use this equipment, P&M

Is it the end of the service period?

NO

YES

70.2
At the end of the service period the C returns to the E, equipment and surplus P&M provided by the E

EMPLOYER'S PLANT AND MATERIALS

70.2
Does the SI state any Equipment is required for the E's use?

NO

YES

70.2
At the end of the service period the C provides items of Equipment for the E's use as stated in the SI

PROVISION OF CONTRACTOR'S EQUIPMENT

70.2
Does the SI state any information or other things are to be provided?

NO

YES

70.2
At the end of the service period the C provides information and other things as stated in the SI

PROVISION OF INFORMATION AND OTHER THINGS

Finish

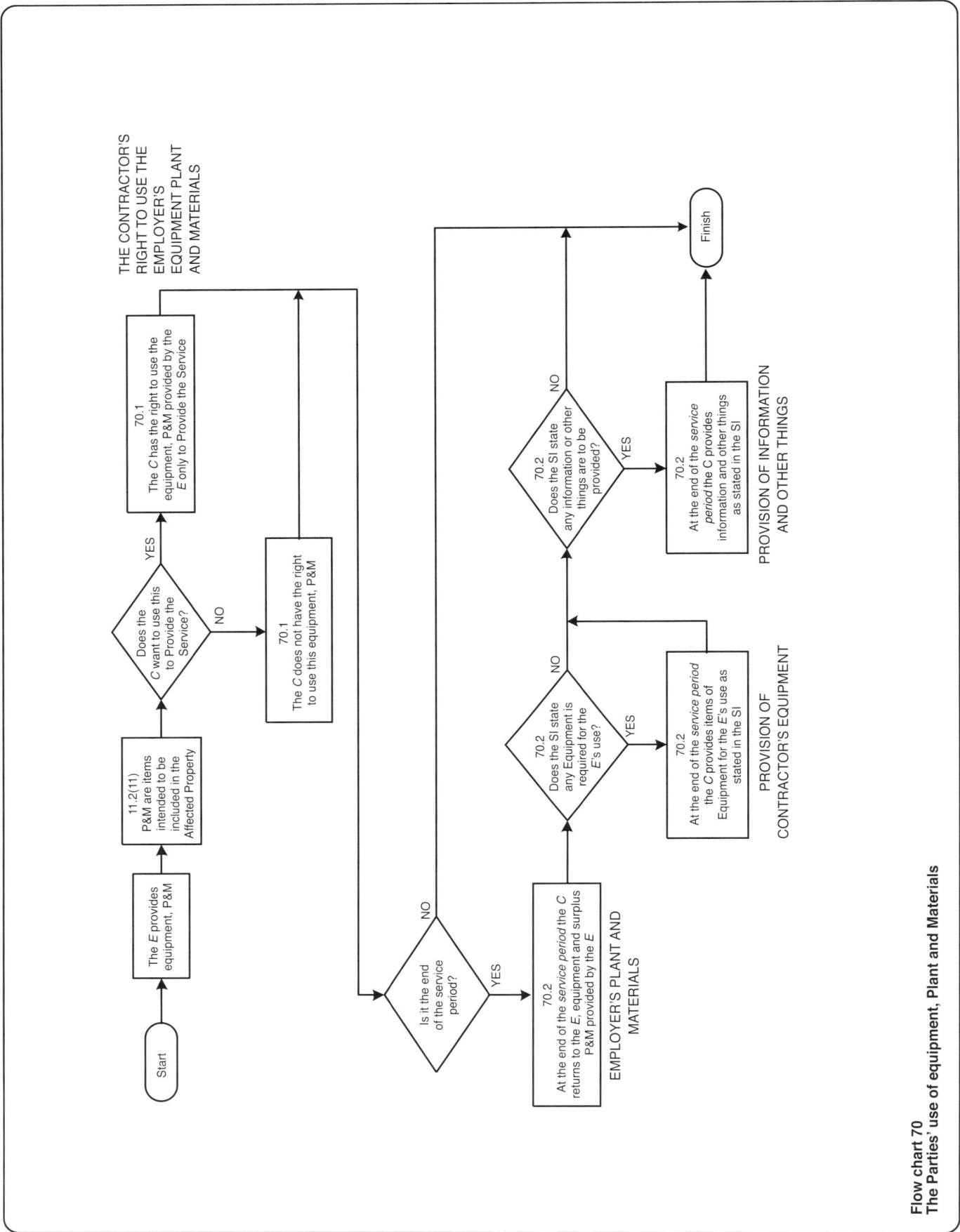

Flow chart 70
The Parties' use of equipment, Plant and Materials

Start

Determine whether the *E* bears the risk of an event

What type of event?

CLAIMS, PROCEEDINGS, ETC

80.1
Claims, proceedings, compensation and costs payable which are

due to?

DUE TO PROVIDING THE SERVICE

80.1
the unavoidable result of the *service* or of Providing the Service

DUE TO NEGLIGENCE ETC

80.1
negligence, breach of statutory duty or interference with any legal right by the *E* or by any person employed or contracted to him except the *C*

DUE TO EMPLOYER'S FAULT

80.1
a fault of the *E* or a fault of his design

DUE TO ANOTHER REASON

EMPLOYER'S RISK

The event is at *E*'s risk

Finish

NOT EMPLOYER'S RISK

The event is not at *E*'s risk

A
Sheet 2

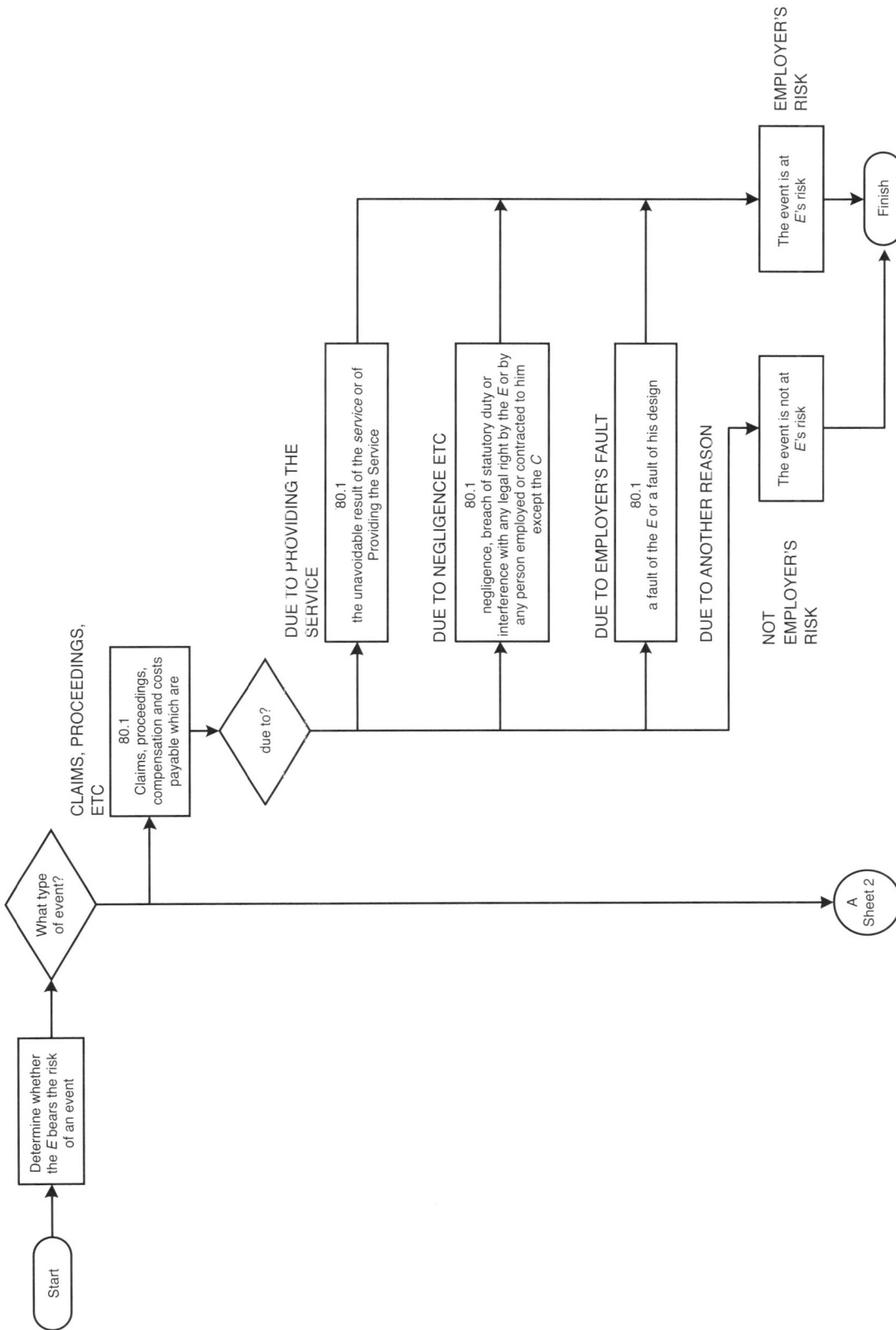

Flow chart 80 Sheet 1 of 3
Employer's risks

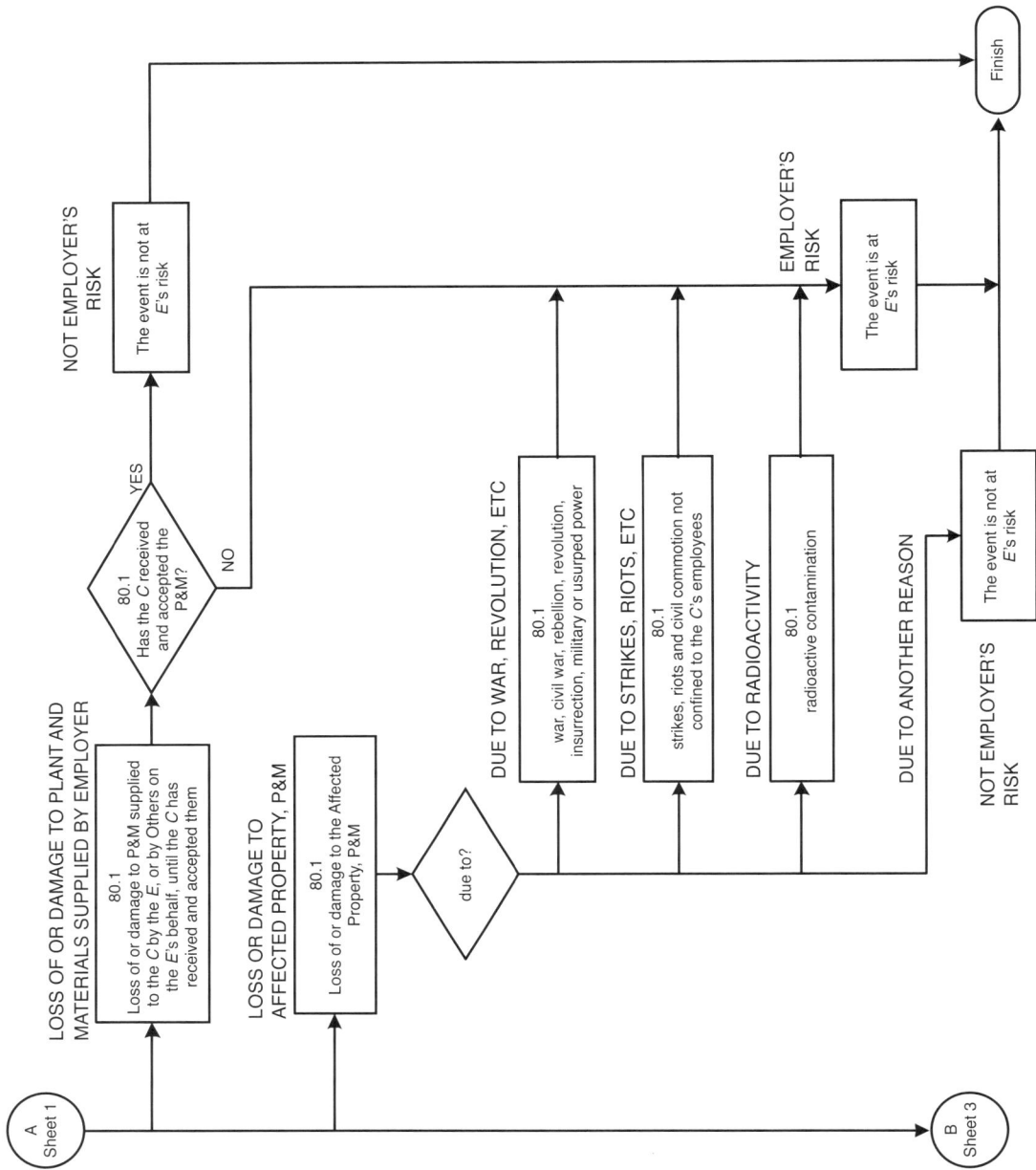

Flow chart 80 Sheet 2 of 3
Employer's risks

LOSS ETC AFTER TERMINATION

B
Sheet 2

80.1
Loss of or wear or damage to any Equipment, P&M retained by the *E* after a termination, except loss, wear or damage due to the activities of the *C* after the termination

OTHER EMPLOYER'S RISK

Other *E*'s risks stated in the CD

NONE OF THE ABOVE APPLY

EMPLOYER'S RISK

The event is at *E*'s risk

NOT EMPLOYER'S RISK

The event is not at *E*'s risk

Finish

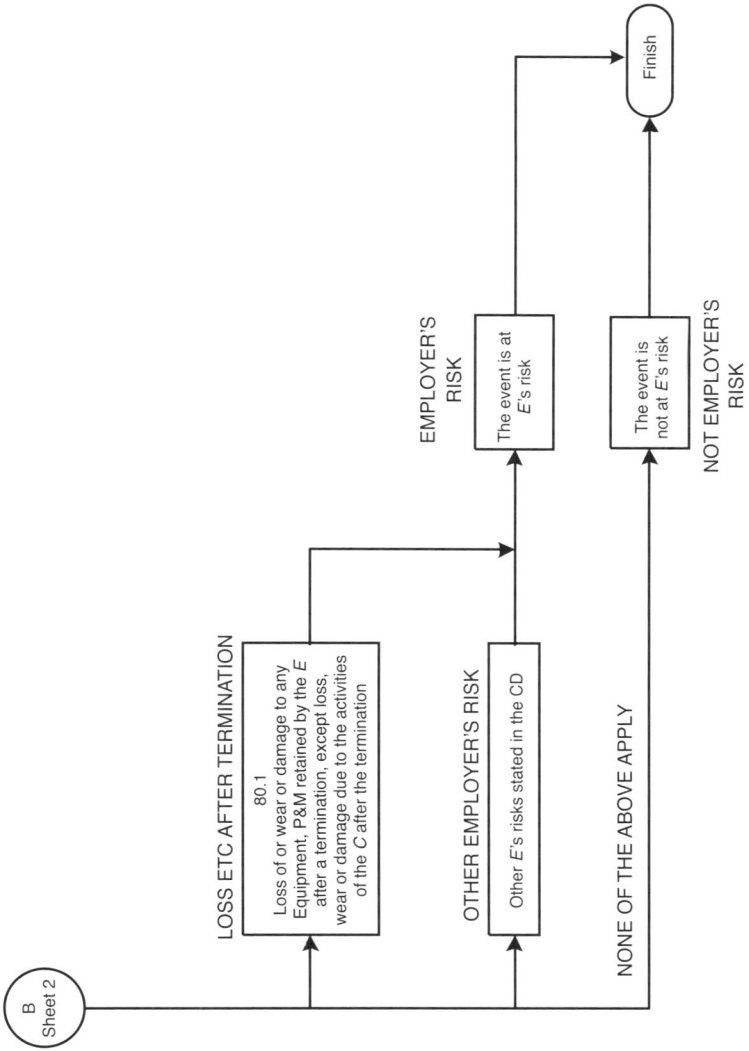

Flow chart 80 Sheet 3 of 3
Employer's risks

BEFORE STARTING DATE

Start

Determine whether the *C* bears the risks of an event

The *starting date* is stated in the CD

81.1
Did the event occur before the *starting date?*

YES

NO

The *service period* is stated in the CD

BEFORE SERVICE PERIOD?

81.1
Did the event occur before the *service period* has ended?

NO

YES

EMPLOYER'S RISK?

FC 80
E's risks

81.1
Is the event a risk carried by the *E*?

YES

NO

NOT A CONTRACTOR'S RISK

Event is not a *C*'s risk

Finish

CONTRACTOR'S RISK

81.1
From the starting date until the end of the *service period* , the risks which are not carried by the *E* are carried by the *C*

Event is a *C*'s risk

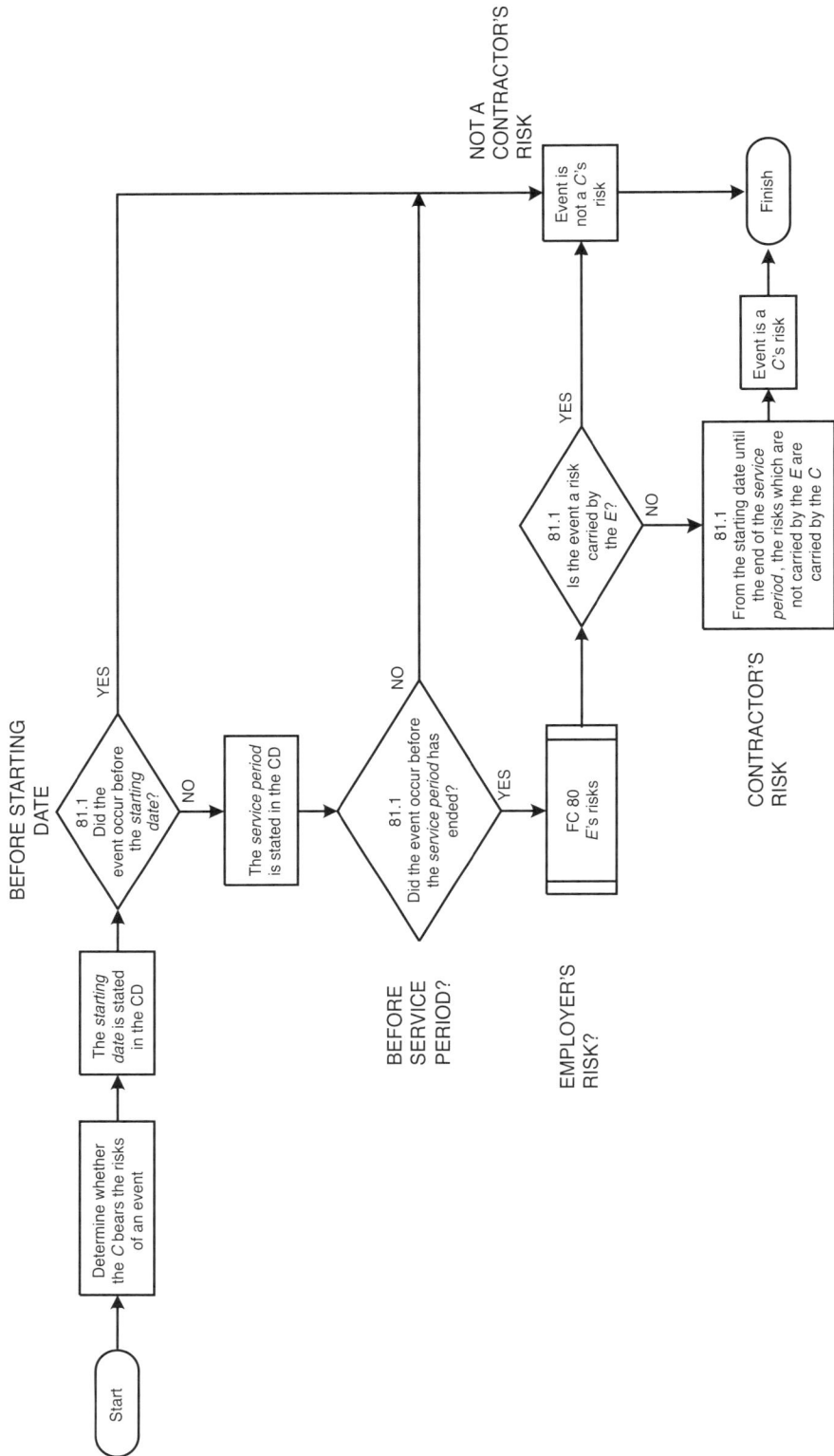

Flow chart 81
Contractor's **risks**

THE PARTIES

11.2(10)
The Parties are
the *E* and the *C*

INDEMNITY

82.1
Each Party indemnifies the other
against claims, proceedings,
compensation and costs due to
an event which is at his risk

SUCH EVENT?

82.1
Has such an event
occurred?

NO

YES

An event occurs for
which the first party
believes the other party
provides an indemnity

ESTABLISH
EVENT RISK

FC 80
Employer's risk

FC 81
Contractor's risk

INDEMNITY PROVIDED

82.1
Each Party indemnifies the other
against claims, proceedings,
compensation and costs due to an
event which is at his risk

CONTRIBUTING EVENT?

82.2
The liability of each Party to indemnify
the other is reduced if events at the
other Party's risk contributed to the
claims, proceedings, compensation
and costs

Are
there any
contributing
events?

NO

YES

CONTRIBUTING
EVENT RISKS

FC 80
Employer's risk

FC 81
Contractor's risk

Are any
contributing events
at the other Party's
risk?

YES

NO

82.2
The liability of each Party to indemnify
the other is reduced in proportion to
the extent that events which were at
the other Party's risk contributed,
taking into account each Party's
responsibilities under this contract

LIABILITY REDUCED
PROPORTIONATELY

Start

Finish

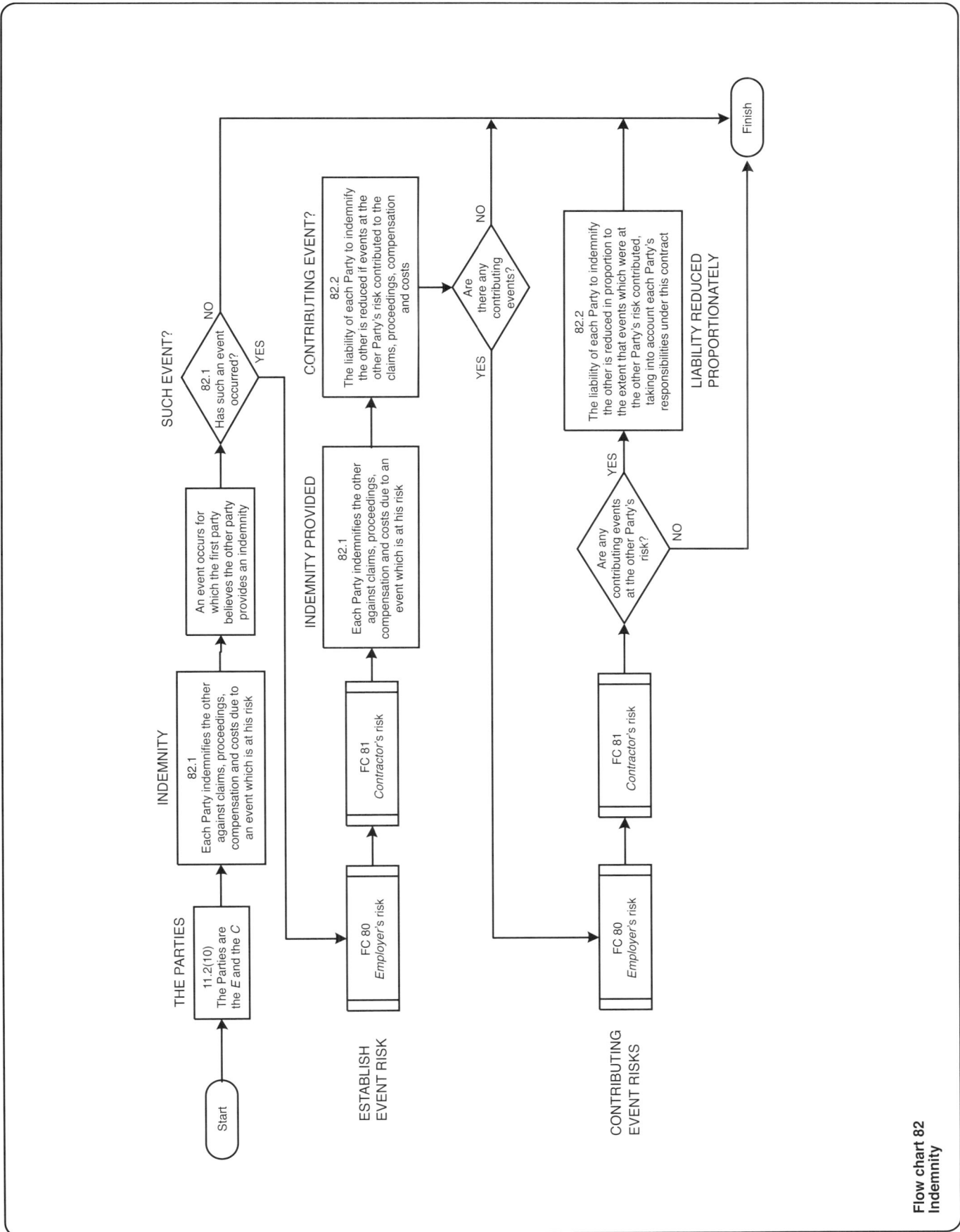

Flow chart 82
Indemnity

INSURANCE TABLE

Insurance against	Minimum amount of cover or minimum level of indemnity
Loss of or damage caused by the C to the E's property	The amount stated in the CD
Loss of or damage to P&M	The replacement cost, including the amount stated in the CD for the replacement of any P&M provided by the E
Loss of or damage to the Equipment	The replacement cost
The C's liability for loss of or damage to property (except the E's property, P&M and Equipment) and liability for bodily injury to or death of a person (not an employee of the C) arising from or in connection with the C's Providing the Service	The amount stated in the CD for any one event with cross liability so that the insurance applies to the Parties separately
Liability for death of or bodily injury to employees of the C arising out of and in the course of their employment in connection with this contract	The greater of the amount required by the applicable law and the amount stated in the CD for any one event

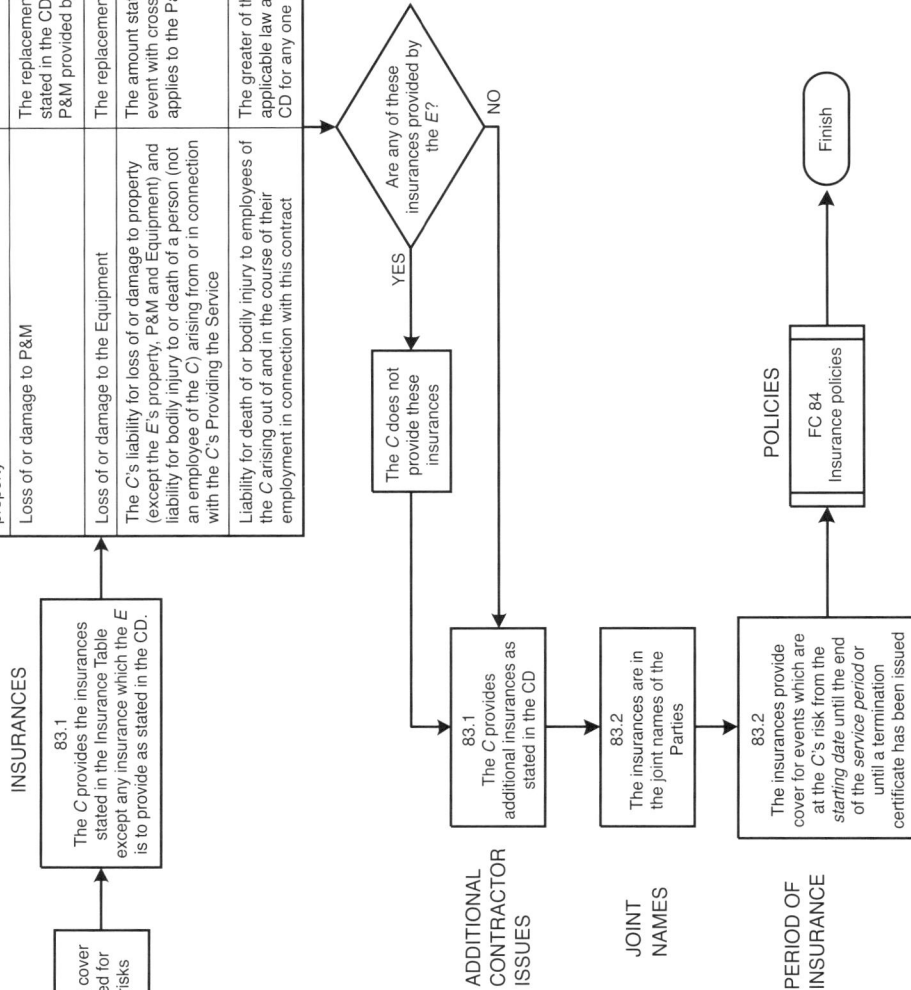

INSURANCES

Start

Insurance cover is provided for certain risks

83.1 The C provides the insurances stated in the Insurance Table except any insurance which the E is to provide as stated in the CD.

Are any of these insurances provided by the E?

YES — NO

The C does not provide these insurances

ADDITIONAL CONTRACTOR ISSUES

83.1 The C provides additional insurances as stated in the CD

JOINT NAMES

83.2 The insurances are in the joint names of the Parties

PERIOD OF INSURANCE

83.2 The insurances provide cover for events which are at the C's risk from the starting date until the end of the service period or until a termination certificate has been issued

POLICIES

FC 84 Insurance policies

Finish

Flow chart 83
Insurance cover

INSURANCE POLICY TO BE EFFECTED

Start

Is an insurance policy to be effected?

NO →

YES ↓

84.2
Insurance policies include a waiver by the insurers of their subrogation rights against directors and other employees of every insured except where there is fraud

84.3
The Parties comply with the terms and conditions of the insurance policies

COMPLIANCE WITH TERMS AND CONDITIONS OF INSURANCE POLICIES

FC 83
Insurance cover

INSURANCE COVER

BY WHOM?

Which Party is responsible for effecting this insurance?

E →
FC 86
Insurance by the E

C ↓

The *starting date* is stated in the CD

84.1
Before the *starting date* and on each renewal of the insurance policy, the C submits to the SM for acceptance certificates which state that the insurance required by this contract is in force.

CONTRACTOR SUBMITS POLICIES FOR ACCEPTANCE

84.1
The certificates are signed by the C's insurer or insurance broker.

84.1
A reason for not accepting the certificates is that they do not comply with this contract

REASON FOR NOT ACCEPTING

Does the C submit?

YES →
FC 13
Submission by C

Is the C's submission accepted?

YES →

NO ↓

NO →
FC 85
If the C does not insure

AMOUNT NOT RECOVERED FROM AN INSURER

Has an amount been recovered from an insurer?

YES ↓

NO →

84.4
Identify whether this is in respect of an event which is at the E's risk or at the C's risk

RISK RESPONSIBILITY

FC 80
Employer's risk

EMPLOYER'S RISK

FC 81
Contractor's risk

CONTRACTOR'S RISK

WHOSE RISK?

Which Party carries the risk?

E →
BORNE BY EMPLOYER
84.4
Any amount not recovered from an insurer is borne by the E for events which are at his risk

C →
BORNE BY CONTRACTOR
84.4
Any amount not recovered from an insurer is borne by the C for events which are at his risk

Finish

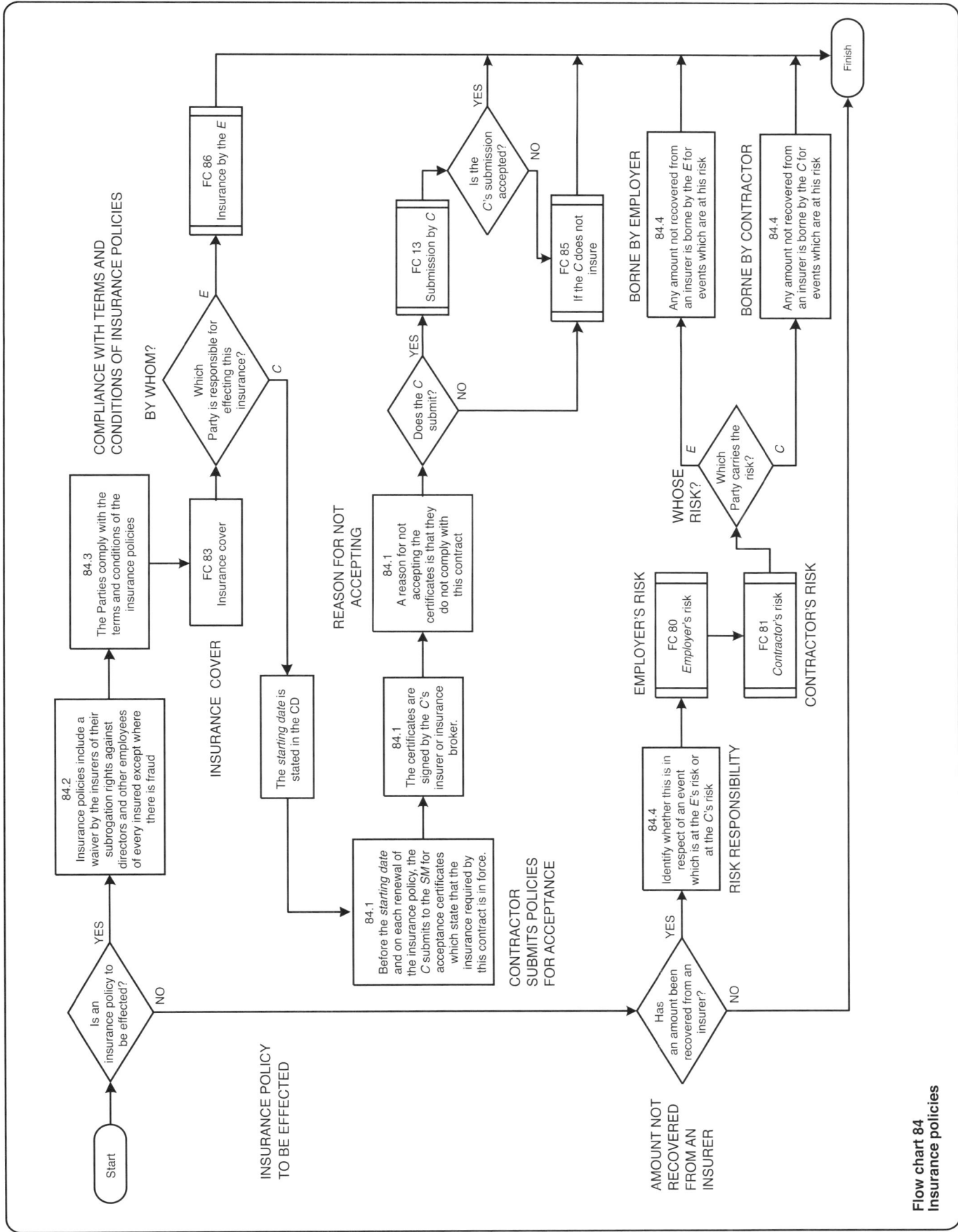

Flow chart 84
Insurance policies

INSURANCE CERTIFICATE
NOT SUBMITTED

Start

85.1
The C has not submitted
a required certificate

85.1
Does the E decide to
insure the risk which
the C should have
insured?

NO

Risk is not
insured

YES

EMPLOYER TAKES OUT INSURANCE

85.1
The E may insure a risk which this contract
requires the C to insure if the C does not
submit a required policy or certificate

85.1
The cost of this
insurance to the E is paid
by the C

FC 50
Assessing the
amount due

Finish

COST OF INSURANCE PAID BY CONTRACTOR

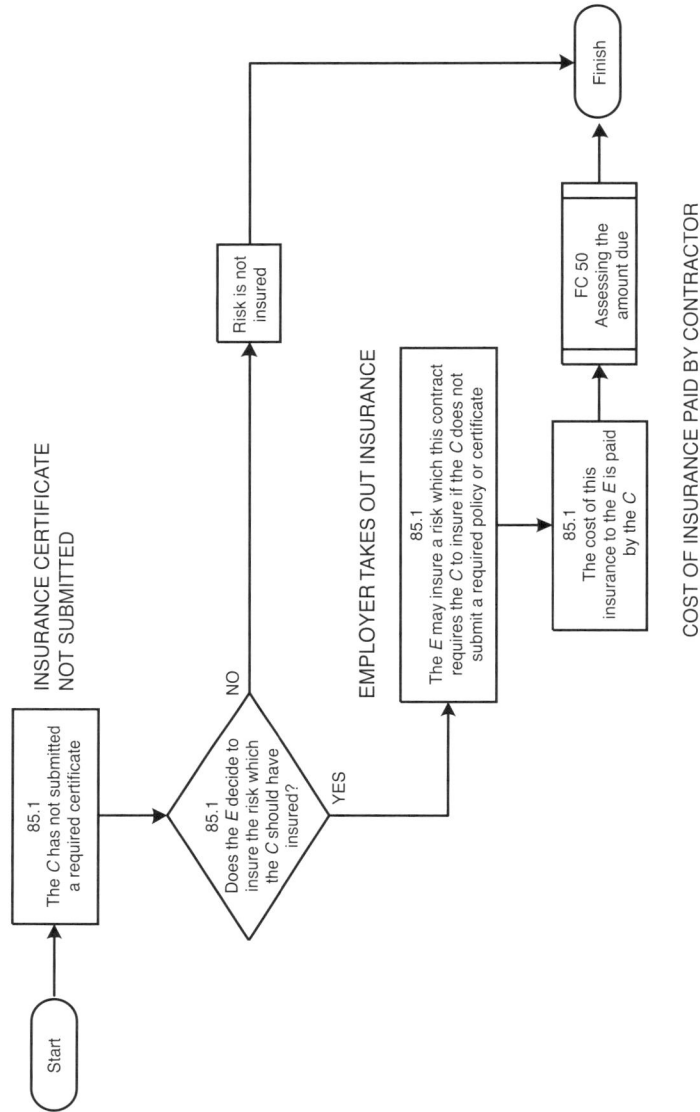

Flow chart 85
If the Contractor does not insure

EMPLOYER INSURANCES

Start

83.1
The *E* is to provide insurances as stated in the CD

POLICIES AND CERTIFICATES SUBMITTED

86.1
The *SM* submits policies and certificates for insurances provided by the *E* to the *C* for acceptance before the *starting date* and afterwards as the *C* instructs

ACCEPTANCE BY CONTRACTOR

86.1
The *C* accepts the policies and certificates if they comply with this contract

EMPLOYER'S RESPONSIBILITY TO INSURE

86.2
The *C*'s acceptance of an insurance policy or certificate provided by the *E* does not change the responsibility of the *E* to provide the insurances stated in the CD

86.3
Have the required policies or certificates been submitted to the *C*?

YES

NO

86.3
Does the *C* decide to insure the risk which the *E* should have insured?

NO

Risk is not insured

YES

CONTRACTOR TAKES OUT INSURANCE

86.3
The *C* may insure a risk which this contract requires the *E* to insure if the *E* does not submit a required policy or certificate

COST OF INSURANCE PAID BY EMPLOYER

86.3
The cost of this insurance to the *C* is paid by the *E*

FC 50
Assessing the amount due

Finish

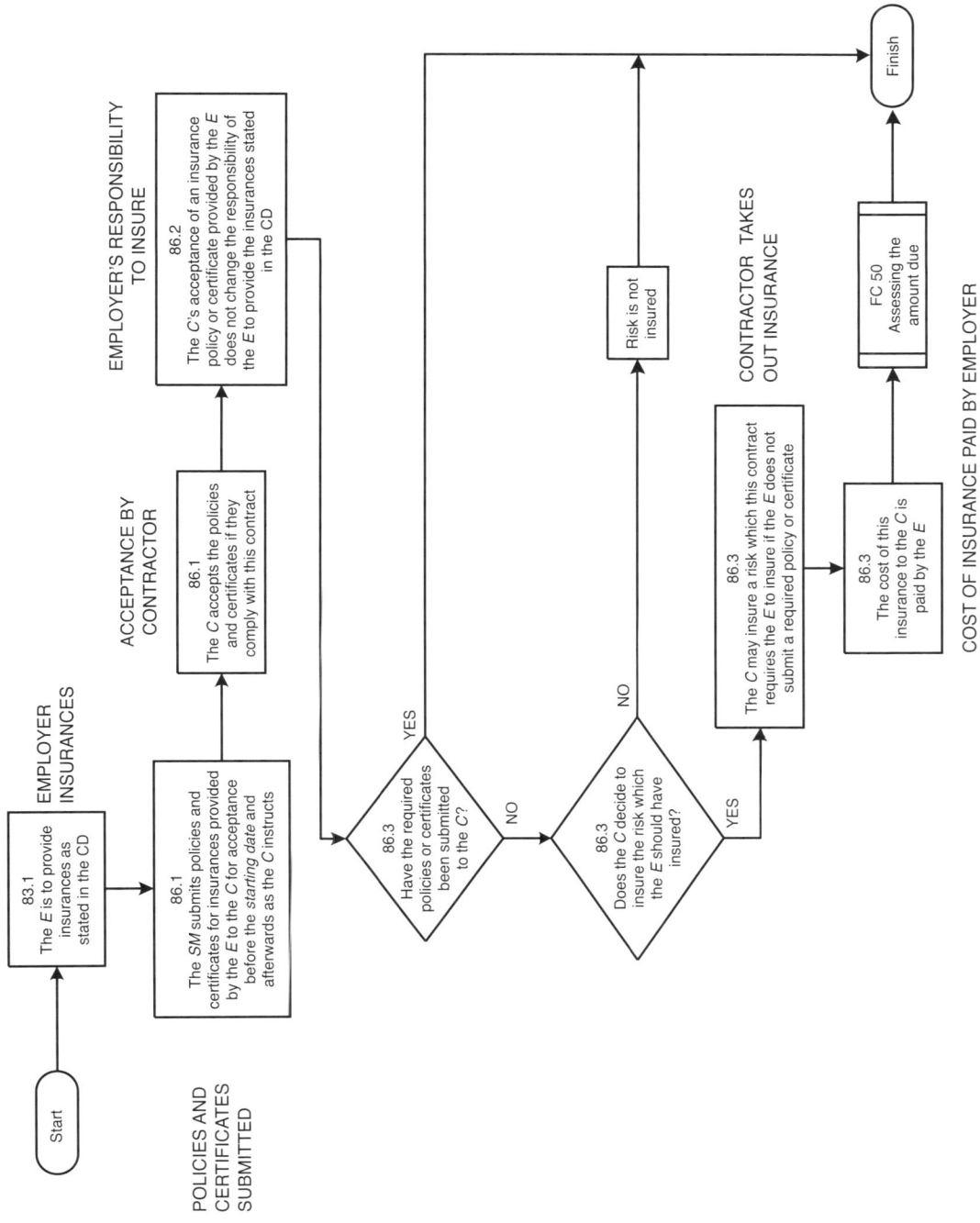

Flow chart 86
Insurance by the *Employer*

PARTY WISHES TO TERMINATE

90.1
If either Party wishes to terminate the C's obligation to Provide the Service, he notifies the SM and the other Party giving details of his reason for terminating

NOTIFICATION

FC 13
Notification with reason

VALID REASONS

FC 91
Reason for termination

Which Party wishes to terminate?

C — **90.2** The C may terminate only for a reason identified in the Termination Table

E — **90.2** The E may terminate for any reason

VALID REASON?

Does the SM decide that the reason complied with this contract?

NO → Termination is not valid → Finish

YES

CONTRACTOR STOPS WORK

90.5
After a termination certificate has been issued the C does no further work necessary to Provide the Service

PROCEDURES FOR TERMINATION

90.3
The procedures for termination are implemented immediately after the SM has issued a termination certificate

FC 92
Procedures on termination

COMPLETION CERTIFICATE

90.1
The SM issues a termination certificate to both Parties promptly if the reason complies with this contract

FINAL PAYMENT

90.4
Within thirteen weeks of termination the SM certifies a final payment to or from the C which is the SM's assessment of the amount due on termination less the total of previous payments

90.4
Payment is made within three weeks of the SM's certificate

FC 93
Payment on termination

90.2
The procedures followed and the amounts due on termination are in accordance with the Termination Table. (See flowcharts 91, 92 & 93 for termination reasons, procedures and payments)

Start

TERMINATION TABLE

Terminating Party	Reason	Procedure	Amount due
The Employer	A reason other than R1–R21	P1, P2 and P4	A1, A2 and A4
	R1–R15, or R18	P1, P2, P3 and P4	A1, A2 and A3
	R17 or R20	P1 and P4	A1 and A2
	R21	P1, P3 and P4	A1 and A2
The Contractor	R1–R10, R16 or R19	P1, P2 and P4	A1, A2 and A4
	R17 or R20	P1, P2 and P4	A1 and A2

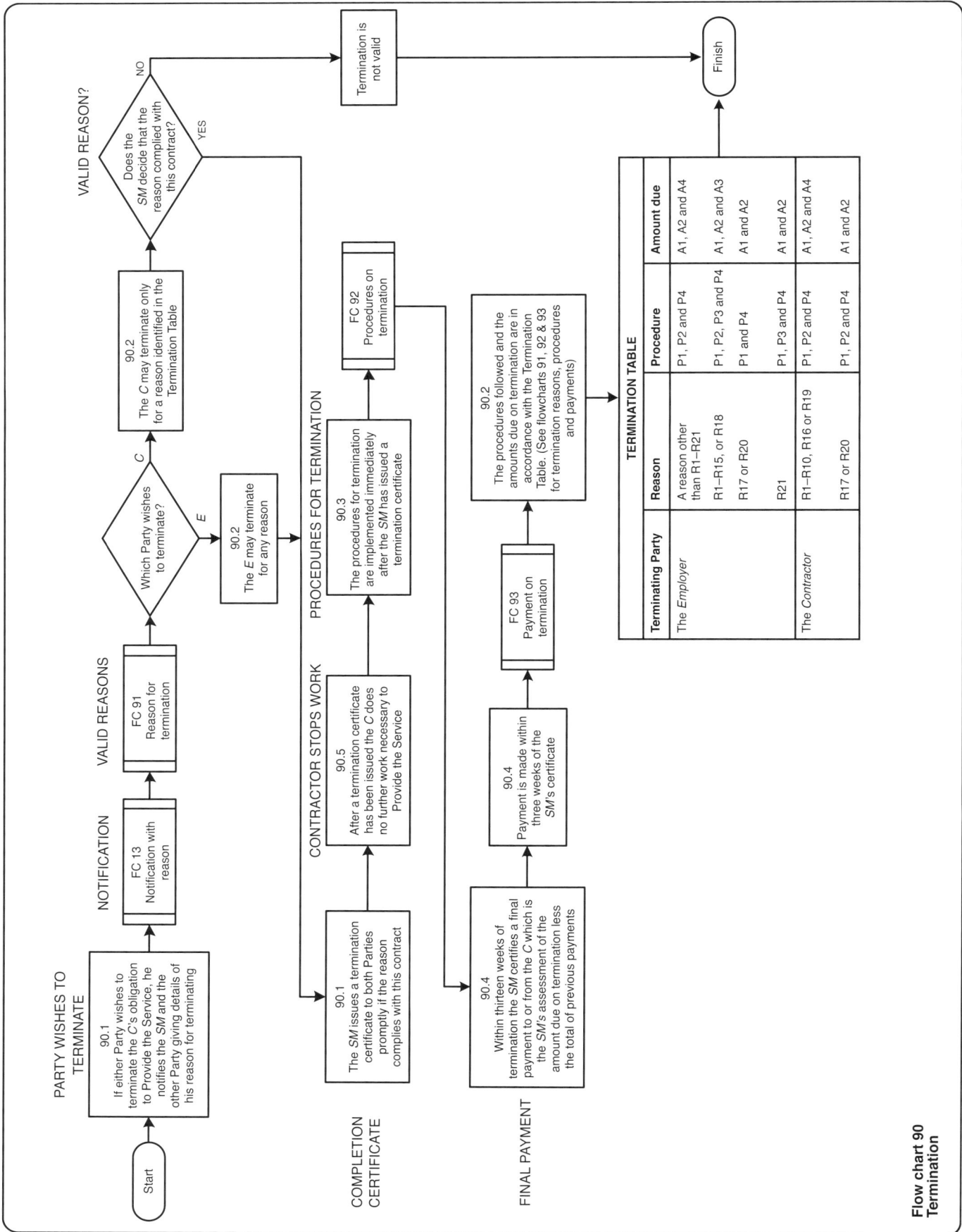

**Flow chart 90
Termination**

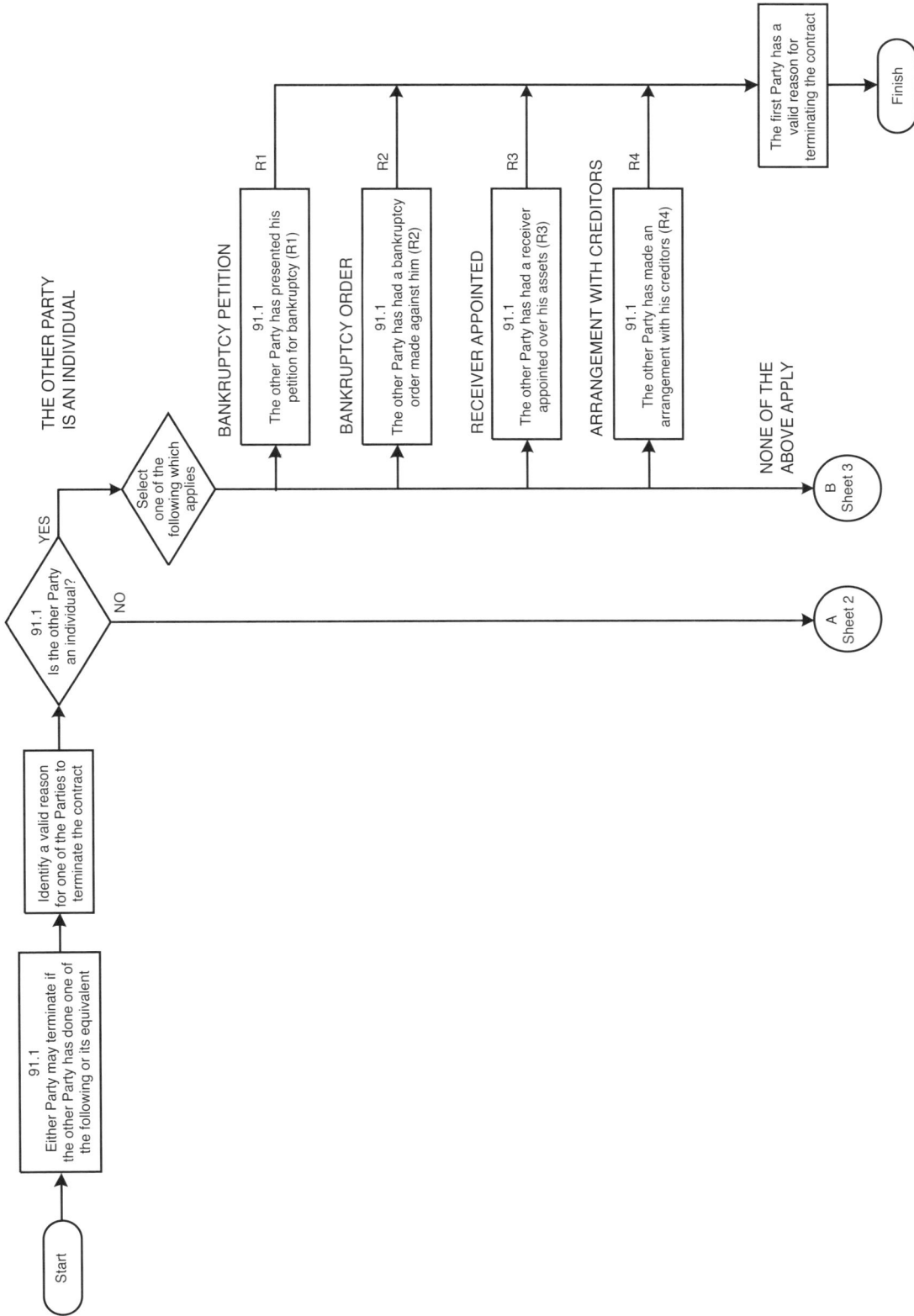

Flow chart 91 Sheet 1 of 5
Reasons for termination

Start

91.1
Either Party may terminate if the other Party has done one of the following or its equivalent

Identify a valid reason for one of the Parties to terminate the contract

91.1
Is the other Party an individual?

YES

NO → A Sheet 2

THE OTHER PARTY
IS AN INDIVIDUAL

Select one of the following which applies

BANKRUPTCY PETITION
91.1
The other Party has presented his petition for bankruptcy (R1)
R1

BANKRUPTCY ORDER
91.1
The other Party has had a bankruptcy order made against him (R2)
R2

RECEIVER APPOINTED
91.1
The other Party has had a receiver appointed over his assets (R3)
R3

ARRANGEMENT WITH CREDITORS
91.1
The other Party has made an arrangement with his creditors (R4)
R4

NONE OF THE
ABOVE APPLY → B Sheet 3

The first Party has a valid reason for terminating the contract

Finish

THE OTHER PARTY
IS A COMPANY OR
PARTNERSHIP

A
Sheet 2

91.1
Is the other Party
a company or
partnership?

YES

NO

Select
one of the
following which
applies

WINDING-UP ORDER

91.1
The other Party has had a winding-up
order made against it (R5)

R5

LIQUIDATOR APPOINTED

91.1
The other Party has had a provisional
liquidator appointed to it (R6)

R6

WINDING-UP RESOLUTION

91.1
The other Party has passed a resolution
for winding-up (other than in order to
amalgamate or reconstruct) (R7)

R7

ADMINISTRATION ORDER

91.1
The other Party has had an administration
order made against it (R8)

R8

RECEIVER APPOINTED

91.1
The other Party has had a receiver,
receiver and manager or administrative
receiver appointed over the whole or a
substantial part of its undertaking or
assets (R9)

R9

ARRANGEMENT WITH CREDITORS

91.1
The other Party has made an
arrangement with its creditors (R10)

R10

The first Party has a
valid reason for
terminating the contract

Finish

NONE OF THE
ABOVE APPLY

B
Sheet 3

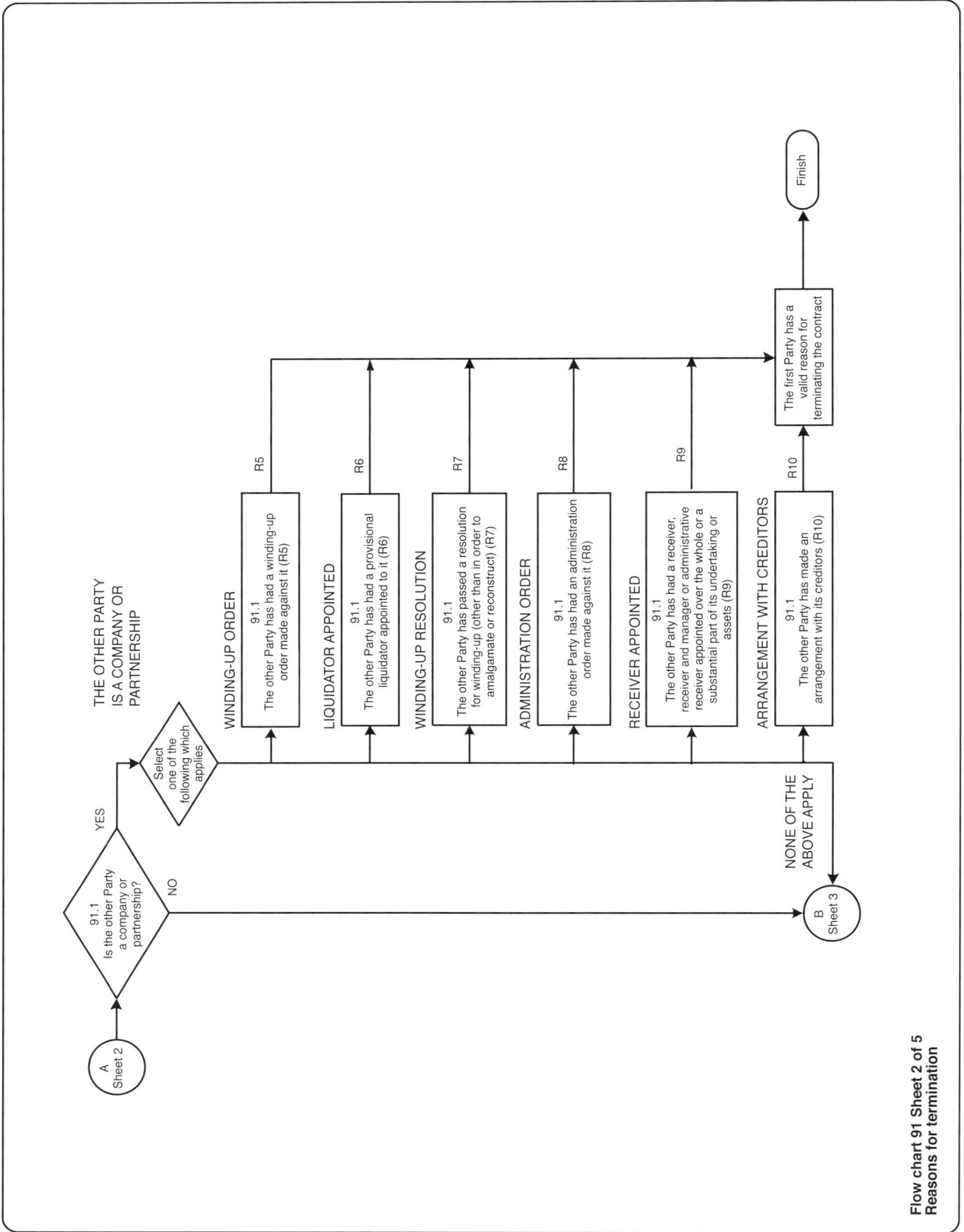

**Flow chart 91 Sheet 2 of 5
Reasons for termination**

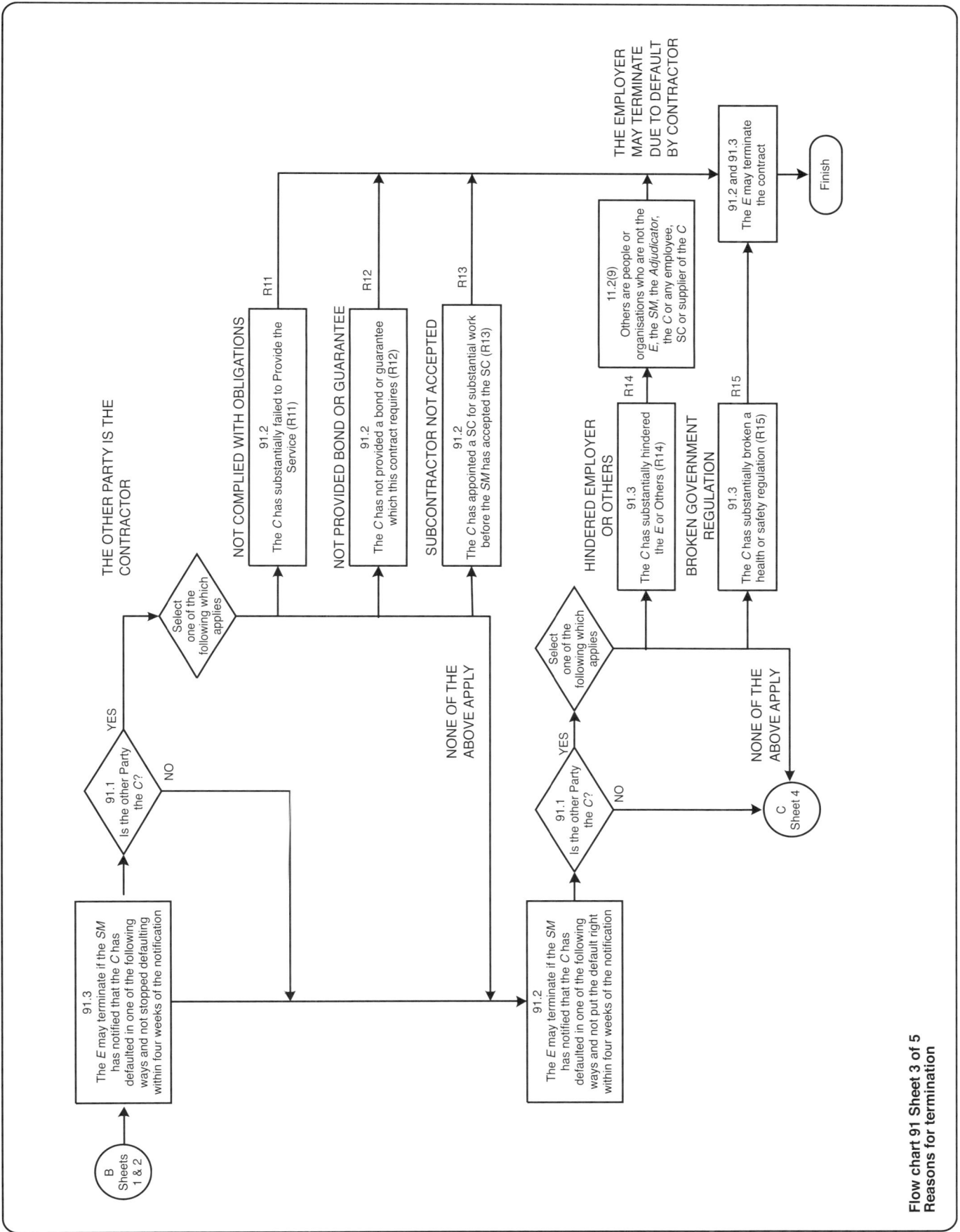

Flow chart 91 Sheet 3 of 5
Reasons for termination

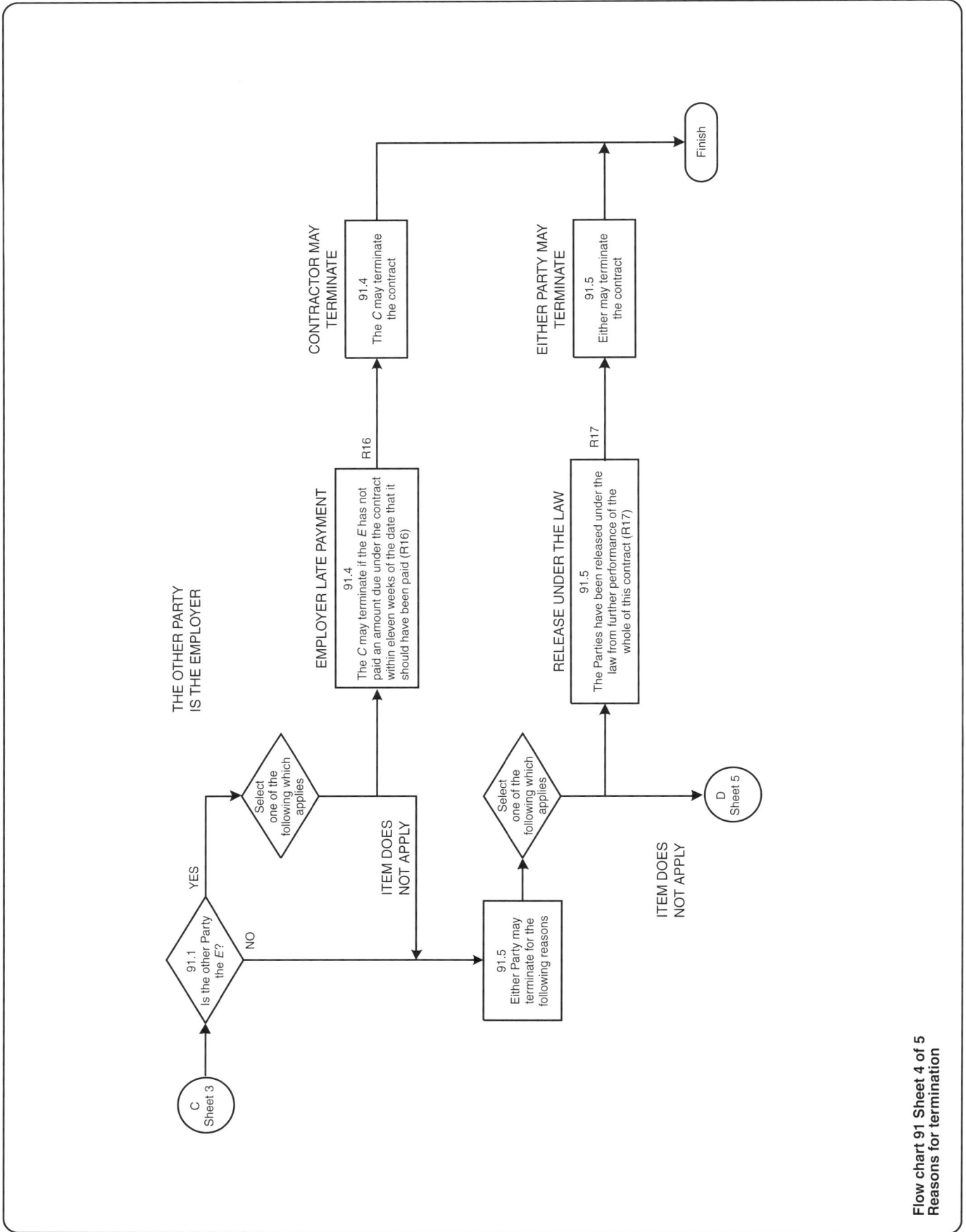

THE OTHER PARTY
IS THE EMPLOYER

C
Sheet 3

91.1
Is the other Party
the *E*?

YES →

NO

**Select
one of the
following which
applies**

CONTRACTOR MAY
TERMINATE

EMPLOYER LATE PAYMENT

91.4
The *C* may terminate if the *E* has not
paid an amount due under the contract
within eleven weeks of the date that it
should have been paid (R16)

R16 →

91.4
The *C* may terminate
the contract

ITEM DOES
NOT APPLY

91.5
Either Party may
terminate for the
following reasons

**Select
one of the
following which
applies**

EITHER PARTY MAY
TERMINATE

RELEASE UNDER THE LAW

91.5
The Parties have been released under the
law from further performance of the
whole of this contract (R17)

R17 →

91.5
Either may terminate
the contract

Finish

ITEM DOES
NOT APPLY

D
Sheet 5

```
D
Sheet 4
```

91.6
Termination of the contract may occur if the *SM* has instructed the *C* to stop or not to start any substantial work or all work and an instruction allowing the work to restart or start has not been given within thirteen weeks

AN INSTRUCTION TO STOP OR NOT TO START WORK IS GIVEN

91.6
Does this situation occur?

YES → Select one of the following which applies

DUE TO ANY OTHER REASON
91.6
Either Party may terminate if the instruction was due to any reason other than reason R18 and R19 (R20)

R20 → Either Party may terminate the contract

DEFAULT BY EMPLOYER
91.6
The *C* may terminate if the instruction was due to a default by the *E* (R19)

R19 → The *C* may terminate the contract

DEFAULT BY CONTRACTOR
91.6
The *E* may terminate if the instruction was due to be a default by the *C* (R18)

R18

NO →

91.7
Termination of the contract may occur if an event which the Parties could not reasonably prevent has substantially affected the *C's* work for a continuous period of more than thirteen weeks

AN EVENT HAS AFFECTED THE CONTRACTOR'S WORK FOR MORE THAN 13 WEEKS

91.7
Does this situation occur?

EVENT AFFECTS WORK
91.7
The *E* may terminate if an event which the Parties could not reasonably prevent has substantially affected the *C's* work for a continuous period of more than thirteen weeks (R21)

R21 →

YES

NO →

Does the E wish to terminate for some other reason?

YES →

EMPLOYER MAY TERMINATE FOR ANY REASON
90.2
The *E* may terminate the contract for any reason (Not R1–R21)

The *E* may terminate the contract

NO →

NO VALID REASON FOR TERMINATION
There is not a valid reason for termination of the contract

Finish

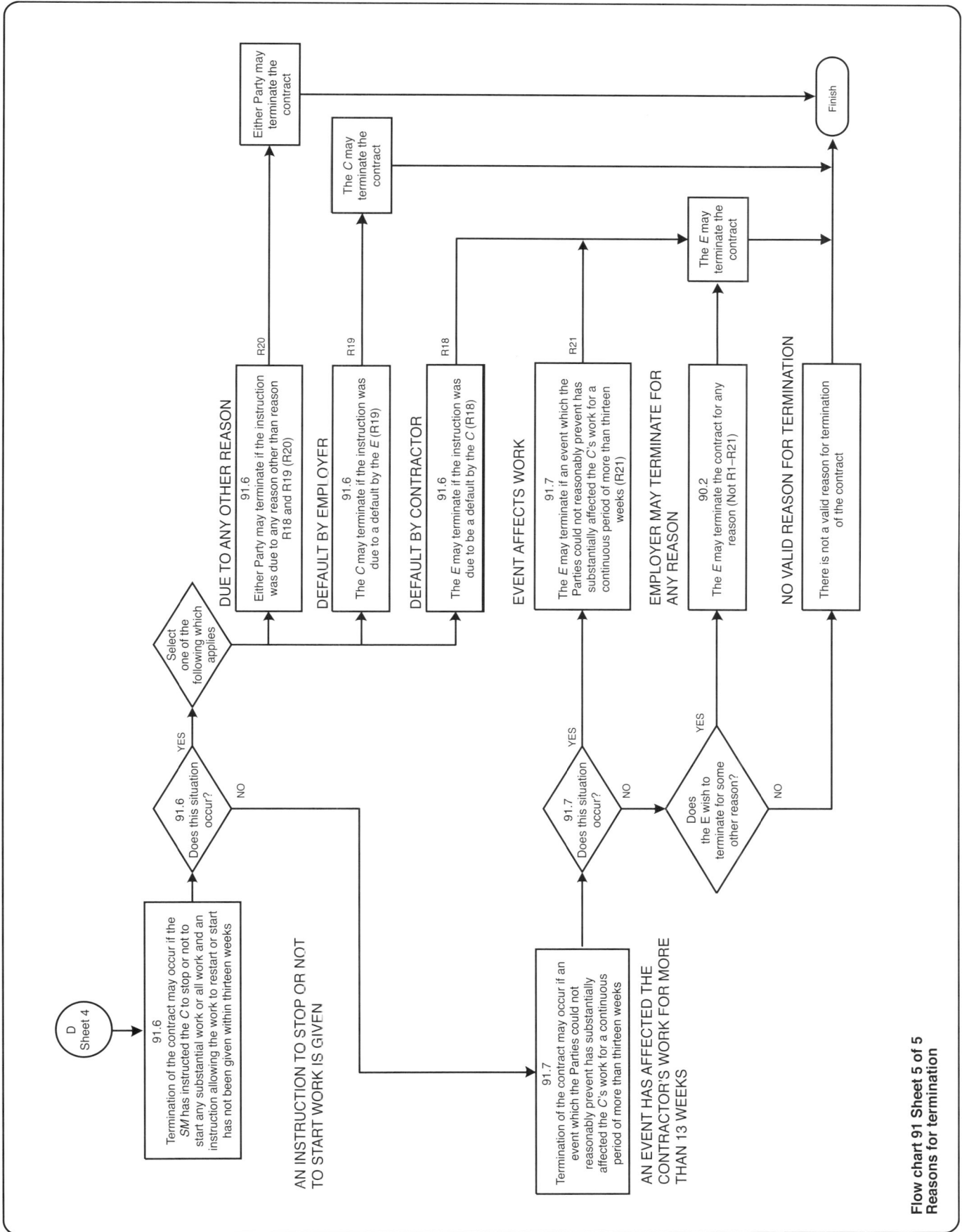

Flow chart 91 Sheet 5 of 5
Reasons for termination

Start

The contract has terminated

PROCEDURE P1

92.1
On termination, the *E* may complete the *service* and may use any P&M provided by the Contractor (P1)

OTHER PROCEDURES

92.2
The procedure on termination also includes one or more of procedures P2 to P4 as set out in the Termination Table

FC 90
Termination Table

Does procedure P2 apply?

YES → 92.2
The *E* may instruct the *C* to remove any Equipment, P&M and assign the benefit of any subcontract or other contract related to performance of this contract to the *E* (P2)

NO

PROCEDURE P2

Does procedure P3 apply?

YES → 92.2
The *E* may use any Equipment to which the *C* has title to complete the *service*. The *C* promptly removes the Equipment when the *SM* notifies him that the *E* no longer requires it to complete the *service* (P3)

NO

PROCEDURE P3

Does procedure P4 apply?

YES → 92.2
The *C* provides to the *E* information and other things which the SI states he is to provide at the end of the *service period*

NO

PROCEDURE P4

Finish

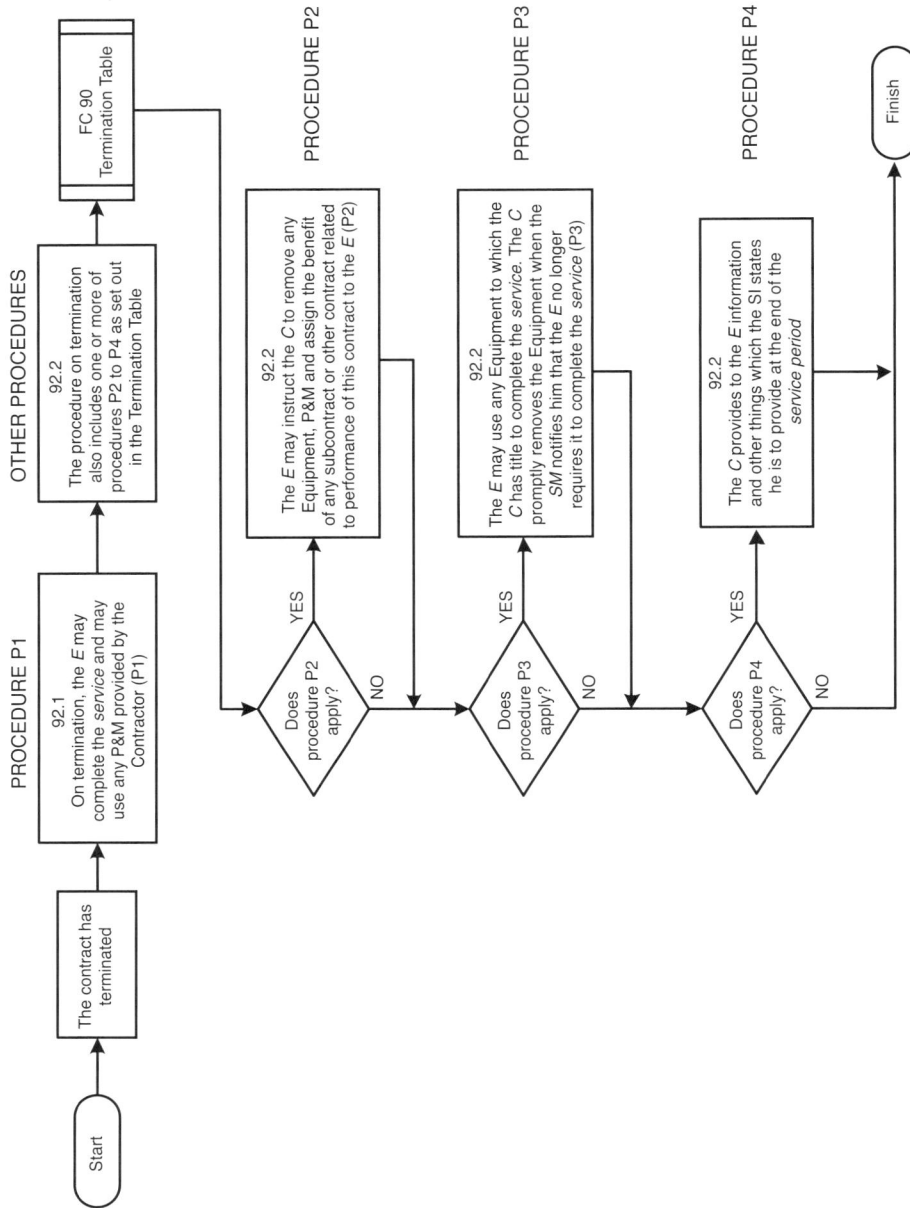

Flow chart 92
Procedures on termination

Start

Which main Option applies?
— C
— A or E

A payment is due on termination

93.1
The amount due on termination includes (A1)
- an amount due assessed as for normal payments,
- the Defined Cost for P&M
  - which have been delivered and retained by the *E* or
  - which the *E* owns and of which the *C* has to accept delivery,
- other Defined Cost reasonably incurred in expectation of completing the whole of the *service* and
- any amounts retained by the *E*

AMOUNT A1

93.3
If there is a termination, the *SM* assesses the *C*'s share after he has certified termination. His assessment uses, as the PSPD, the total Defined Cost which the *C* has paid and which he is committed to pay for work done before termination. The assessment uses as the total of the Prices
- the quantity of the work which the *C* has completed for each item on the Price List multiplied by the rate and
- a proportion of each lump sum which is the proportion of the work covered by the item which the *C* has completed.
The *SM*'s assessment of the *C*'s share is added to the amount due to the *C* if there has been a saving, or deducted if there has been an excess

CONTRACTOR'S SHARE

93.2
The amount due on termination also includes one or more amounts A2 to A4 as set out in the Termination Table

OTHER AMOUNTS

FC 90 Termination Table

Include amount A2?
— YES
— NO

93.2
The forecast Defined Cost of removing the Equipment (A2)

AMOUNT A2

REMOVING EQUIPMENT

Include amount A3?
— YES
— NO

93.2
A deduction of the forecast of the additional cost to the *E* of completing the whole of the *service* (A3)

AMOUNT A3

ADDITIONAL COST TO COMPLETE

Include amount A4?
— YES
— NO

Which main Option applies?
— A or C
— E

93.2
A *direct fee percentage* applied to any excess of the total of the Prices at the Contract Date over the PSPD (A4)

AMOUNT A4

ADDITIONAL FEE

93.2
The *direct fee percentage* applied to any excess of the first forecast of the Defined Cost for the *service* over the PSPD less the Fee (A4)

AMOUNT A4

ADDITIONAL FEE

Finish

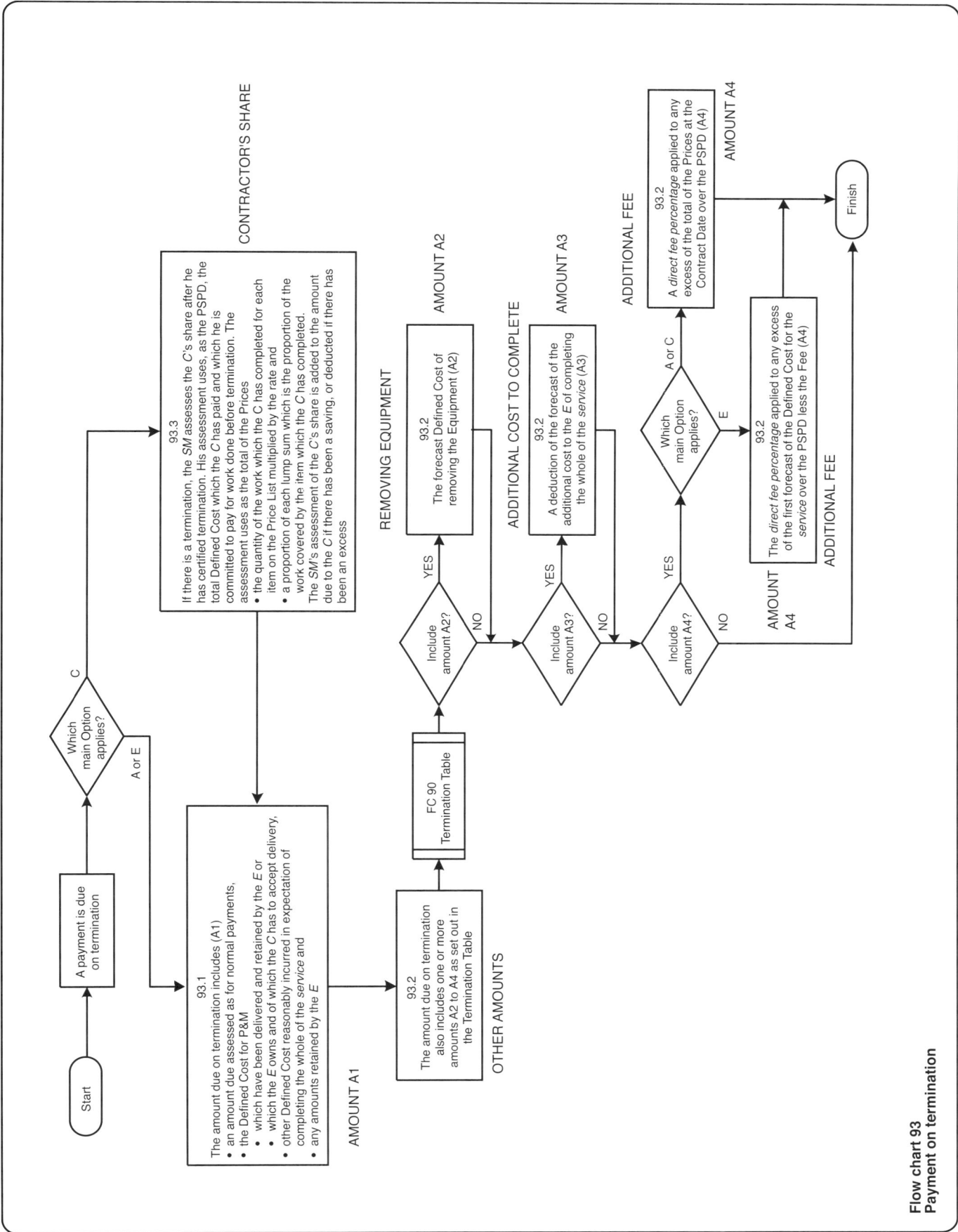

Flow chart 93
Payment on termination

DISPUTE ARISES

Start

A dispute has arisen

DISPUTE RESOLUTION

W1.1
Any dispute arising under or in connection with this contract is referred to and decided by the *Adjudicator*

THE PARTIES

11.2(10)
The Parties are the *E* and the *C*

APPOINTED UNDER NEC ADJUDICATOR'S CONTRACT

W1.2(1)
The Parties appoint the *Adjudicator* under the NEC Adjudicator's Contract current at the *starting date*

ADJUDICATOR NOT ARBITRATOR

W1.2(2)
The *Adjudicator* acts impartially and decides the dispute as an independent adjudicator and not as an arbitrator

The *starting date* and the *Adjudicator nominating body* are stated in the CD

IDENTIFIED IN THE CD?

W1.2(3)
Is the *Adjudicator* identified in the CD?

NO

YES

THE ADJUDICATOR

W1.2(3)
Has the *Adjudicator* resigned or become unable to act?

RESIGNED OR UNABLE TO ACT?

YES

NO

CHOSEN JOINTLY?

W1.2(3)
Do the Parties choose an adjudicator jointly?

YES

NO

NEW ADJUDICATOR

W1.2(3)
The chosen adjudicator becomes the *Adjudicator*

W1.2(3)
The *Adjudicator nominating body* chooses an adjudicator within four days of the request

NOMINATED

W1.2(3)
If the Parties have not chosen an adjudicator, either Party may ask the *Adjudicator nominating body* to choose one

REPLACEMENT?

W1.2(4)
Does the *Adjudicator* replace a previous adjudicator?

YES

NO

INHERITS ANY UNDECIDED DISPUTES

W1.2(4)
A replacement *Adjudicator* has the power to decide a dispute referred to his predecessor but not decided at the time when the predecessor resigned or became unable to act. He deals with an undecided dispute as if it had been referred to him on the date he was appointed

W1.2(5)
The Adjudicator, his employees and agents are not liable to the Parties for any action or failure to take action in an adjudication unless the action or failure to take action was in bad faith

NOT LIABLE UNLESS ACTS IN BAD FAITH

ADJUDICATION

A
Sheet 2

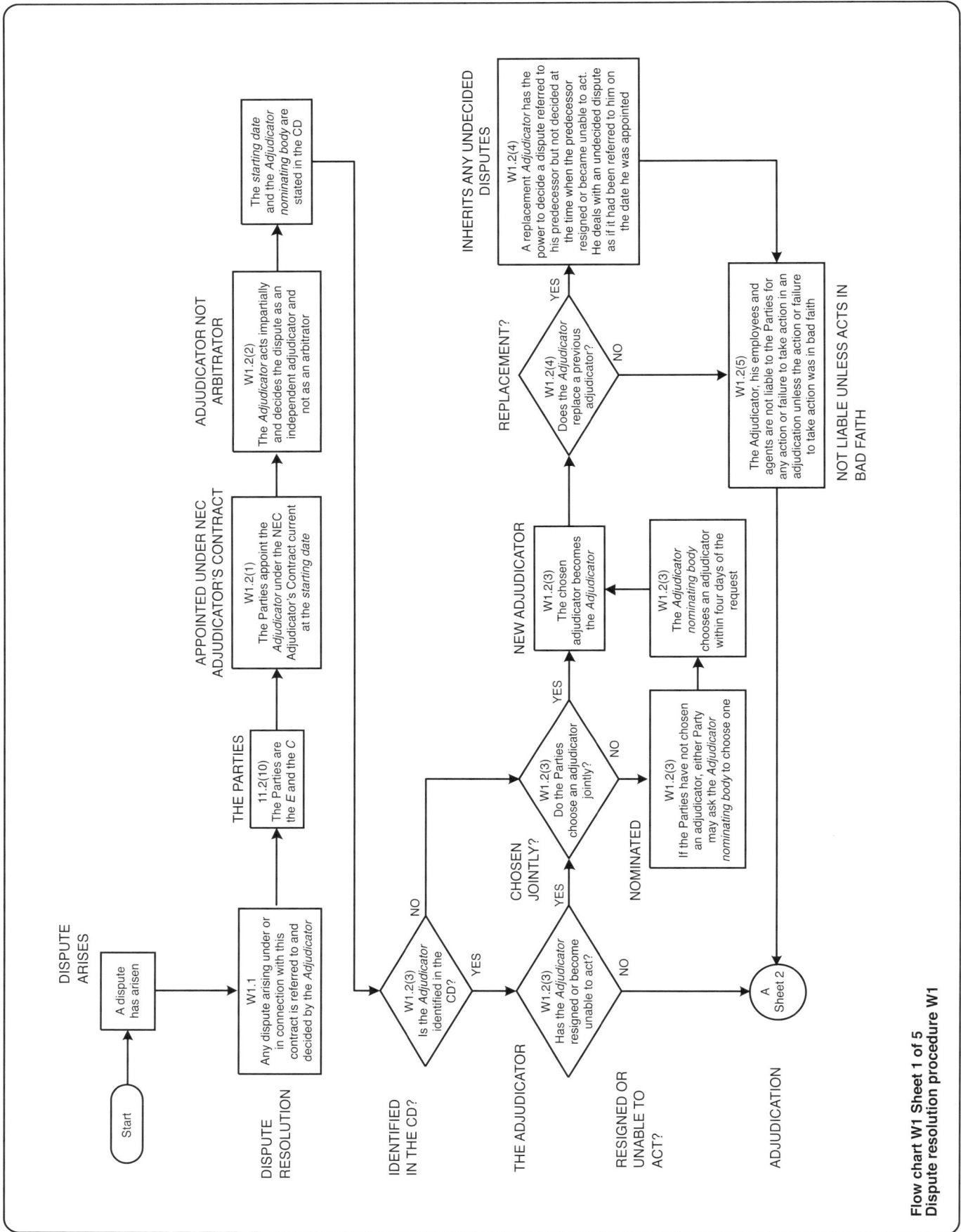

Flow chart W1 Sheet 1 of 5
Dispute resolution procedure W1

ADJUDICATION TABLE

Dispute about	Which Party may refer it to the *Adjudicator*?	When may it be referred to the *Adjudicator*?
An action of the *SM*	The *C*	Between two and four weeks after the *C*'s notification of the dispute to the *E* and the *SM*, the notification itself being made not more than four weeks after the *C* becomes aware of the action
The *SM* not having taken an action	The *C*	Between two and four weeks after the *C*'s notification of the dispute to the *E* and the *SM*, the notification itself being made not more than four weeks after the *C* becomes aware that the action was not taken
A quotation for a CE which is treated as having been accepted	The *E*	Between two and four weeks after the *SM*'s notification of the dispute to the *E* and the *C*, the notification itself being made not more than four weeks after the quotation was treated as accepted
Any other matter	Either Party	Between two and four weeks after notification of the dispute to the other Party and the *SM*

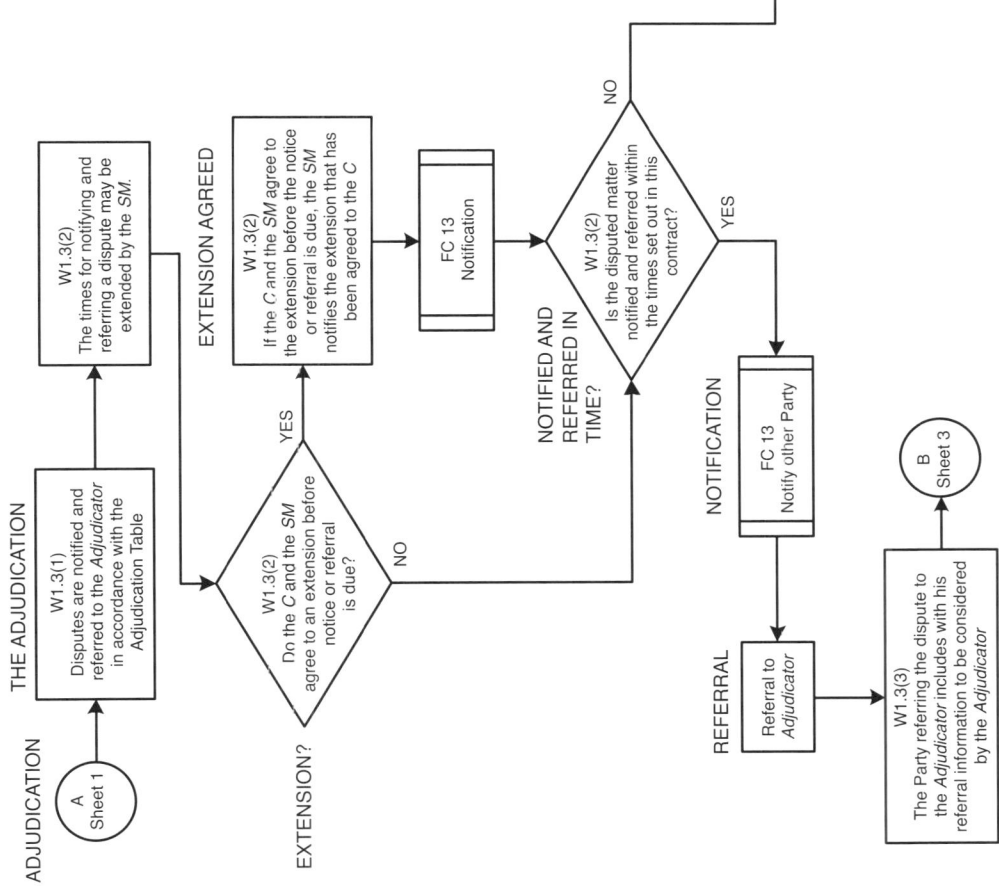

ADJUDICATION

A
Sheet 1

THE ADJUDICATION

W1.3(1)
Disputes are notified and referred to the *Adjudicator* in accordance with the Adjudication Table

W1.3(2)
The times for notifying and referring a dispute may be extended by the *SM*.

EXTENSION?

W1.3(2)
Do the *C* and the *SM* agree to an extension before notice or referral is due?

YES

EXTENSION AGREED

W1.3(2)
If the *C* and the *SM* agree to the extension before the notice or referral is due, the *SM* notifies the extension that has been agreed to the *C*

NO

FC 13
Notification

NOTIFIED AND REFERRED IN TIME?

W1.3(2)
Is the disputed matter notified and referred within the times set out in this contract?

NO

NOT ADJUDICABLE

W1.3(2)
If a disputed matter is not notified and referred within the times set out in this contract, neither Party may subsequently refer the disputed matter to the *Adjudicator* or the tribunal

COMMUNICATIONS SHARED

Finish

YES

NOTIFICATION

FC 13
Notify other Party

REFERRAL

Referral to *Adjudicator*

W1.3(3)
The Party referring the dispute to the *Adjudicator* includes with his referral information to be considered by the *Adjudicator*

B
Sheet 3

Flow chart W1 Sheet 2 of 5
Dispute resolution procedure W1

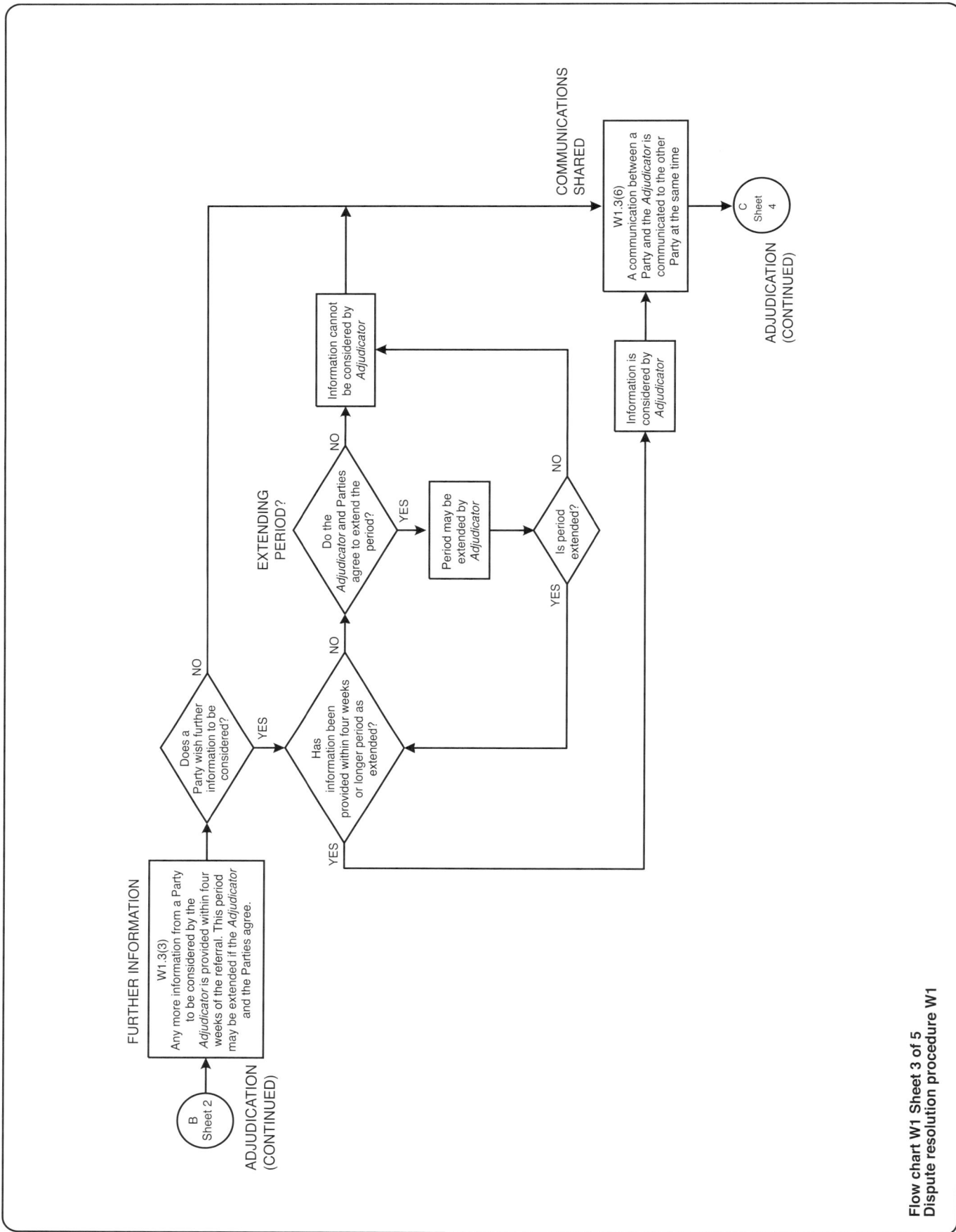

FURTHER INFORMATION

B Sheet 2

ADJUDICATION (CONTINUED)

W1.3(3)
Any more information from a Party to be considered by the *Adjudicator* is provided within four weeks of the referral. This period may be extended if the *Adjudicator* and the Parties agree.

Does a Party wish further information to be considered?

EXTENDING PERIOD?

Do the *Adjudicator* and Parties agree to extend the period?

Information cannot be considered by *Adjudicator*

Period may be extended by *Adjudicator*

Is period extended?

Has information been provided within four weeks or longer period as extended?

Information is considered by *Adjudicator*

COMMUNICATIONS SHARED

W1.3(6)
A communication between a Party and the *Adjudicator* is communicated to the other Party at the same time

C Sheet 4

ADJUDICATION (CONTINUED)

Flow chart W1 Sheet 3 of 5
Dispute resolution procedure W1

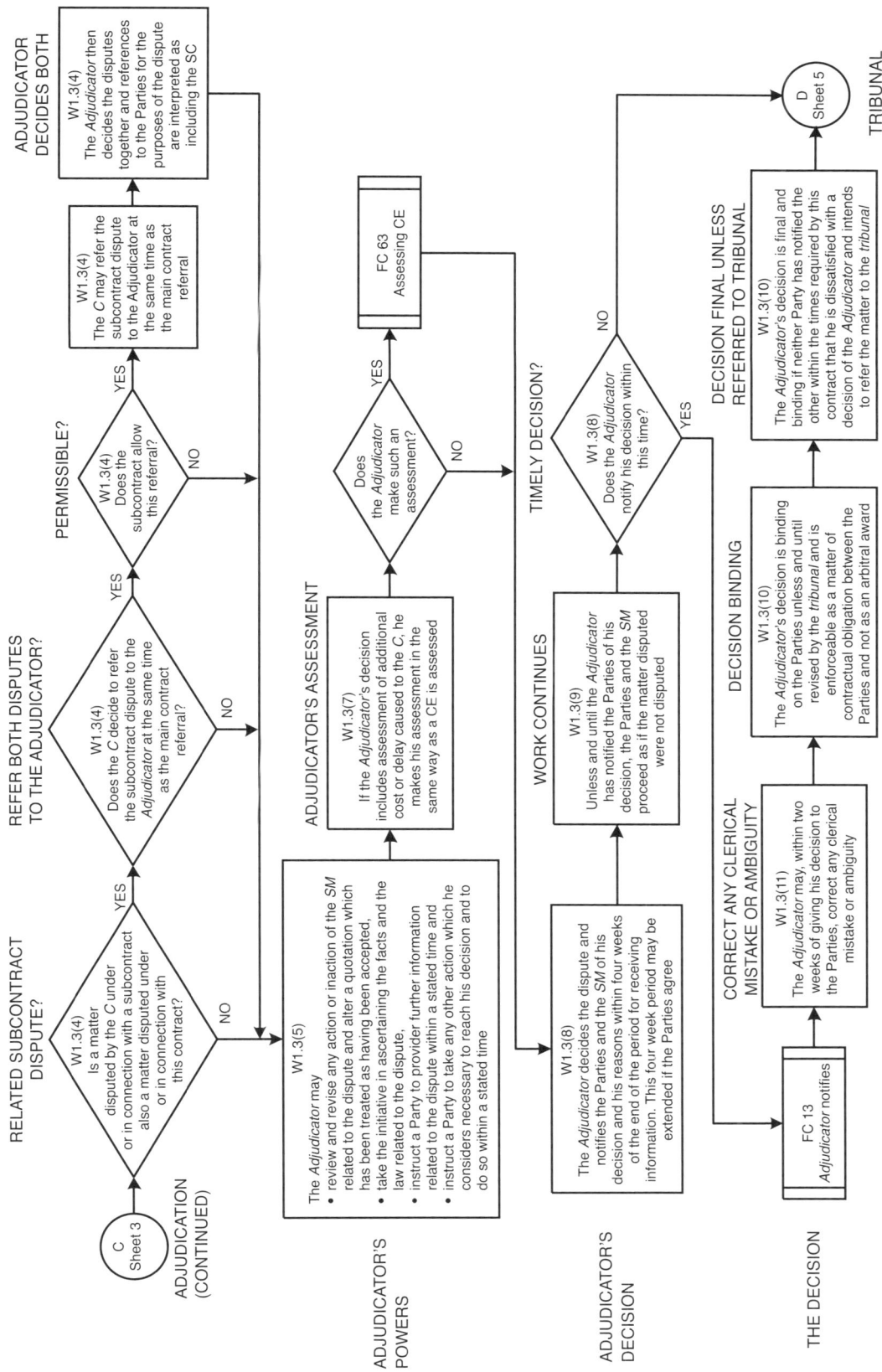

RELATED SUBCONTRACT DISPUTE?

C Sheet 3

ADJUDICATION (CONTINUED)

W1.3(4)
Is a matter disputed by the *C* under or in connection with a subcontract also a matter disputed under or in connection with this contract?

NO →

YES ↓

REFER BOTH DISPUTES TO THE ADJUDICATOR?

W1.3(4)
Does the *C* decide to refer the subcontract dispute to the *Adjudicator* at the same time as the main contract referral?

NO →

YES ↓

PERMISSIBLE?

W1.3(4)
Does the subcontract allow this referral?

NO →

YES ↓

W1.3(4)
The *C* may refer the subcontract dispute to the *Adjudicator* at the same time as the main contract referral

ADJUDICATOR DECIDES BOTH

W1.3(4)
The *Adjudicator* then decides the disputes together and references to the Parties for the purposes of the dispute are interpreted as including the SC

ADJUDICATOR'S POWERS

W1.3(5)
The *Adjudicator* may
• review and revise any action or inaction of the *SM* related to the dispute and alter a quotation which has been treated as having been accepted,
• take the initiative in ascertaining the facts and the law related to the dispute,
• instruct a Party to provider further information related to the dispute within a stated time and
• instruct a Party to take any other action which he considers necessary to reach his decision and to do so within a stated time

ADJUDICATOR'S ASSESSMENT

W1.3(7)
If the *Adjudicator's* decision includes assessment of additional cost or delay caused to the *C*, he makes his assessment in the same way as a CE is assessed

Does the *Adjudicator* make such an assessment?

YES → **FC 63 Assessing CE**

NO ↓

ADJUDICATOR'S DECISION

W1.3(8)
The *Adjudicator* decides the dispute and notifies the Parties and the *SM* of his decision and his reasons within four weeks of the end of the period for receiving information. This four week period may be extended if the Parties agree

WORK CONTINUES

W1.3(9)
Unless and until the *Adjudicator* has notified the Parties of his decision, the Parties and the *SM* proceed as if the matter disputed were not disputed

TIMELY DECISION?

W1.3(8)
Does the *Adjudicator* notify his decision within this time?

NO →

YES ↓

CORRECT ANY CLERICAL MISTAKE OR AMBIGUITY

W1.3(11)
The *Adjudicator* may, within two weeks of giving his decision to the Parties, correct any clerical mistake or ambiguity

FC 13 Adjudicator notifies

THE DECISION

DECISION BINDING

W1.3(10)
The *Adjudicator's* decision is binding on the Parties unless and until revised by the *tribunal* and is enforceable as a matter of contractual obligation between the Parties and not as an arbitral award

DECISION FINAL UNLESS REFERRED TO TRIBUNAL

W1.3(10)
The *Adjudicator's* decision is final and binding if neither Party has notified the other within the times required by this contract that he is dissatisfied with a decision of the *Adjudicator* and intends to refer the matter to the *tribunal*

D Sheet 5

TRIBUNAL

DISPUTES REFERRED FIRST TO THE ADJUDICATOR

W1.4(1)
A Party does not refer any dispute under or in connection with this contract to the *tribunal* unless it has first been referred to the *Adjudicator* in accordance with this contract

(D Sheet 4)

DECISION IN TIME?

W1.4(3)
Has the *Adjudicator* notified his decision in time?

A PARTY DISSATISFIED

W1.4(2)
If, after the *Adjudicator* notifies his decision, a Party is dissatisfied, he may notify the other Party that he intends to refer it to the *tribunal*

DECISION NOT NOTIFIED

W1.4(3)
If the *Adjudicator* does not notify his decision within the time provided by this contract, a Party may notify the other Party that he intends to refer the dispute to the *tribunal*

NOTIFICATION OF REFERRAL

FC 13
Notification of referral to the *tribunal*

IF THE TRIBUNAL IS ARBITRATION

W1.4(5)
If the *tribunal* is arbitration, the arbitration procedure, the place where the arbitration is to be held and the method of choosing the arbitrator are those stated in the CD

TRIBUNAL'S POWERS

W1.4(4)
The *tribunal* has the powers to reconsider any decision of the *Adjudicator* and review and revise any action or inaction of the *SM* related to the dispute

ADMISSIBLE EVIDENCE

W1.4(4)
A Party is not limited in the *tribunal* proceedings to the information, evidence or arguments put to the *Adjudicator*

Has this dispute been referred to the *Adjudicator*?

PERIOD FOR NOTIFICATION

W1.4(2)
A Party may not refer a dispute to the *tribunal* unless this notification is given within four weeks of notification of the *Adjudicator's* decision

W1.4(2)
Is a Party dissatisfied with the *Adjudicator's* decision?

PERIOD FOR NOTIFICATION

W1.4(3)
A Party may not refer a dispute to the *tribunal* unless this notification is given within four weeks of the date by which the *Adjudicator* should have notified his decision

NOTIFY IN TIME?

Does a Party notify within the time?

NO REFERRAL TO TRIBUNAL

This dispute is not referred to the *tribunal*

ADJUDICATOR NOT CALLED AS WITNESS

W1.4(6)
A Party does not call the *Adjudicator* as a witness in *tribunal* proceedings

TRIBUNAL DECIDES

W1.4(4)
The *tribunal* settles the dispute referred to it

(Finish)

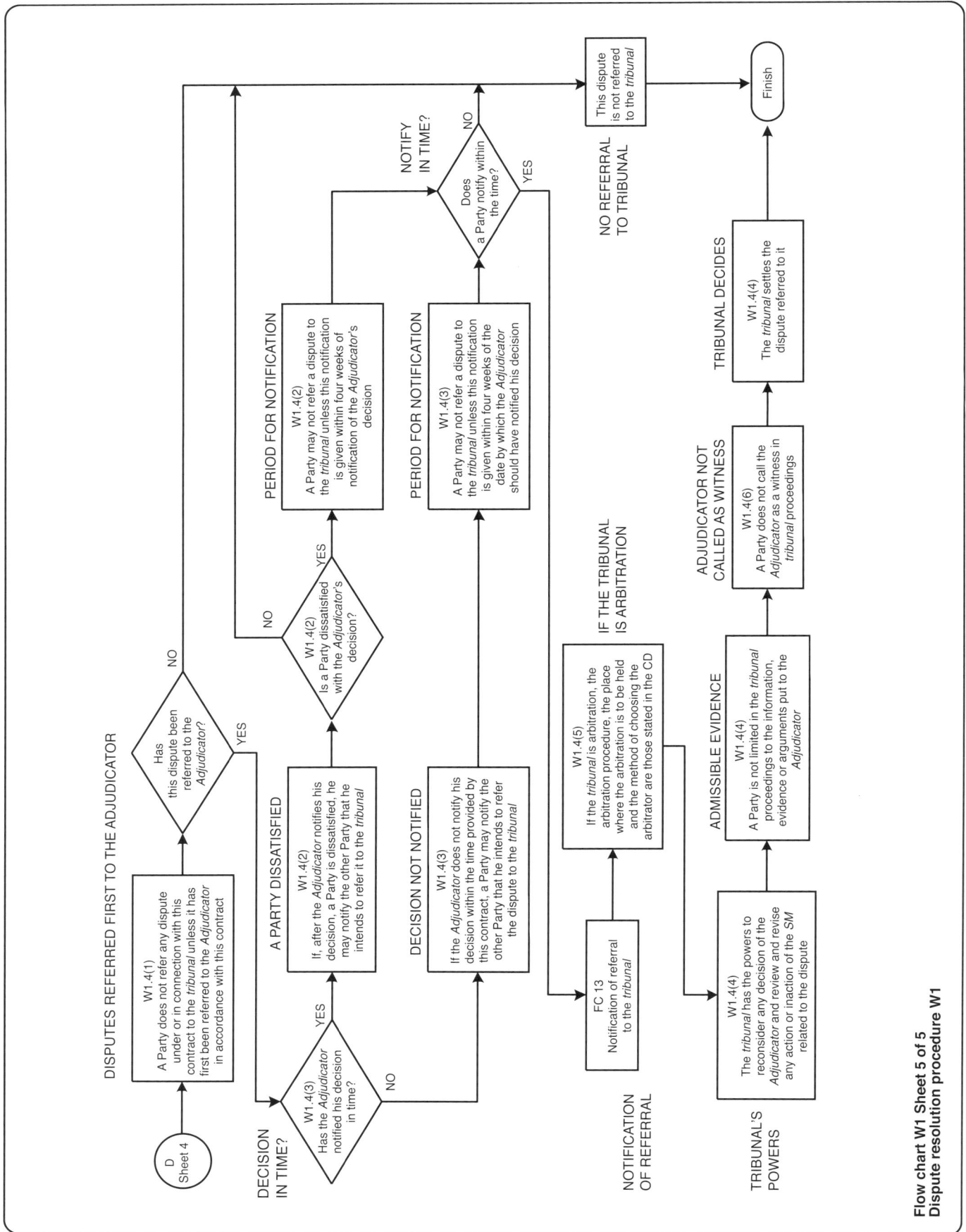

Flow chart W1 Sheet 5 of 5
Dispute resolution procedure W1

Flow chart W2 Sheet 1 — Dispute resolution procedure W2

Start

DISPUTE ARISES — A dispute has arisen

11.2(11) — The Parties are the *E* and the *C*

DEFINITIONS — The *starting date* and the *Adjudicator nominating body* are stated in the CD

W2.1(2) — In this Option, time periods stated in days exclude Christmas Day, Good Friday and bank holidays

DISPUTE RESOLUTION

W2.1(1) — Any dispute arising under or in connection with this contract is referred to and decided by the *Adjudicator*. A Party may refer a dispute to the *Adjudicator* at any time

APPOINTED UNDER NEC ADJUDICATOR'S CONTRACT

W2.2(1) — The Parties appoint the *Adjudicator* under the NEC Adjudicator's Contract current at the *starting date*

ADJUDICATOR NOT ARBITRATOR

W2.2(2) — The *Adjudicator* acts impartially and decides the dispute as an independent adjudicator and not as an arbitrator

IDENTIFIED IN THE CD?

W2.2(3) — Is the *Adjudicator* identified in the CD? — NO / YES

THE ADJUDICATOR

W2.2(3) — Has the *Adjudicator* resigned or become unable to act? — YES / NO

RESIGNED OR UNABLE TO ACT?

CHOSEN JOINTLY?

W2.2(3) — Do the Parties choose an adjudicator jointly? — YES / NO

APPOINT NEW ADJUDICATOR

B Sheets 2–4

NEW ADJUDICATOR

W2.2(3) — The chosen adjudicator becomes the *Adjudicator*

W2.2(3) — The *Adjudicator nominating body* chooses an adjudicator within four days of the request

NOMINATED

W2.2(3) — A Party may ask the *Adjudicator nominating body* to choose an adjudicator

REPLACEMENT?

W2.2(4) — Does the *Adjudicator* replace a previous adjudicator? — YES / NO

INHERITS ANY UNDECIDED DISPUTES

W2.2(4) — A replacement Adjudicator has the power to decide a dispute referred to his predecessor but not decided at the time when his predecessor resigned or became unable to act. He deals with an undecided dispute as if it had been referred to him on the date he was appointed.

W2.2(5) — The *Adjudicator*, his employees and agents are not liable to the Parties for any action or failure to take action in an adjudication unless the action or failure to take action was in bad faith

NOT LIABLE UNLESS ACTS IN BAD FAITH

A Sheet 2

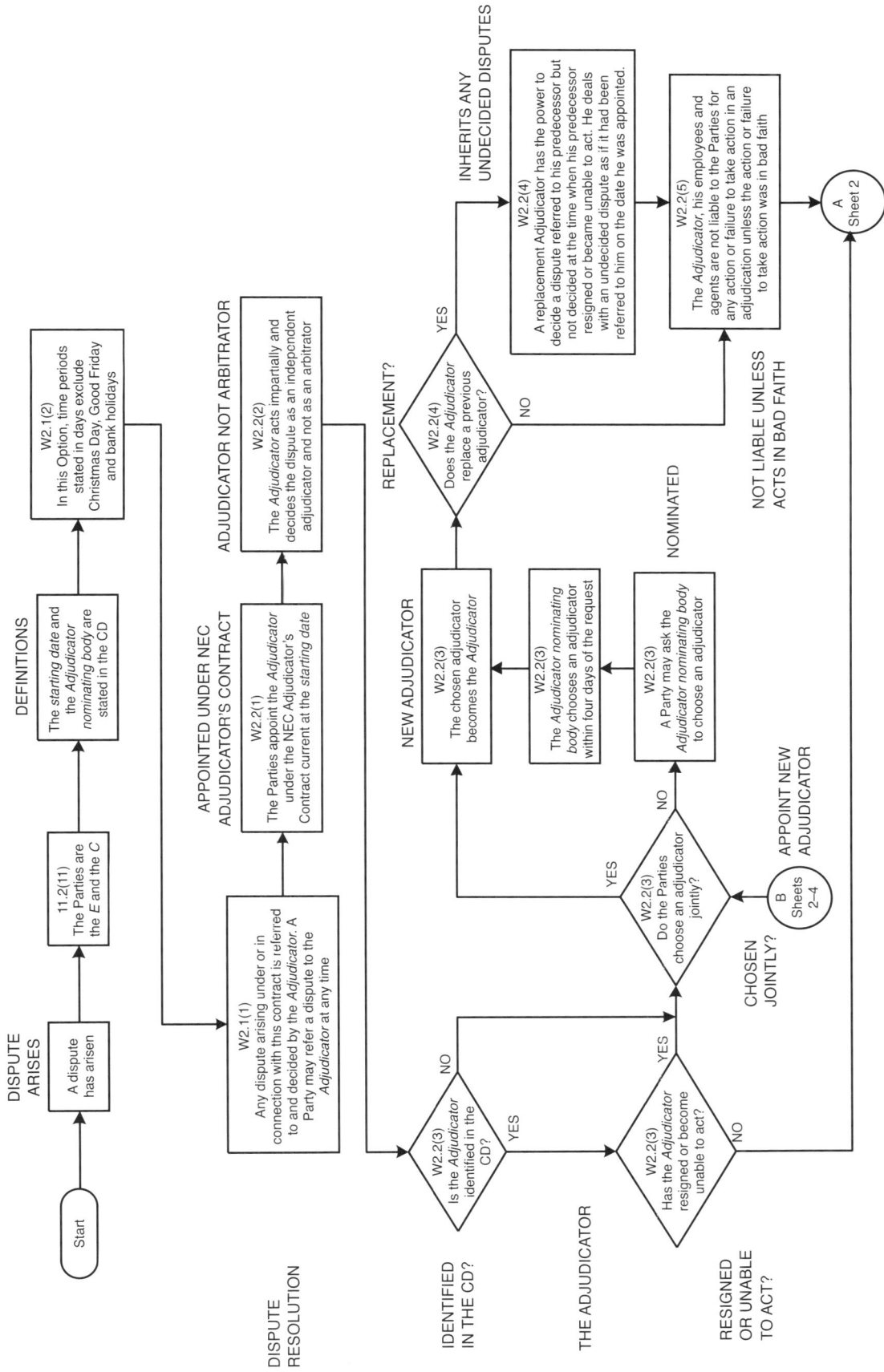

Flow chart W2 Sheet 1 of 6
Dispute resolution procedure W2

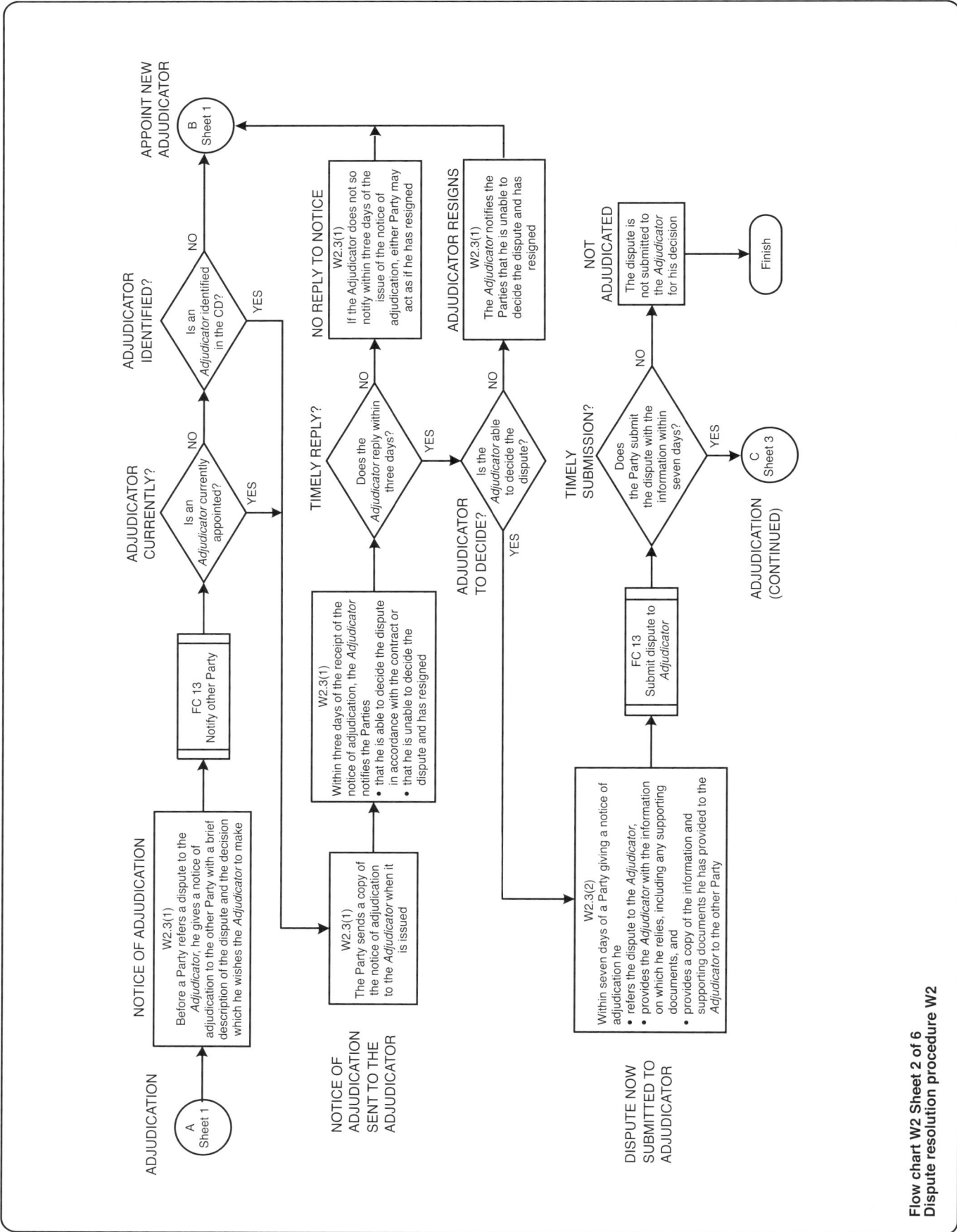

ADJUDICATION

A
Sheet 1

NOTICE OF ADJUDICATION

W2.3(1)

Before a Party refers a dispute to the *Adjudicator*, he gives a notice of adjudication to the other Party with a brief description of the dispute and the decision which he wishes the *Adjudicator* to make

FC 13
Notify other Party

ADJUDICATOR CURRENTLY?

Is an *Adjudicator* currently appointed?

NO / YES

ADJUDICATOR IDENTIFIED?

Is an *Adjudicator* identified in the CD?

NO / YES

APPOINT NEW ADJUDICATOR

B
Sheet 1

NOTICE OF ADJUDICATION SENT TO THE ADJUDICATOR

W2.3(1)

The Party sends a copy of the notice of adjudication to the *Adjudicator* when it is issued

W2.3(1)

Within three days of the receipt of the notice of adjudication, the *Adjudicator* notifies the Parties
• that he is able to decide the dispute in accordance with the contract or
• that he is unable to decide the dispute and has resigned

TIMELY REPLY?

Does the *Adjudicator* reply within three days?

NO / YES

NO REPLY TO NOTICE

W2.3(1)

If the *Adjudicator* does not so notify within three days of the issue of the notice of adjudication, either Party may act as if he has resigned

ADJUDICATOR TO DECIDE?

Is the *Adjudicator* able to decide the dispute?

NO / YES

ADJUDICATOR RESIGNS

W2.3(1)

The *Adjudicator* notifies the Parties that he is unable to decide the dispute and has resigned

DISPUTE NOW SUBMITTED TO ADJUDICATOR

W2.3(2)

Within seven days of a Party giving a notice of adjudication he
• refers the dispute to the *Adjudicator*,
• provides the *Adjudicator* with the information on which he relies, including any supporting documents, and
• provides a copy of the information and supporting documents he has provided to the *Adjudicator* to the other Party

FC 13
Submit dispute to *Adjudicator*

TIMELY SUBMISSION?

Does the Party submit the dispute with the information within seven days?

NO / YES

NOT ADJUDICATED

The dispute is not submitted to the *Adjudicator* for his decision

Finish

ADJUDICATION (CONTINUED)

C
Sheet 3

FURTHER INFORMATION

W2.3(2)
Any further information from a Party to be considered by the *Adjudicator* is provided within fourteen days from the submission. This period may be extended if the *Adjudicator* and the Parties agree

C Sheet 3

ADJUDICATION (CONTINUED)

Does a Party wish further information to be considered?

YES / NO

Has information been provided within fourteen days or longer period as extended?

YES / NO

EXTENDING PERIOD?

Do the *Adjudicator* and Parties agree to extend the period?

NO / YES

Period may be extended by *Adjudicator*

Is period extended?

NO / YES

Information cannot be considered by *Adjudicator*

Information is considered by *Adjudicator*

D Sheet 4

ADJUDICATION (CONTINUED)

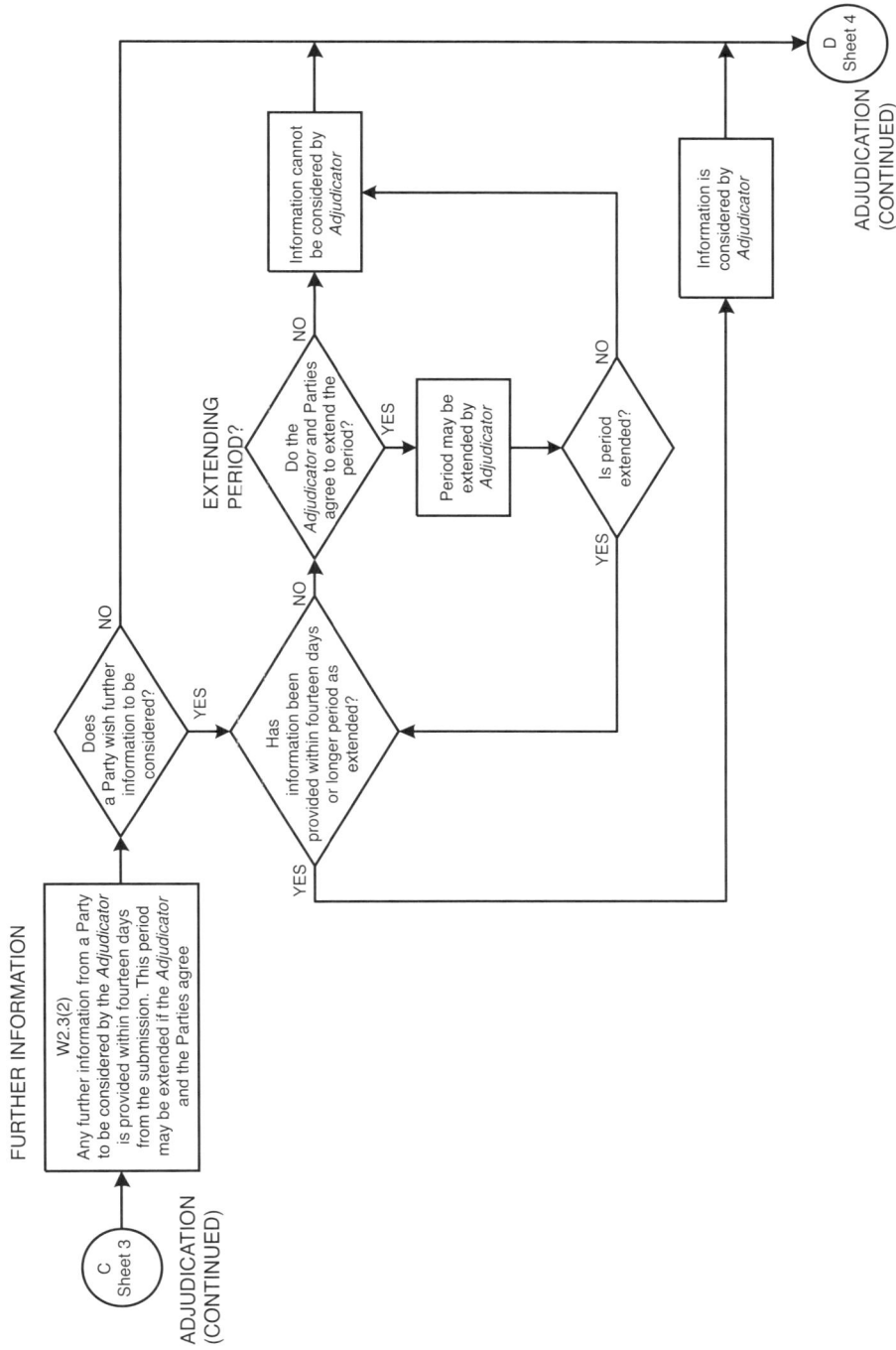

**Flow chart W2 Sheet 3 of 6
Dispute resolution procedure W2**

REFER BOTH DISPUTES TO THE ADJUDICATOR?

RELATED SUBCONTRACT DISPUTE?

D
Sheet 3

ADJUDICATION (CONTINUED)

W2.3(3)
Is a matter disputed by the *C* under or in connection with a subcontractor also a matter disputed under or in connection with this contract?

YES

NO

W2.3(3)
Does the *C* decide to refer the subcontract disputes to the *Adjudicator* at the same time as the main contract referral?

YES

NO

SUBCONTRACTOR CONSENTS?

W2.3(3)
Does the SC consent to the joint referral?

YES

NO

ADJUDICATOR DECIDES BOTH

W2.3(3)
The *Adjudicator* then decides the disputes together and references to the Parties for the purposes of the dispute are interpreted as including the SC

ADJUDICATOR'S POWERS

W2.3(4)
The *Adjudicator* may
• revise and review any action or inaction of the *SM* related to the dispute and alter a quotation which has been treated as having been accepted,
• take the initiative in ascertaining the facts and the law related to the dispute,
• instruct a Party to provider further information related to the dispute within a stated time and
• instruct a Party to take any other action which he considers necessary to reach his decision and to do so within a stated time

COMMUNICATIONS SHARED

W2.3(6)
A communication between a Party and the *Adjudicator* is communicated to the other Party at the same time

PARTY NOT COMPLYING

W2.3(5)
If a Party does not comply with any instruction within the time stated by the *Adjudicator*, the *Adjudicator* may continue the adjudication and make his decision based upon the information and evidence he has received

ADJUDICATOR CONTINUES?

W2.3(5)
Does the *Adjudicator* continue?

NO

YES

B
Sheet 1

APPOINT NEW ADJUDICATOR

ADJUDICATOR'S ASSESSMENT

W2.3(7)
If the *Adjudicator's* decision includes assessment of additional cost or delay caused to the *C*, he makes his assessment in the same way as a CE is assessed

COMPENSATION EVENT ASSESSED

Does the *Adjudicator* make such an assessment?

YES

NO

FC 60
Assessing CE

ADJUDICATOR'S DECISION

W2.3(7)
If the *Adjudicator's* decision changes an amount notified as due, payment of the sum decided by the *Adjudicator* is due no later than seven days from the date of the decision or the final date for payment of the notified amount, whichever is the later

Does the *Adjudicator* make such a decision?

YES

NO

FC 51
Payment

E
Sheet 5

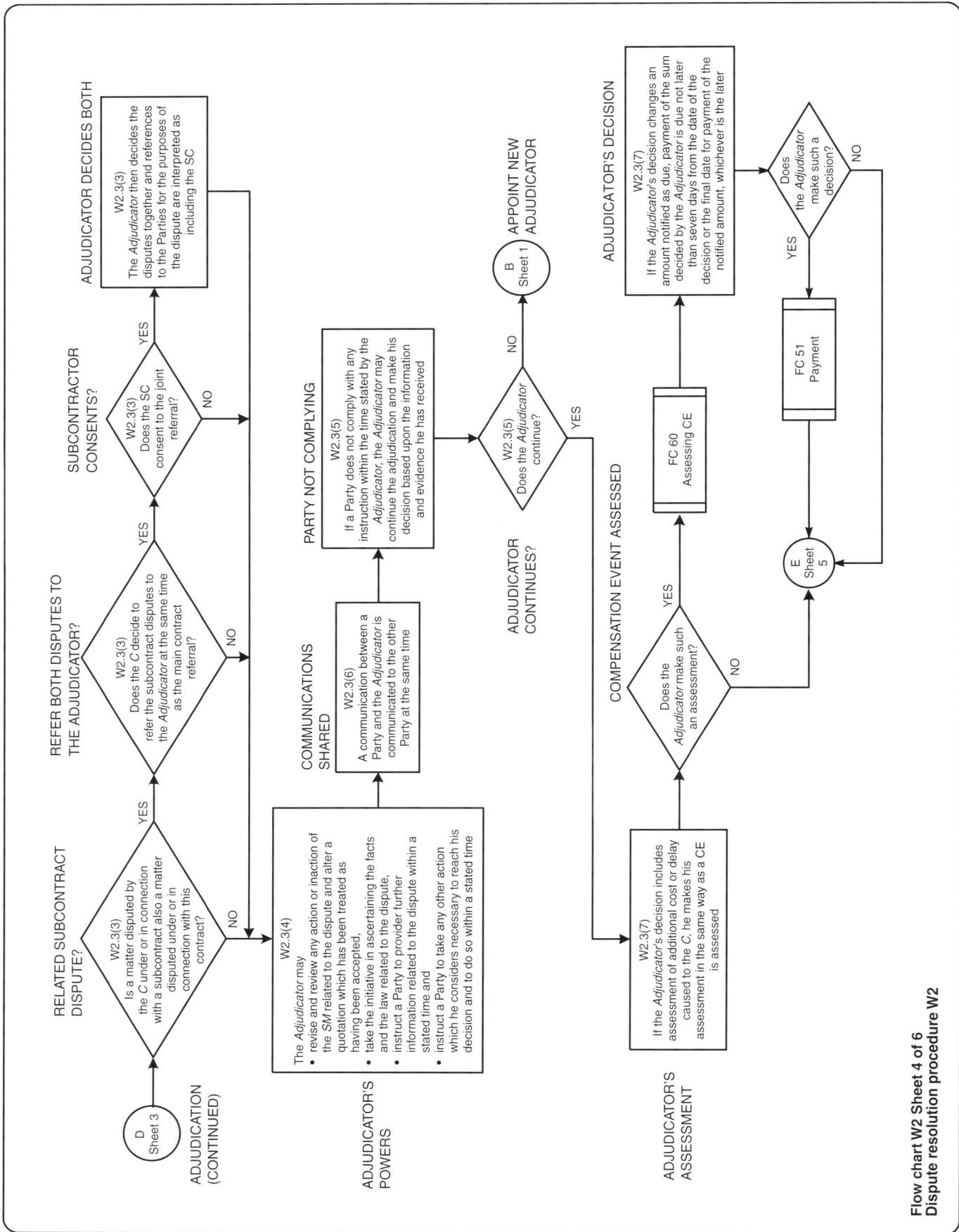

Flow chart W2 Sheet 4 of 6
Dispute resolution procedure W2

ADJUDICATION (CONTINUED)

WORK CONTINUES

W2.3(9)
Unless and until the *Adjudicator* has notified the Parties of his decision, the Parties and the *SM* proceed as if the matter disputed was not disputed

(E Sheet 4)

ADJUDICATOR'S DECISION

W2.3(8)
The *Adjudicator* decides the dispute and notifies the Parties and the *SM* of his decision and his reasons within twenty eight days of the dispute being referred to him. The *Adjudicator* may in his decision allocate his fees and expenses between the Parties

PARTIES EXTENDS?

W2.3(8)
Do the Parties agree to extend the period?

NO

YES

W2.3(8)
The Parties may extend the period by any other agreed period

PERIOD EXTENDED

REFERRER EXTENDS?

W2.3(8)
Does the referring Party consent to extend the period?

NO

YES

W2.3(8)
The referring Party may extend the period by up to fourteen days

AGREED?

W2.3(10)
Do the Parties and the *Adjudicator* agree to extend the period?

NO

YES

W2.3(10)
Either Party may act as if the *Adjudicator* has resigned

(B Sheet 1)

APPOINT NEW ADJUDICATOR

FURTHER EXTENSION

W2.3(10)
The Parties and the *Adjudicator* may agree to extend the period for making his decision

DECISION MADE AND NOTIFIED IN TIME?

W2.3(10)
Does the *Adjudicator* make his decision and notify it to the Parties within the extended period?

NO

YES

DECISION MADE AND NOTIFIED IN TIME?

W2.3(10)
Does the *Adjudicator* make his decision and notify it to the Parties within the time provided by this contract?

NO

YES

DECISION

FC 13
Adjudicator notifies

CORRECT ANY CLERICAL MISTAKE OR AMBIGUITY

W2.3(12)
The *Adjudicator* may, within five days of giving his decision to the Parties, correct the decision to remove a clerical or typographical error arising by accident or omission

DECISION BINDING

W2.3(11)
The *Adjudicator's* decision is binding on the Parties unless and until revised by the *tribunal* and is enforceable as a matter of contractual obligation between the Parties and not as an arbitral award

DECISION FINAL UNLESS REFERRED TO TRIBUNAL

W2.3(11)
The *Adjudicator's* decision is final and binding if neither Party has notified the other within the times required by this contract that he is dissatisfied with a matter decided by the *Adjudicator* and intends to refer the matter to the *tribunal*

(F Sheet 6)

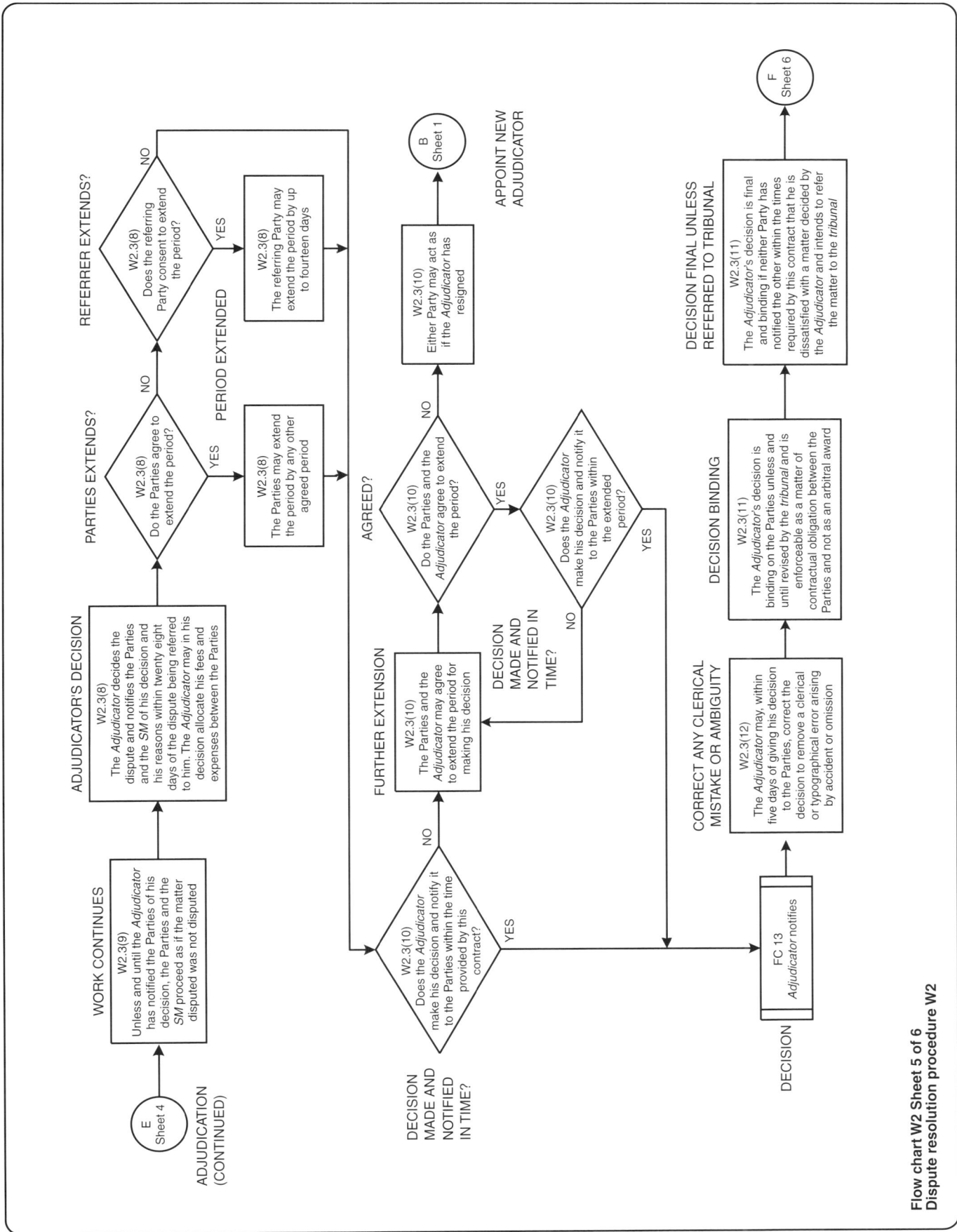

Flow chart W2 Sheet 5 of 6
Dispute resolution procedure W2

DISPUTES DECIDED FIRST BY THE ADJUDICATOR

F Sheet 5

ADJUDICATOR'S DECISION

W2.4(1)
A Party does not refer any dispute under or in connection with this contract to the *tribunal* unless it has first been decided by the *Adjudicator* in accordance with this contract

Has this dispute been decided by the *Adjudicator*?
NO / YES

PARTY DISSATISFIED WITH ADJUDICATOR'S DECISION

W2.4(2)
If, after the *Adjudicator* notifies his decision, a Party is dissatisfied, that Party may notify the other Party of the matter which he disputes and state that he intends to refer it to the *tribunal*

PARTY DISSATISFIED?

W2.4(2)
Is a Party dissatisfied with the *Adjudicator's* decision?
NO / YES

W2.4(2)
The dispute may not be referred to the *tribunal* unless this notification is given within four weeks of notification of the *Adjudicator's* decision

PERIOD FOR NOTIFICATION

NOTIFY IN TIME?
Does a Party notify within the time?
NO / YES

This dispute is not referred to the *tribunal*

NO REFERRAL TO TRIBUNAL

Finish

NOTIFICATION OF REFERRAL

FC 13
Notification of referral to the *tribunal*

IF TRIBUNAL ARBITRATION

W2.4(4)
If the *tribunal* is arbitration, the *arbitration procedure*, the place where the arbitration is to be held and the method of choosing the arbitrator are those stated in the CD

TRIBUNAL'S POWERS

W2.4(3)
The *tribunal* has the powers to reconsider any decision of the *Adjudicator* and to review and revise any action or inaction of the *SM* related to the dispute

ADMISSIBLE EVIDENCE

W2.4(3)
A Party is not limited in *tribunal* proceedings to the information or arguments put to the *Adjudicator*

ADJUDICATOR NOT CALLED AS WITNESS

W2.4(5)
A Party does not call the *Adjudicator* as a witness in *tribunal* proceedings

TRIBUNAL DECIDES

W2.4(3)
The *tribunal* settles the dispute referred to it

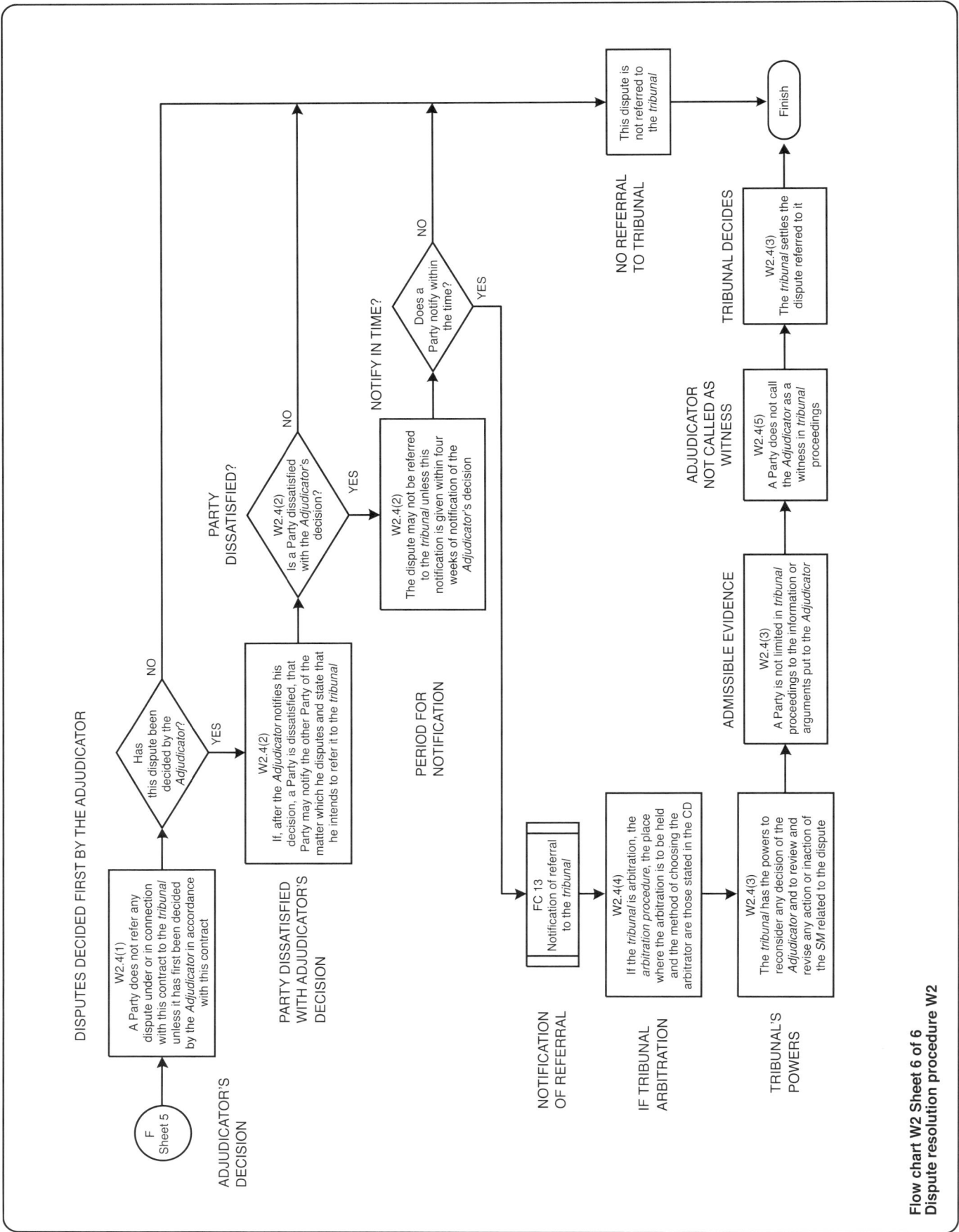

Flow chart W2 Sheet 6 of 6
Dispute resolution procedure W2

Start

Assessment of the amount due or the total of the Prices adjusted for inflation

Which main Option applies?

A or C

E

The indices, proportions and *base date* are defined in the CD

Calculate the PAF for an assessment date?

YES

NO

X1.1(a)
The Base Date Index (B) is the latest available index before the *base date*

BASE DATE INDEX

X1.1(b)
The Latest Index (L) is the latest available index before the assessment of an amount due

LATEST INDEX

X1.1(c)
The PAF is the total of the products of each of the proportions stated in the CD multiplied by (L−B)/B for the index linked to it

PRICE ADJUSTMENT FACTOR

INDEX CHANGED

Has an index been changed after it has been used for a PAF?

YES

NO

X1.2
If an index is changed after it has been used in calculating a PAF, the calculation is repeated and a correction included in the next assessment of the amount due

CORRECTION IN NEXT ASSESSMENT

COMPENSATION EVENT

Assess CEs?

YES

NO

X1.3
The Defined Cost for CEs is assessed using the
• Defined Cost current at the time of assessing the CE adjusted to *base date* by dividing by one plus the PAF for the last assessment of the amount due and
• Defined Cost at *base date* levels for amounts calculated from rates and prices in the Price List

DEFINED COST OF COMPENSATION EVENTS ASSESSED AT BASE DATE LEVELS

Calculate price adjustment

Which main Option applies?

A

C

X1.4
Each amount due includes an amount for price adjustment which is the sum of
• the change in the PSPD since the last assessment of the amount due multiplied by the PAF for the date of the current assessment,
• the amount for price adjustment included in the previous amount due and
• correcting amounts, not included elsewhere, which arise from changes to indices used for assessing previous amounts for price adjustment

X1.5
Each time the amount due is assessed, an amount for price adjustment is added to the total of the Prices which is the sum of
• the change in the PSPD since the last assessment of the amount due multiplied by (PAF/(1+PAF)) where PAF is the PAF for the date of the current assessment and
• correcting amounts, not included elsewhere, which arise from changes to indices used for assessing previous amounts for price adjustment

PRICE ADJUSTMENT INCLUDED IN THE AMOUNT DUE

PRICE ADJUSTMENT ADDED TO THE TOTAL OF THE PRICES

Finish

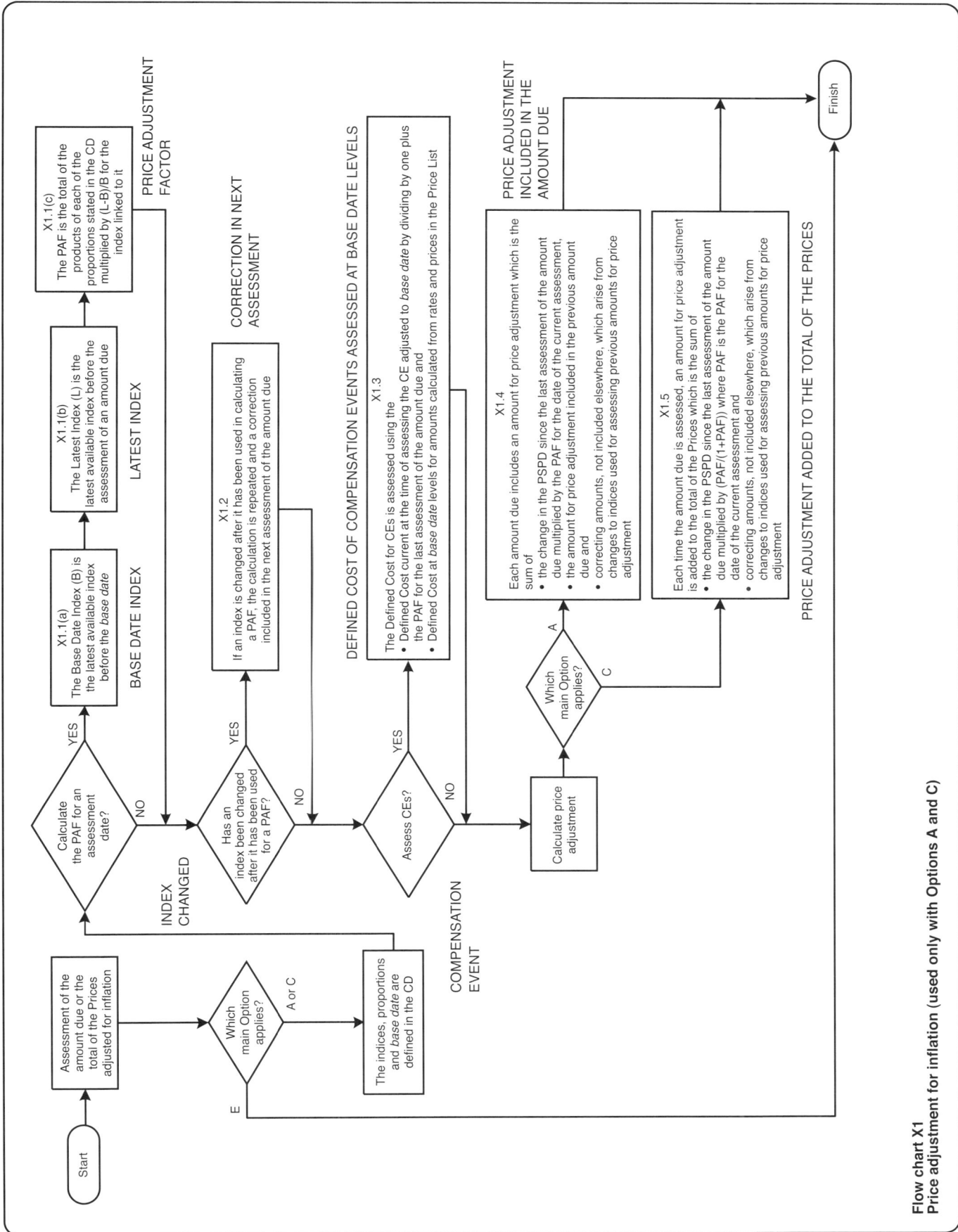

Flow chart X1
Price adjustment for inflation (used only with Options A and C)

CHANGE IN THE LAW IS COMPENSATION EVENT

Start

X2.1
A change in the law of the country in which the Affected Property is located is a CE if it occurs after the Contract Date

CONTRACT DATE

11.2(3)
The Contract Date is the date when this contract came into existence

CHANGE IN LAW?

Does change in the law occur?
— NO
— YES

SERVICE MANAGER MAY NOTIFY COMPENSATION EVENT

X2.1
The *SM* may notify the *C* of a CE for a change in the law and instruct him to submit quotations

NOTIFIED BY SERVICE MANAGER?

Does the *SM* notify a CE?
— NO
— YES

NOTIFIED BY CONTRACTOR?

Does the *C* believe the event is a CE?
— NO
— YES

FC 61
Notifying CEs 61.3

TIMELY NOTIFICATION

61.3
Does the *C* notify a CE in time?
— NO
— YES

Finish

COMPENSATION EVENT

FC 61
Notify CE X2.1

PRICES MAY BE REDUCED

X2.1
If the effect of a CE which is a change in the law is to reduce the total Defined Cost, the Prices are reduced

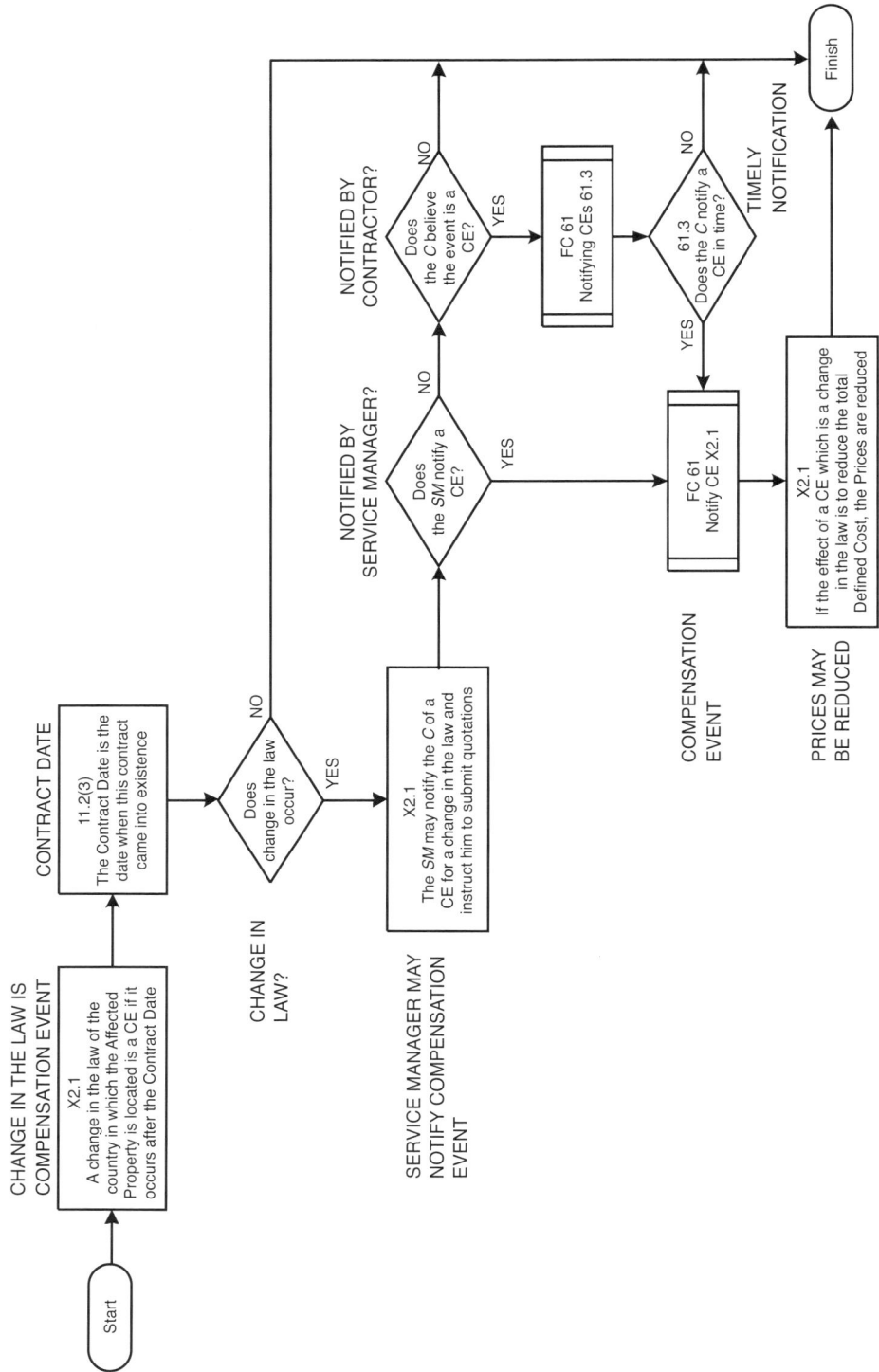

Flow chart X2
Changes in the law

www.neccontract.com

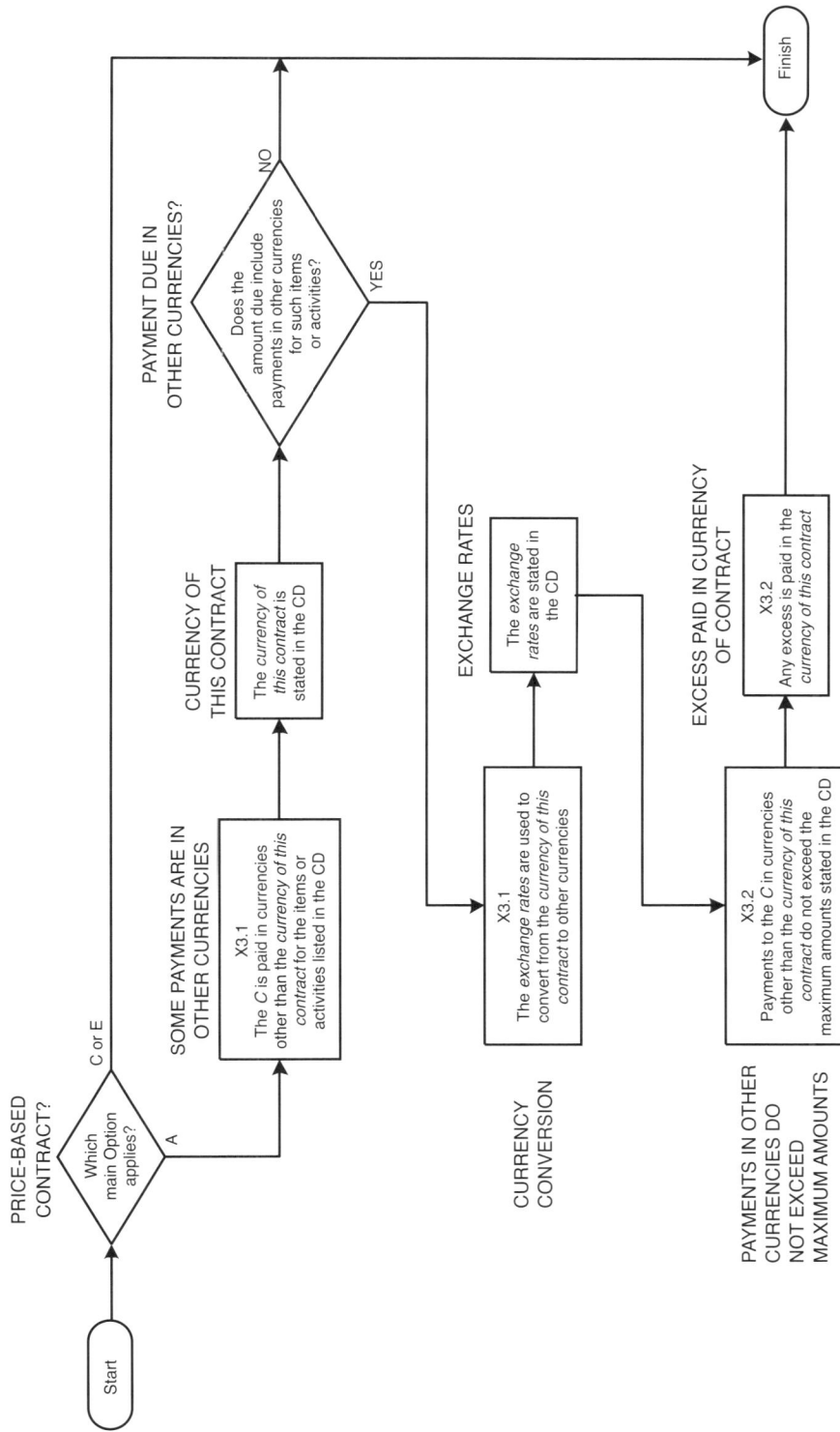

Flow chart X3
Multiple currencies (used only with Option A)

Start

This contract includes provision for a parent company guarantee

X4.1
Does a parent company own the C?

NO

YES

PARENT COMPANY GUARANTEE NEEDED

X4.1
The C gives to the E a guarantee by the parent company of the C's performance in the form set out in the SI

CONTRACT DATE

11.2(3)
The Contract Date is the date when this contract came into existence

GUARANTEE GIVEN BY CONTRACT DATE?

Is the guarantee given by the Contract Date?

YES

NO

GUARANTEE GIVEN WITHIN FOUR WEEKS

X4.1
The guarantee is given to the E within four weeks of the Contract Date

Finish

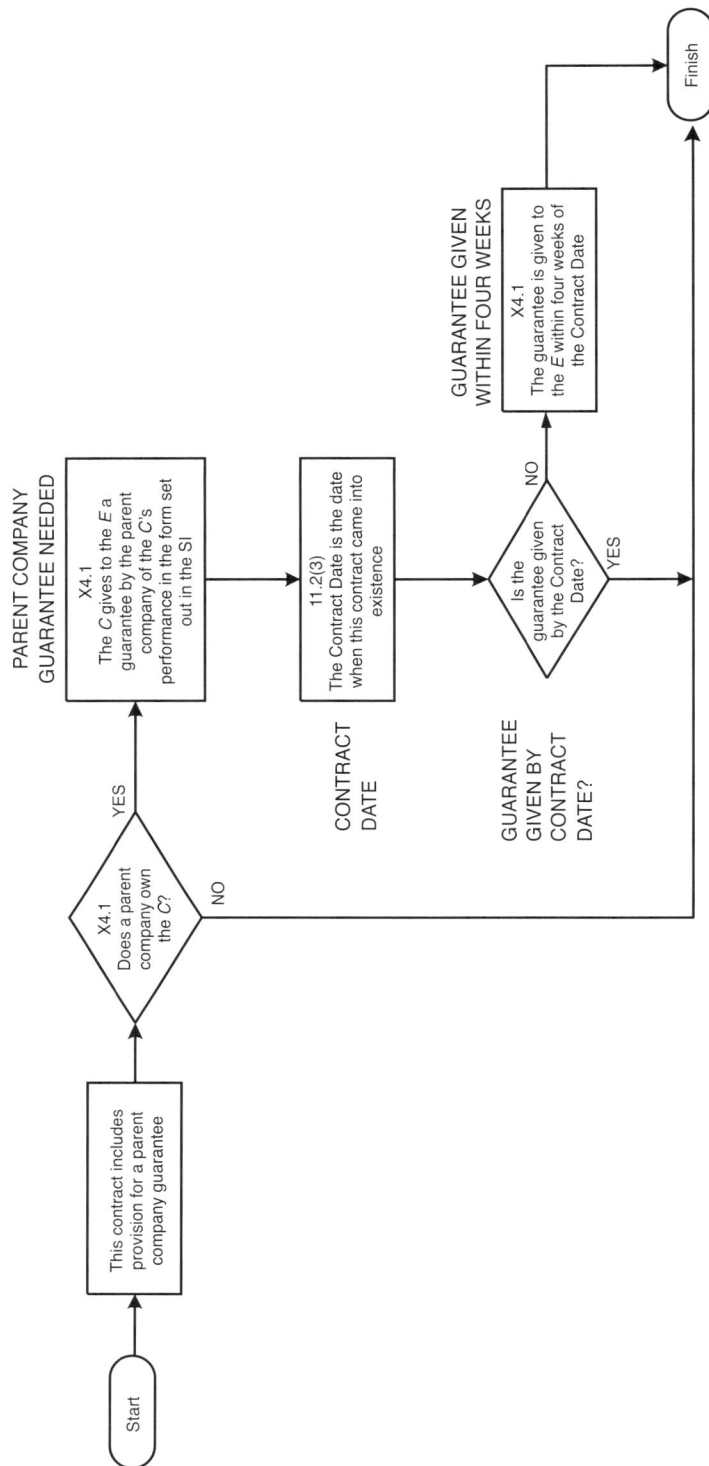

Flow chart X4
Parent company guarantee

SCHEDULE OF PARTNERS

Start

The Partnering Option is required

X12.1(1)
The Partners are those named the Schedule of Partners

X12.1(1)
The *Client* is a Partner

The *Client* is stated in the CD

OWN CONTRACT

X12.1(2)
An Own Contract is a contract between two Partners which includes this Option

CORE GROUP

X12.1(3)
The Core Group comprises the Partners listed in the Schedule of Core Group Members

X12.1(4)
Partnering information is information which specifies how the Partners work together

PARTNERING INFORMATION

Has an instruction been given providing the Partners Information?

YES

X12.1(4)
Partnering Information is in an instruction given in accordance with this contract

NO

X12.1(4)
Partnering Information is in documents which the CD states it is in

CLIENT AND PARTNER OBJECTIVES

X12.2(1)
Each Partner works with the other Partners to achieve the *Client's objective* stated in the CD and the objectives of every other Partner stated in the Schedule of Partners

KEY PERFORMANCE INDICATOR

X12.1(5)
A Key Performance Indicator is an aspect of performance for which a target is stated in the Schedule of Partners

PARTNER REPRESENTATIVES

X12.2(2)
Each Partner nominates a representative to act for him in dealings with other Partners

CORE GROUP SELECTION

X12.2(4)
The Partners select the members of the Core Group. The Core Group decides how they will work and decides the dates when each member joins and leaves the Core Group

Does the Partnering Information state who instead of the *Client's* representative will lead the Core Group?

YES

X12.2(4)
The person stated in the Partnering Information leads the Core Group

NO

X12.2(4)
The *Client's* representative leads the Core Group

CORE GROUP ACTS AND DECIDES ON BEHALF OF PARTNERS

X12.2(3)
The Core Group acts and takes decisions on behalf of the Partners on those matters stated in the Partnering Information

SCHEDULES

X12.2(5)
The Core Group keeps the Schedule of Core Group Members and the Schedule of Partners up to date

Has either the Schedule of Core Group members or the Schedule of Partners been revised?

YES

X12.2(5)
The Core Group issues copies of them to the Partners each time either is revised

NO

LEGAL PARTNERSHIP

X12.1(6)
This Option does not create a legal partnership between Partners who are not one of the Parties in this contract

X12.3(1)
The Partners work together as stated in the Partnering Information and in a spirit of mutual trust and co-operation

PARTNERS PROVIDE INFORMATION

X12.3(2)
A Partner may ask another Partner to provide information which he needs to carry out the work in his Own Contract and the other Partner provides it

Does the other Partner provide the Information?

NO

FC 16
Early Warning

YES

A
Sheet 2

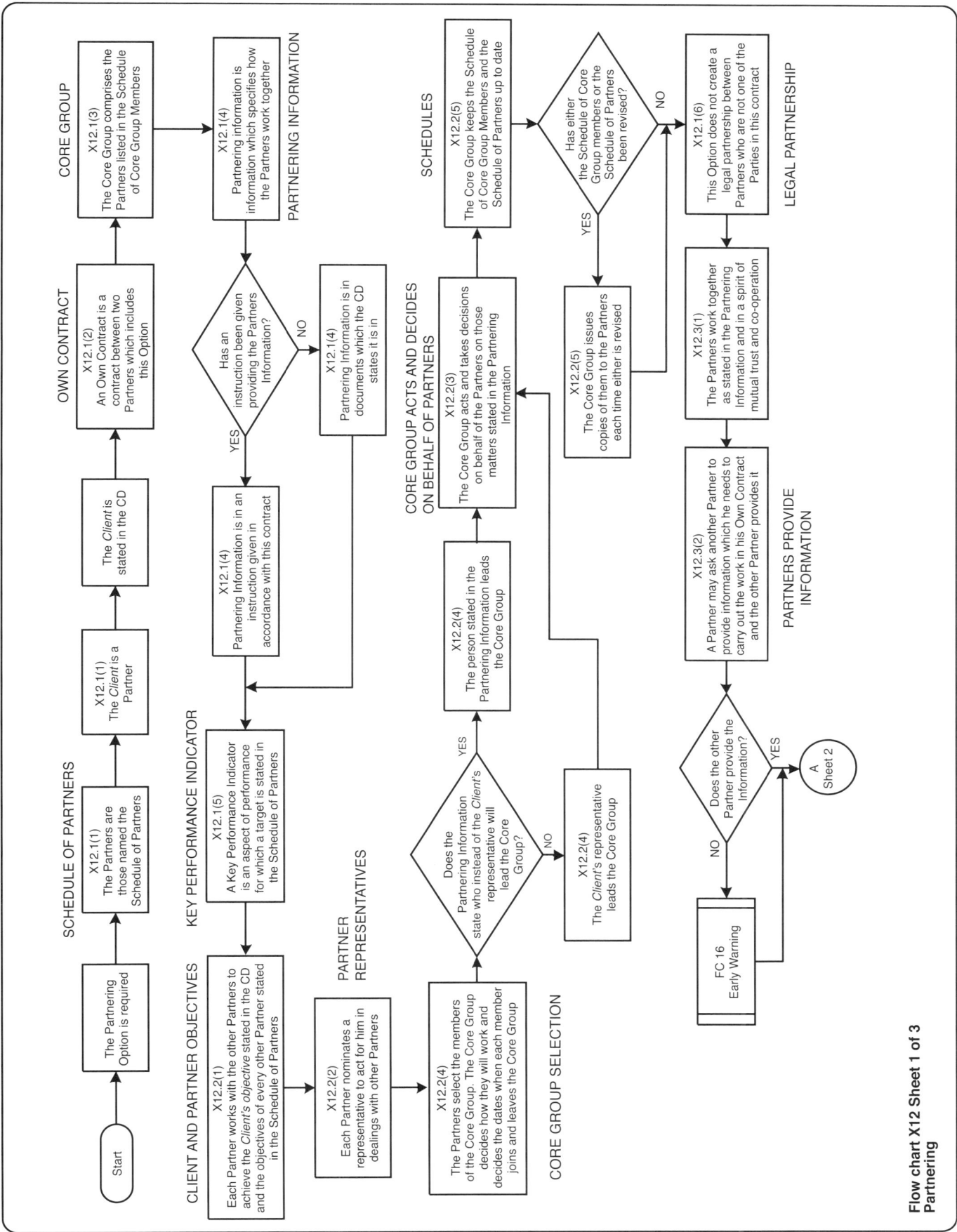

**Flow chart X12 Sheet 1 of 3
Partnering**

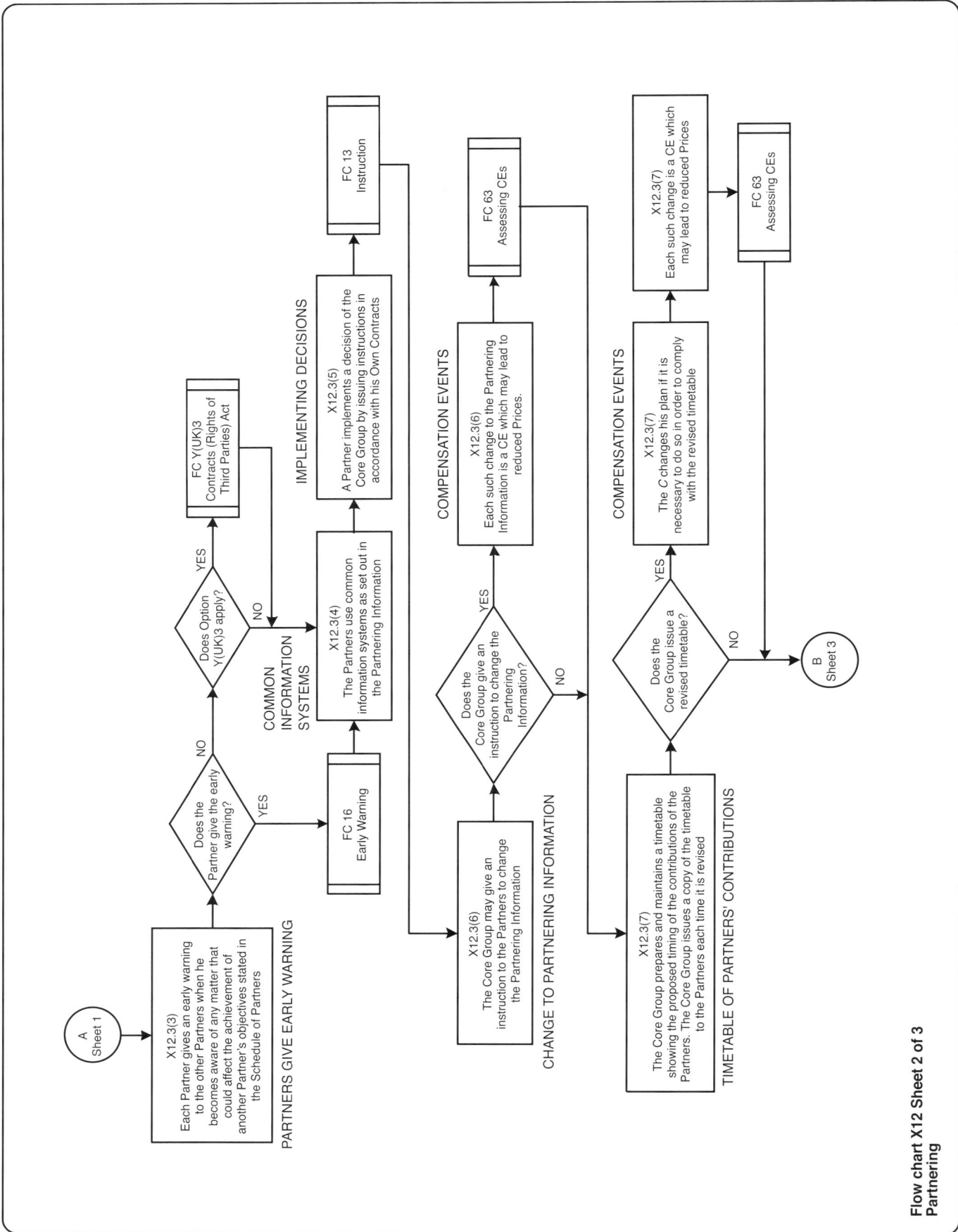

Flow chart X12 Sheet 2 of 3
Partnering

PARTNERS GIVE ADVICE,
INFORMATION AND OPINION

X12.3(8)

A Partner gives advice, information and opinion to the
Core Group and to other Partners when asked to do so
by the Core Group. This advice, information and opinion
relates to work that another Partner is to carry out under
its Own Contract and is given fully, openly and objectively.
The Partners show contingency and risk allowances
in information about costs, prices and timing for future work

B
Sheet 2

SUBCONTRACTING

X12.3(9)

A Partner notifies the
Core Group before
subcontracting any work

FC 13
Notification

ACHIEVEMENT
OF TARGET

X12.4(1)

A Partner is paid the amount stated in the
Schedule of Partners if the target stated for
a Key Performance Indicator is improved
upon or achieved

Has the
target been
improved upon or
achieved?

YES

NO

X12.4(1)

Payment of the amount is due when the
target has been improved upon or
achieved and is made as part of the
amount due in the Partners Own Contract

PAYMENT
DUE

FC 50
Assessing the
Amount Due

X12.4(2)

The *Client* may add a Key Performance
Indicator or associated payment to the Schedule
of Partners but may not delete or reduce a
payment stated in the Schedule of Partners

ADJUSTING KEY PERFORMANCE
INDICATORS

Finish

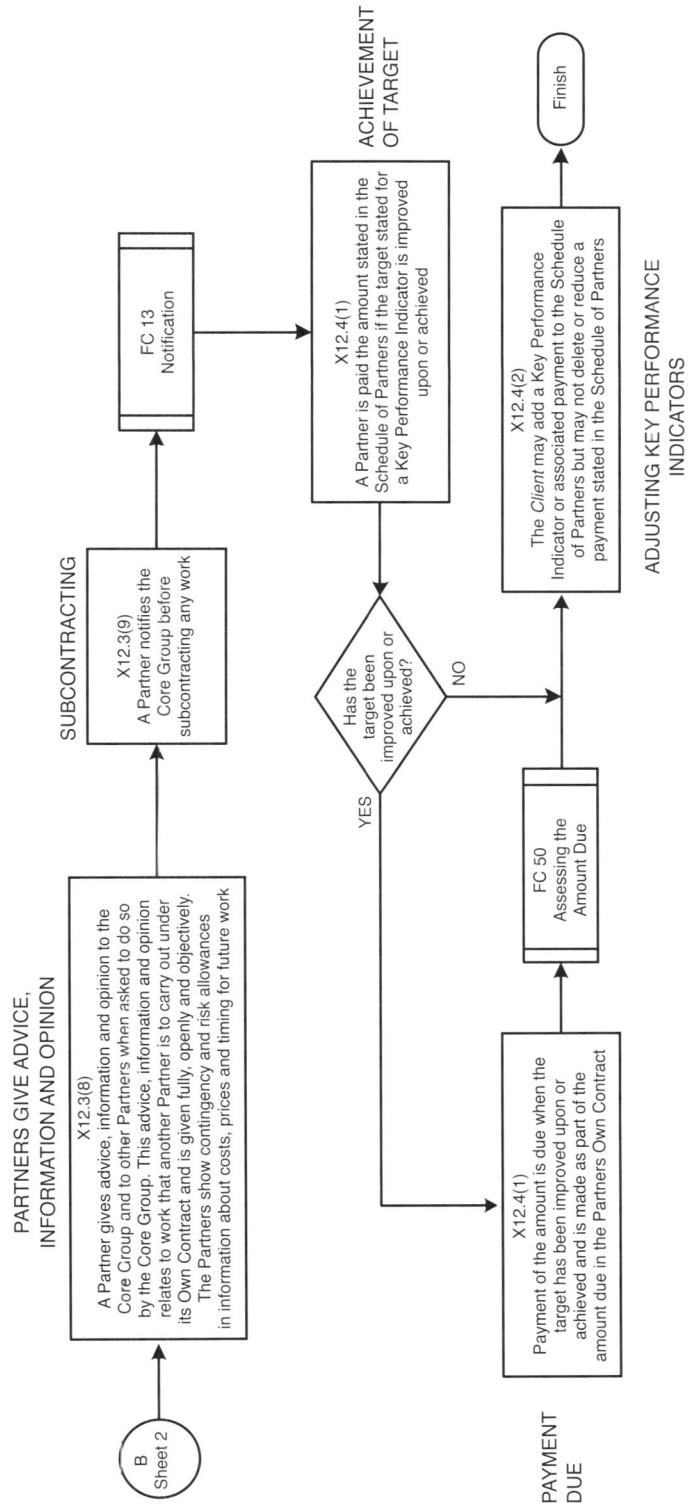

Flow chart X12 Sheet 3 of 3
Partnering

PERFORMANCE BOND

X13.1
The C gives the E a performance bond, provided by a bank or insurer which the SM has accepted, for the amount stated in the CD and in the form set out in the SI

A performance bond is required

Start

CONTRACT DATE

11.2(3)
The Contract Date is the date when this contract came into existence

BOND GIVEN BY THE CONTRACT DATE?

Is the bond given by the Contract Date?

NO

YES

X13.1
The performance bond is given to the E within four weeks of the Contract Date

Is the bond given within four weeks?

YES

NO

FC 91
Termination 91.2

REASON FOR NOT ACCEPTING

X13.1
A reason for not accepting the bank or insurer is that its commercial position is not strong enough to carry the bond

SUBMISSION FOR ACCEPTANCE

FC 13
Submission for acceptance

ACCEPTED?

Does the SM accept the performance bond?

NO

YES

The C submits an alternative proposal

Finish

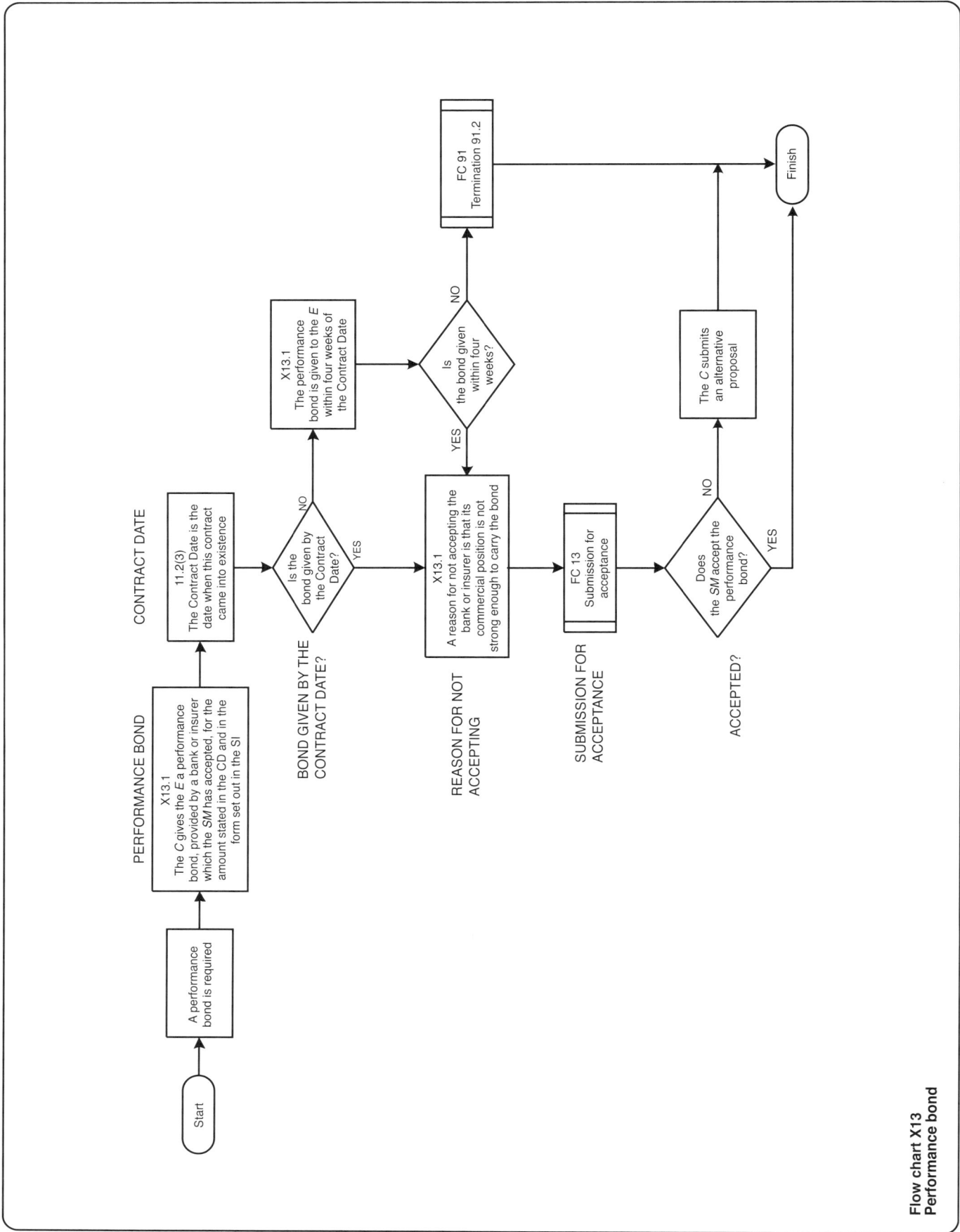

Flow chart X13
Performance bond

Start → Part of the *service* is not adequate → The *service* and *service level table* are stated in the CD → Does any part of the *service* not meet the *service level*?

YES → X17.1
If a part of the *service* does not meet the service level stated in the *service level table*, the *C* pays the amount of low service damages stated in the *service level table*

NO → Finish

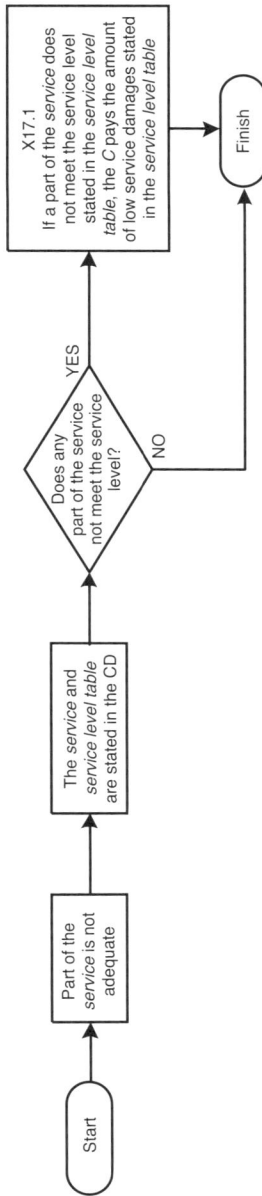

Flow chart X17
Low service damages

Start

A matter has arisen which may make the C liable to the E

The *end of liability date* is stated in the CD

Has the matter been notified to the C before *end of liability date*?

NO → X18.5
The C is not liable to the E for a matter unless it is notified to the C before the *end of liability date*

YES

Has loss of or damage to the E's property occurred?

YES → FC 81
Contractor's risks

X18.2
For any one event, the liability of the C to the E for loss of or damage to the E's property is limited to the amount stated in the CD

NO

Have Defects arisen due to the C's plan?

YES → FC 42
Correcting Defects

FC 44
Uncorrected work

X18.3
The C's liability to the E for Defects due to his design of an item of Equipment is limited to the amount stated in the CD

NO

Has the E an indirect or consequential loss?

YES → X18.1
The C's liability to the E for the E's indirect or consequential loss is limited to the amount stated in the CD

NO

X18.4
The excluded matters are amounts payable by the C as stated in this contract for
• loss of or damage to the E's property,
• low performance damages if Option X17 applies,
• delay damages if Option X19 applies and
• C's share if Option C applies

Is it an excluded matter?

NO → X18.4
The C's total liability to the E for all matters arising under or in connection with this contract, other than the excluded matters, is limited to the amount stated in the CD

X18.4
The C's total liability applies in contract, tort or delict and otherwise to the extent allowed under the *law of the contract*

YES

The *law of the contract* is stated in the CD

Finish

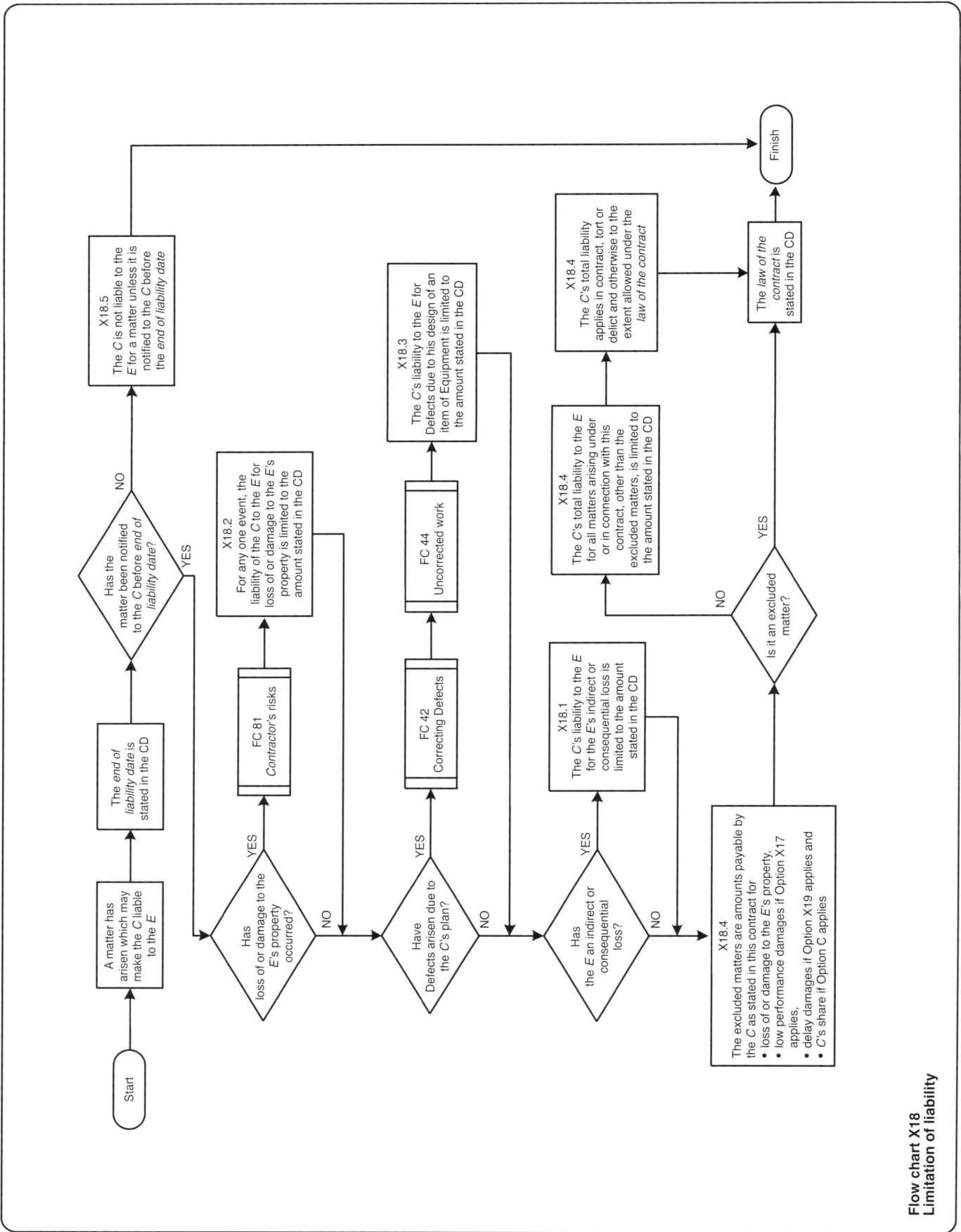

Flow chart X18
Limitation of liability

TASK

X19.1(1)
A Task is work within the *service* which the *C* may instruct the *SM* to carry out within a stated period of time

TASK ORDER

X19.1(2)
A Task Order is the *SM*'s instruction to carry out a Task

11.2(12)
The Price List is the *price list* unless later changed in accordance with this contract

What is the issue?

INSTRUCTING TASK ORDER

Task Order to be instructed

Is it after the end of the *service period*?

YES → **X19.4**
No Task Order is issued after the end of the *service period*

NO → The *SM* may issue a Task Order to the *C*

X19.4
The *C* does not start any work included in the Task until the *SM* has instructed him to carry out the Task and does the work so that Task Completion is on or before the Task Completion Date

X19.4
If Task Completion is after the end of the *service period*, the *service period* is extended until Task Completion. The *SM* does not issue a Task Order during this extended period

TASK COMPLETION

X19.1(3)
Task Completion is when the *C* has done all the work in the Task and corrected Defects which would have prevented the *E* or Others from using the Affected Property and Others from doing their work

X19.4
The *SM* may issue an instruction changing a Task Order

TASK COMPLETION DATE

X19.1(4)
Task Completion Date is the date for completion stated in the Task Order unless later changed in accordance with this contract

X19.2
When a Task Order is issued
- the priced list of items for the Task is inserted in the Price List, and
- the work involved is added to the Service Information.
An instruction to carry out a Task is not a compensation event.

DELAY DAMAGES

X19.3
If Task Completion is later than the Task Completion Date, the *C* pays delay damages at the rate stated in the Task Order from the Task Completion Date until Task Completion

Defining the Task Order
(See procedure on sheets 2 and 3)

The Programme
(See procedure on sheets 4 and 5)

Finish

TASK ORDER COMPENSATION EVENTS

Possible CE → Task Order Compensation Event
(See procedure on sheets 6–8)

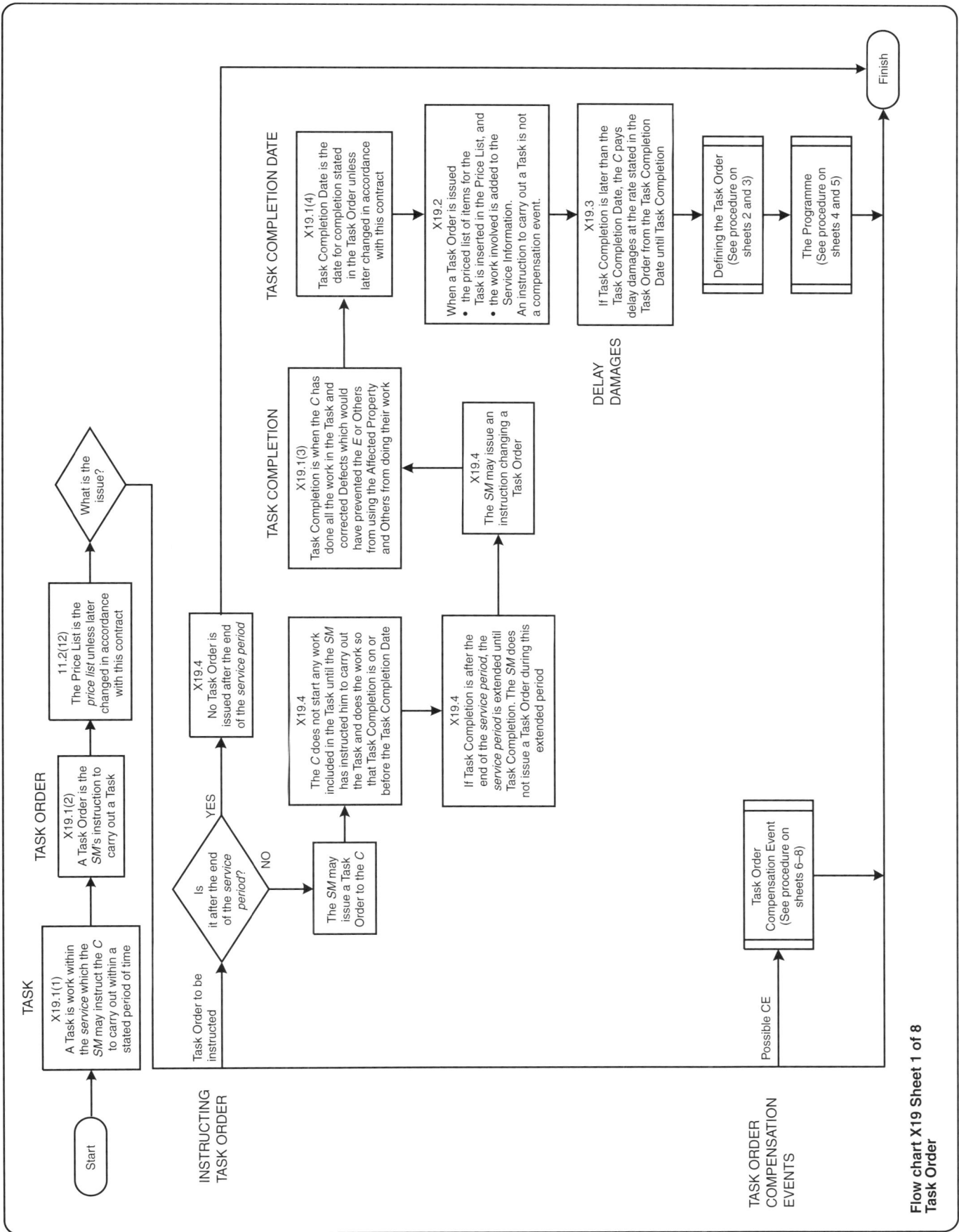

Flow chart X19 Sheet 1 of 8
Task Order

Start

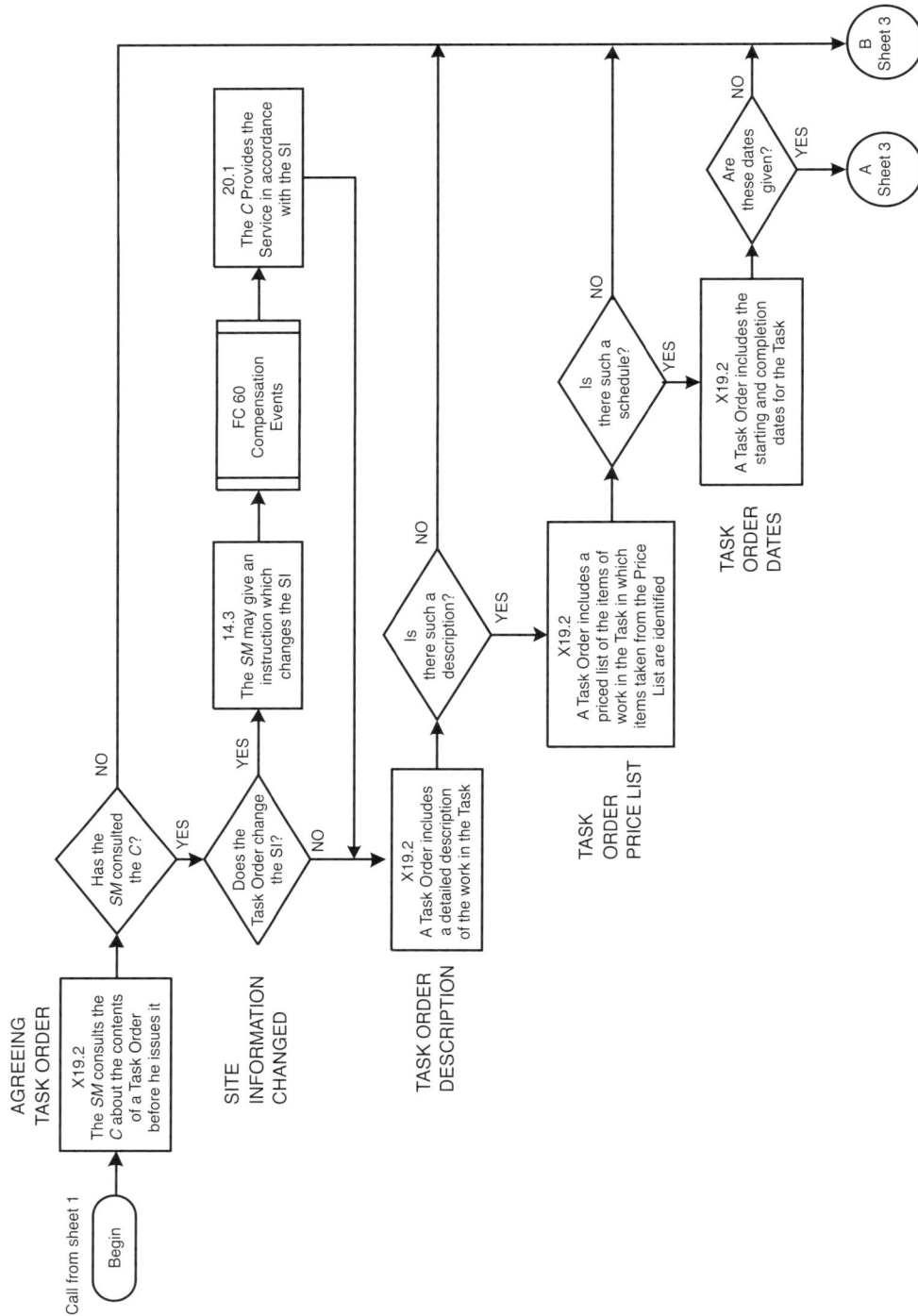

AGREEING
TASK ORDER

Call from sheet 1

Begin

X19.2
The *SM* consults the
C about the contents
of a Task Order
before he issues it

Has the
SM consulted
the *C*?
NO / YES

SITE
INFORMATION
CHANGED

Does the
Task Order change
the SI?
YES / NO

14.3
The *SM* may give an
instruction which
changes the SI

FC 60
Compensation
Events

20.1
The *C* Provides the
Service in accordance
with the SI

TASK ORDER
DESCRIPTION

X19.2
A Task Order includes
a detailed description
of the work in the Task

Is
there such a
description?
NO / YES

TASK
ORDER
PRICE LIST

X19.2
A Task Order includes a
priced list of the items of
work in the Task in which
items taken from the Price
List are identified

Is
there such a
schedule?
NO / YES

TASK
ORDER
DATES

X19.2
A Task Order includes the
starting and completion
dates for the Task

Are
these dates
given?
NO / YES

B
Sheet 3

A
Sheet 3

Flow chart X19 Sheet 2 of 8
Task Order

TASK ORDER DAMAGES

A Sheet 2

X19.2
A Task Order includes the amount of delay damages for late completion of the Task

↓

Are delay damages given?

— NO → (up to B Sheet 2)

— YES →

X19.3
The delay damages in a Task Order, if any, are not more than the estimated cost to the *E* of late completion of the Task

↓

Does amount exceed limit?

— YES → (up to B Sheet 2)

— NO →

TASK ORDER PRICES

Which main Option applies?

— A or C →

X19.2
A Task Order includes the total of the Prices for the Task

↓

FC 54
The Price List

↓

X19.3
The Prices for items in the Task price list which are not taken from the Price List are assessed in the same way as CEs

— E →

X19.2
A Task Order includes the forecast total of the Prices for the Task

↓ (to FC 54)

FC 63
Assessing CEs

↓

Are the total of the Prices given?

— NO → (up to FC 63)

— YES →

Return

Return to sheet 1

B Sheet 2 →

A Task Order cannot be issued → **Finish**

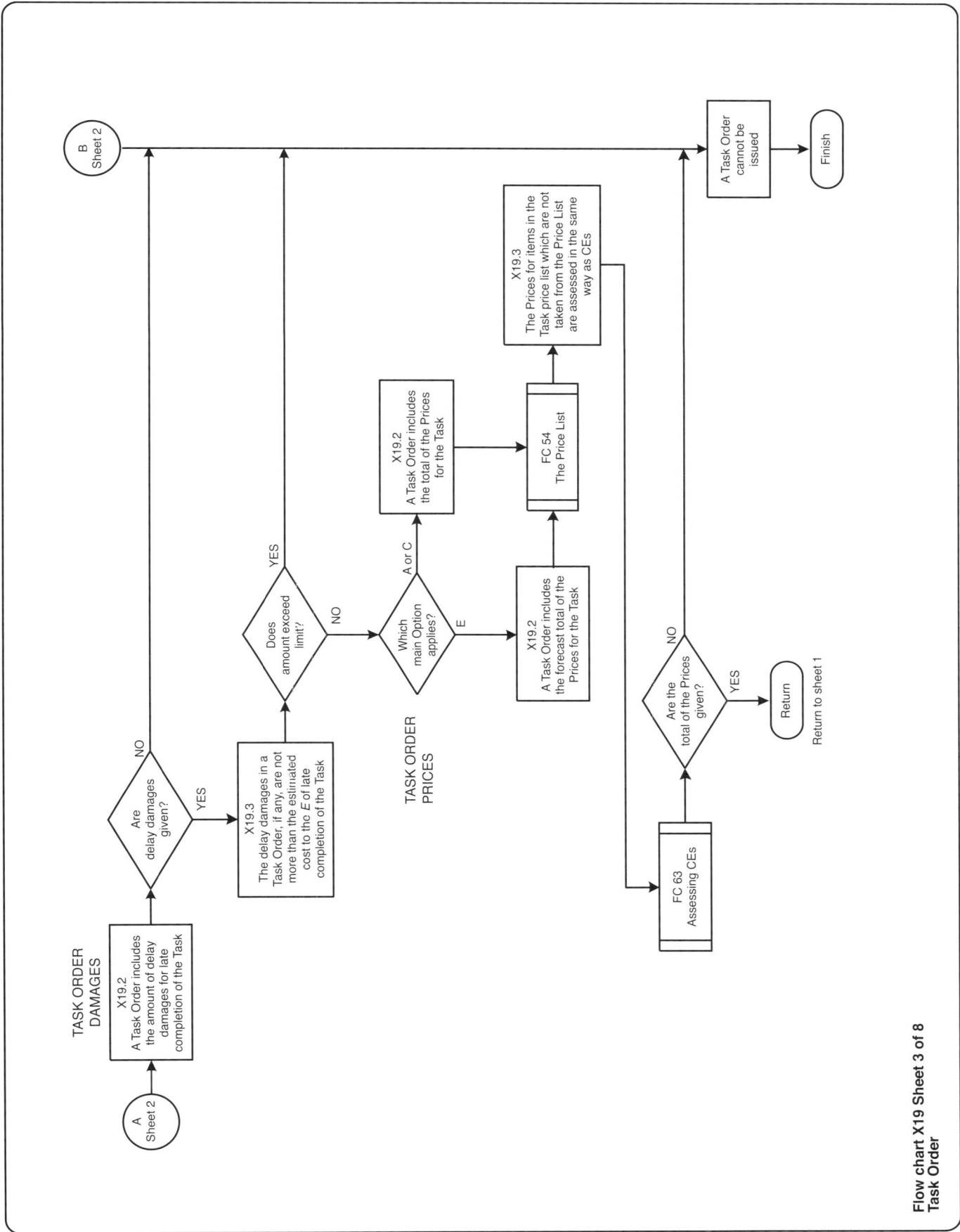

Flow chart X19 Sheet 3 of 8
Task Order

TASK ORDER PROGRAMME

Called from Sheet 1

Begin

X19.5
The C submits a Task Order programme to the SM for acceptance within the period stated in the CD

X19.6
The C shows on each Task Order programme which he submits for acceptance

- the Task starting date and the Task Completion Date,
- planned Task Completion,
- the order and timing of the operations which the C plans to do in order to complete the Task,
- provisions for
  - float,
  - time risk allowances,
  - health and safety requirements and
  - the procedures set out in this contract,
- the dates when, in order to Provide the Service in accordance with his Task Order programme, the C will need
  - access to the Affected Property,
  - acceptances,
  - P&M, equipment and other things to be provided by the E and
  - information from Others and
- other information which the SI requires the C to show on a Task Order programme submitted for acceptance

INFORMATION TO BE SHOWN ON TASK ORDER PROGRAMME

TIMELY SUBMISSION

Does the C submit a Task Order programme for acceptance on time?

NO → **FC 16**
SM gives C early warning

YES ↓

X19.7
Within one week of the C submitting a Task Order programme to him for acceptance, the SM either accepts the programme or notifies the C of his reasons for not accepting it

PERIOD FOR REPLY

FC 13
Submission for acceptance

SUBMISSION

Return
Return to sheet 1

X19.7
A reason for not accepting the Task Order programme is that
- the C's plans which it shows are not practicable,
- it does not show the information which this contract requires or
- it does not comply with the SI

REASONS FOR NOT ACCEPTING THE PROGRAMME

Revising the C's programme
See procedure sheet 5

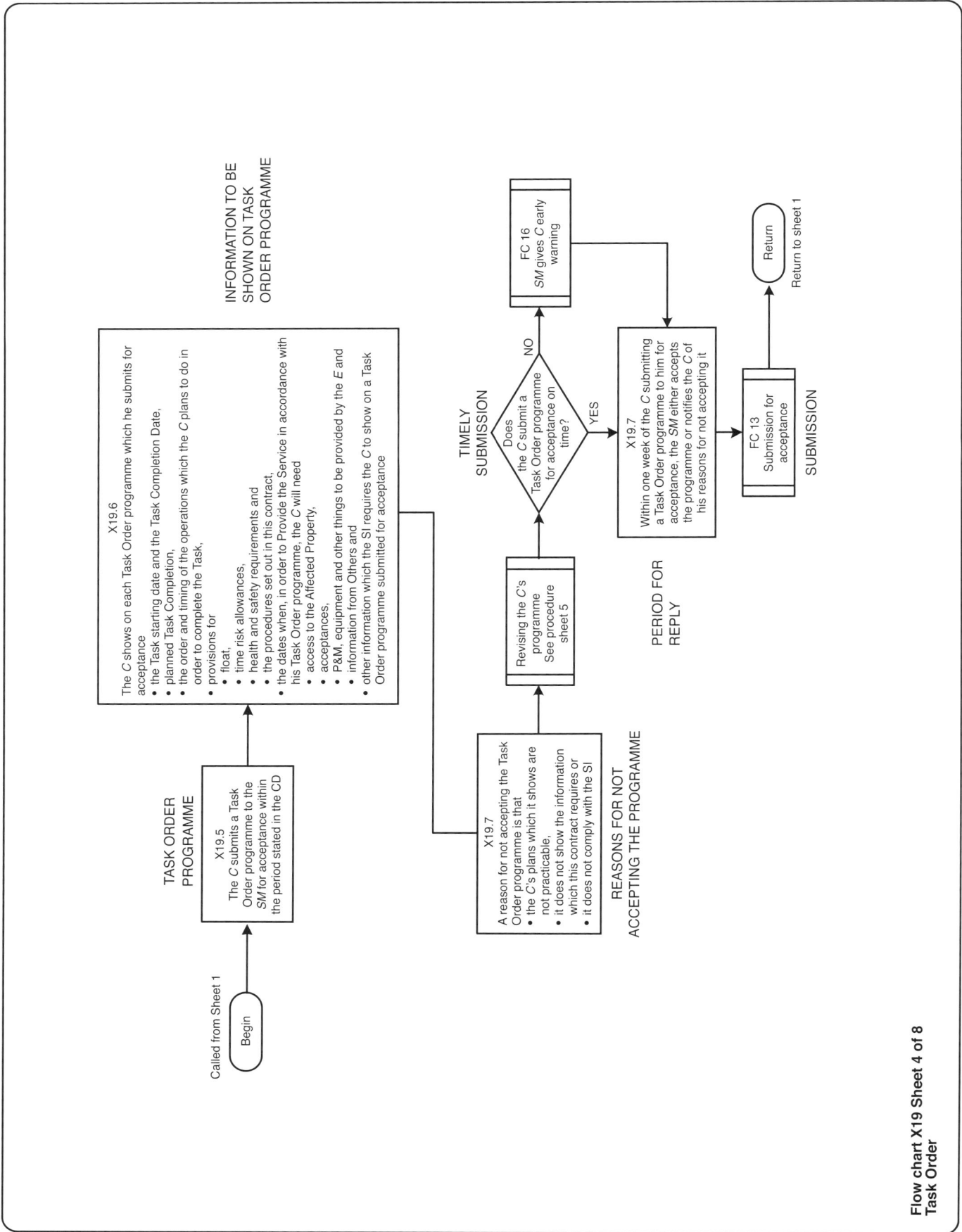

Flow chart X19 Sheet 4 of 8
Task Order

Called from sheet 4

Begin

A revised Task Order programme is to be submitted

X19.9
The C submits a revised Task Order programme to the SM for acceptance

SERVICE MANAGER INSTRUCTS A REVISED TASK ORDER PROGRAMME TO BE SUBMITTED

Does the SM instruct the C to submit a revised programme?

YES

X19.9
The C submits a revised Task Order programme within the *period for reply* after the SM has instructed him to

PERIOD FOR SUBMISSION

NO

The *period for reply* is stated in the CD

CONTRACTOR CHOOSES TO SUBMIT A REVISED TASK ORDER PROGRAMME

Does the C choose to submit a revised programme?

YES

X19.9
The C submits a revised Task Order programme when he chooses to

NO

X19.8
The C shows on each revised Task Order programme
• the actual progress achieved on each operation and its effect upon the timing of the remaining work,
• the effects of implemented CEs,
• how the C plans to deal with any delays and to correct notified Defects and
• any other changes which the C proposes to make to the Task Order programme

INFORMATION TO BE SHOWN ON REVISED TASK ORDER PROGRAMME

X19.9
The latest programme accepted by the SM supersedes previous accepted programmes

Return

Return to sheet 4

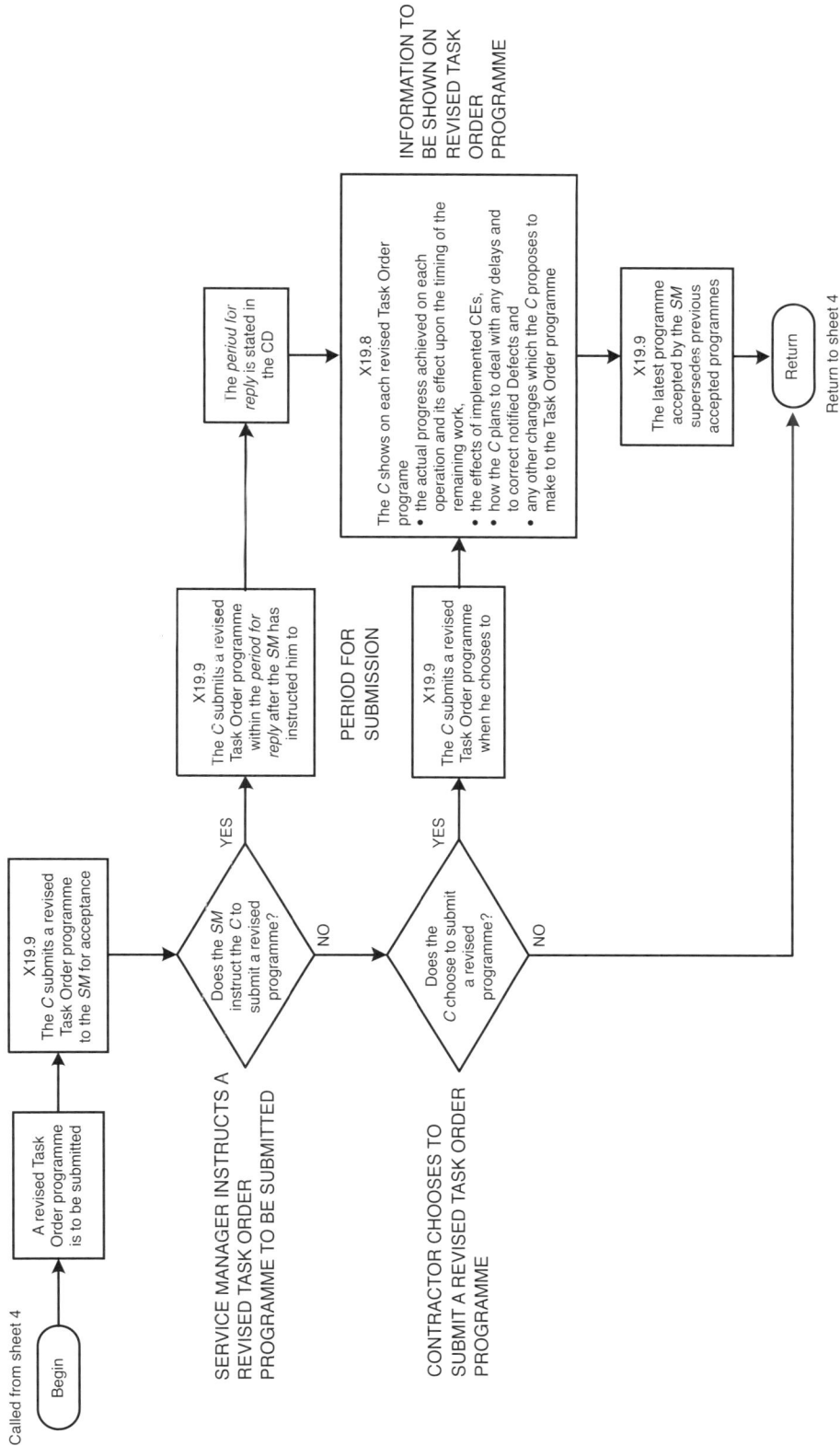

Flow chart X19 Sheet 5 of 8
Task Order

Called from sheet 1

Begin

A possible CE has been identified

POSSIBLE COMPENSATION EVENT

What type of event?

CHANGE TO SERVICE INFORMATION

X19.10(1)

X19.10(1)
The *SM* gives an instruction changing a Task Order

X — Sheet 8

COMPENSATION EVENT ARISING FROM AN INSTRUCTION OR CHANGED DECISION

NO ACCESS OR USE OF SITE

X19.10(2)

X19.10(2)
The *C* receives the Task Order after the starting date stated in the Task Order

SOMETHING NOT PROVIDED

X19.10(3)

X19.10(3)
The *E* does not provide right of access to Affected Property in accordance with the latest accepted Task Order programme

STOP OR NOT START

X19.10(4)

X19.10(4)
The *E* does not provide something which he is to provide as stated in the SI in accordance with the latest accepted Task Order programme

Y — Sheet 8

OTHER COMPENSATION EVENTS

C — Sheet 7

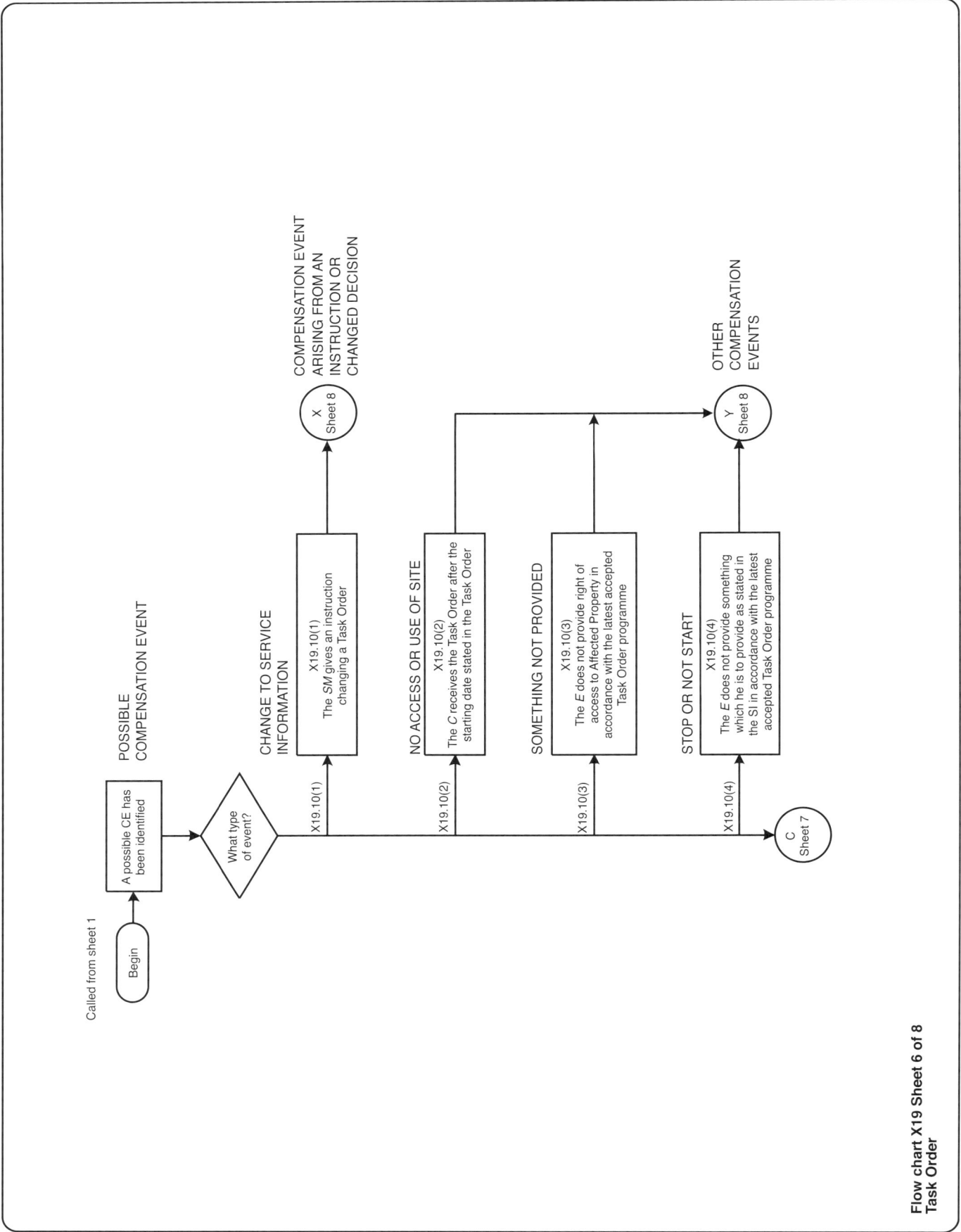

**Flow chart X19 Sheet 6 of 8
Task Order**

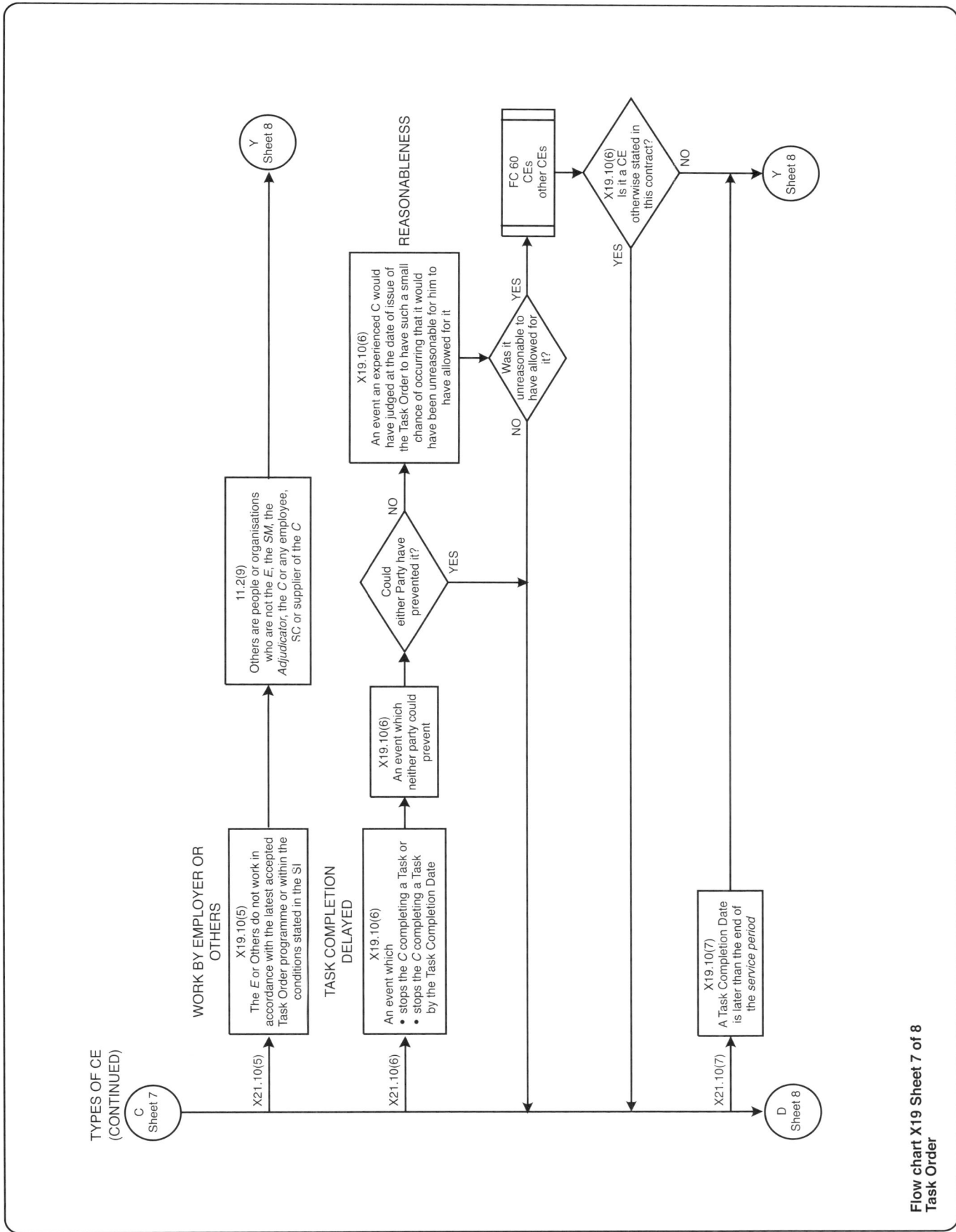

TYPES OF CE
(CONTINUED)

(C
Sheet 7)

**WORK BY EMPLOYER OR
OTHERS**

X21.10(5) →

X19.10(5)
The *E* or Others do not work in
accordance with the latest accepted
Task Order programme or within the
conditions stated in the SI

11.2(9)
Others are people or organisations
who are not the *E*, the *SM*, the
Adjudicator, the *C* or any employee,
SC or supplier of the *C*

→ (Y
Sheet 8)

**TASK COMPLETION
DELAYED**

X21.10(6) →

X19.10(6)
An event which
• stops the *C* completing a Task or
• stops the *C* completing a Task
  by the Task Completion Date

X19.10(6)
An event which
neither party could
prevent

Could
either Party have
prevented it?

YES →

NO ↓

X19.10(6)
An event an experienced *C* would
have judged at the date of issue of
the Task Order to have such a small
chance of occurring that it would
have been unreasonable for him to
have allowed for it

REASONABLENESS

Was it
unreasonable to
have allowed for
it?

NO →

YES ↓

FC 60
CEs
other CEs

X19.10(6)
Is it a CE
otherwise stated in
this contract?

YES ↓

NO →

→ (Y
Sheet 8)

X21.10(7) →

X19.10(7)
A Task Completion Date
is later than the end of
the *service period*

(D
Sheet 8)

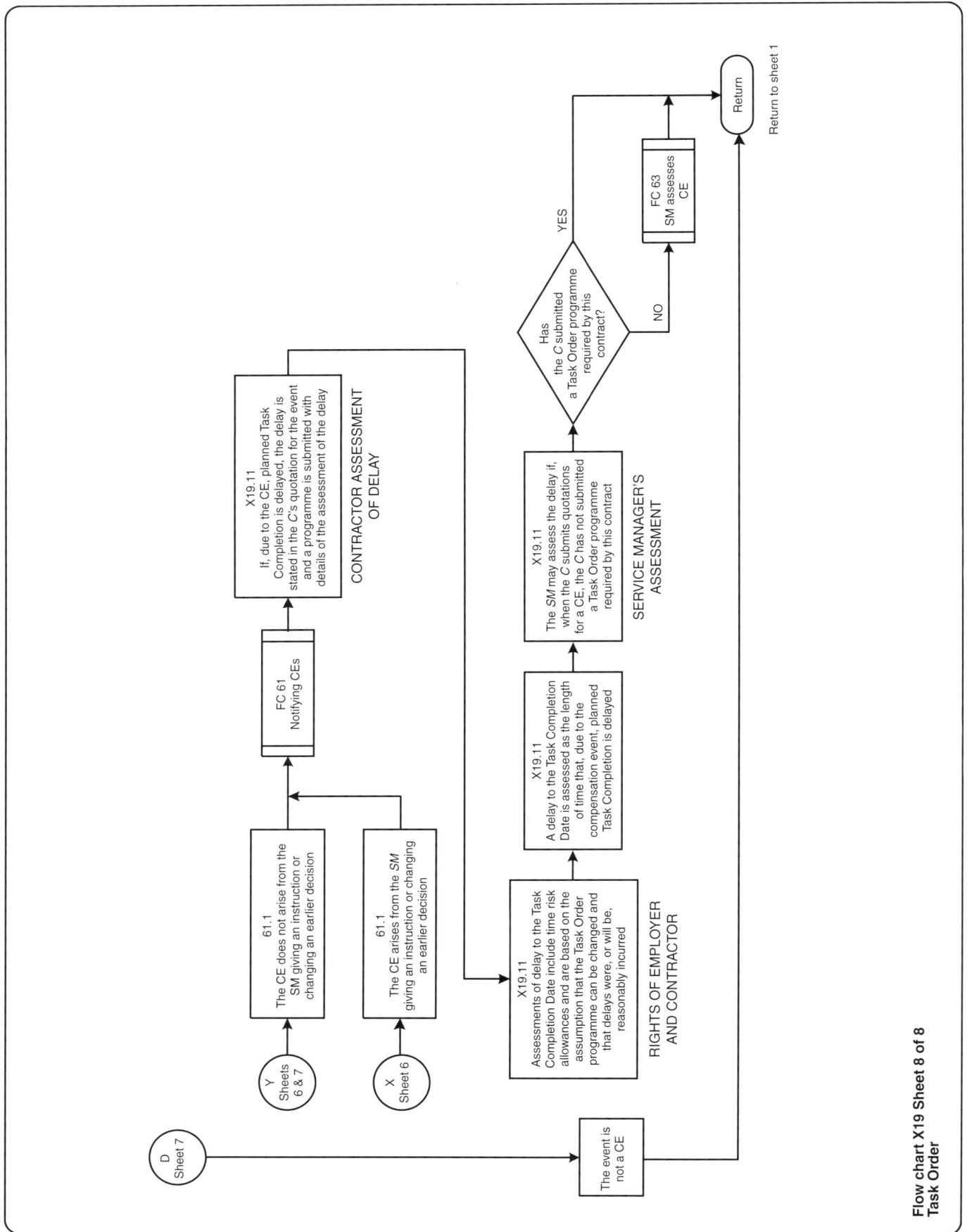

CONTRACTOR ASSESSMENT OF DELAY

X19.11
If, due to the CE, planned Task Completion is delayed, the delay is stated in the C's quotation for the event and a programme is submitted with details of the assessment of the delay

FC 61
Notifying CEs

61.1
The CE does not arise from the SM giving an instruction or changing an earlier decision

61.1
The CE arises from the SM giving an instruction or changing an earlier decision

Y
Sheets 6 & 7

X
Sheet 6

RIGHTS OF EMPLOYER AND CONTRACTOR

X19.11
Assessments of delay to the Task Completion Date include time risk allowances and are based on the assumption that the Task Order programme can be changed and that delays were, or will be, reasonably incurred

X19.11
A delay to the Task Completion Date is assessed as the length of time that, due to the compensation event, planned Task Completion is delayed

SERVICE MANAGER'S ASSESSMENT

X19.11
The *SM* may assess the delay if, when the *C* submits quotations for a CE, the *C* has not submitted a Task Order programme required by this contract

Has the *C* submitted a Task Order programme required by this contract?

YES

NO

FC 63
SM assesses CE

Return

Return to sheet 1

D
Sheet 7

The event is not a CE

Flow chart X19 Sheet 8 of 8
Task Order

www.neccontract.com

Start

X20.1
A Key Performance Indicator is an aspect of performance by the *C* for which a target is stated in the Incentive Schedule. The Incentive Schedule is the *incentive schedule* unless later changed in accordance with this contract

X20.2
From the *starting date* until the end of the *service period*, the *C* reports to the *SM* his performance against each of the Key Performance Indicators. Reports are provided at the intervals stated in the CD and include the forecast final measurement against each indicator

X20.3
If the *C*'s forecast final measurement against a Key Performance Indicator will not achieve the target stated in the Incentive Schedule, he submits to the *SM* his proposals for improving performance

Has the target stated for a Key Performance Indicator been improved upon or achieved?

YES → **X20.4**
The *C* is paid the amount stated in the Incentive Schedule if the target stated for a Key Performance Indicator is improved upon or achieved. Payment of the amount is due when the target has been improved upon or achieved

NO →

Does the *E* wish to add a Key Performance Indicator?

YES → **Does it delete or reduce a payment stated in the Incentive Schedule?**

NO →

Does it delete or reduce a payment stated in the Incentive Schedule?

NO → **X20.5**
The *E* may add a Key Performance Indicator and associated payment to the Incentive Schedule

YES → **X20.5**
The *E* may not add a Key Performance Indicator and associated payment to the Incentive Schedule

Finish

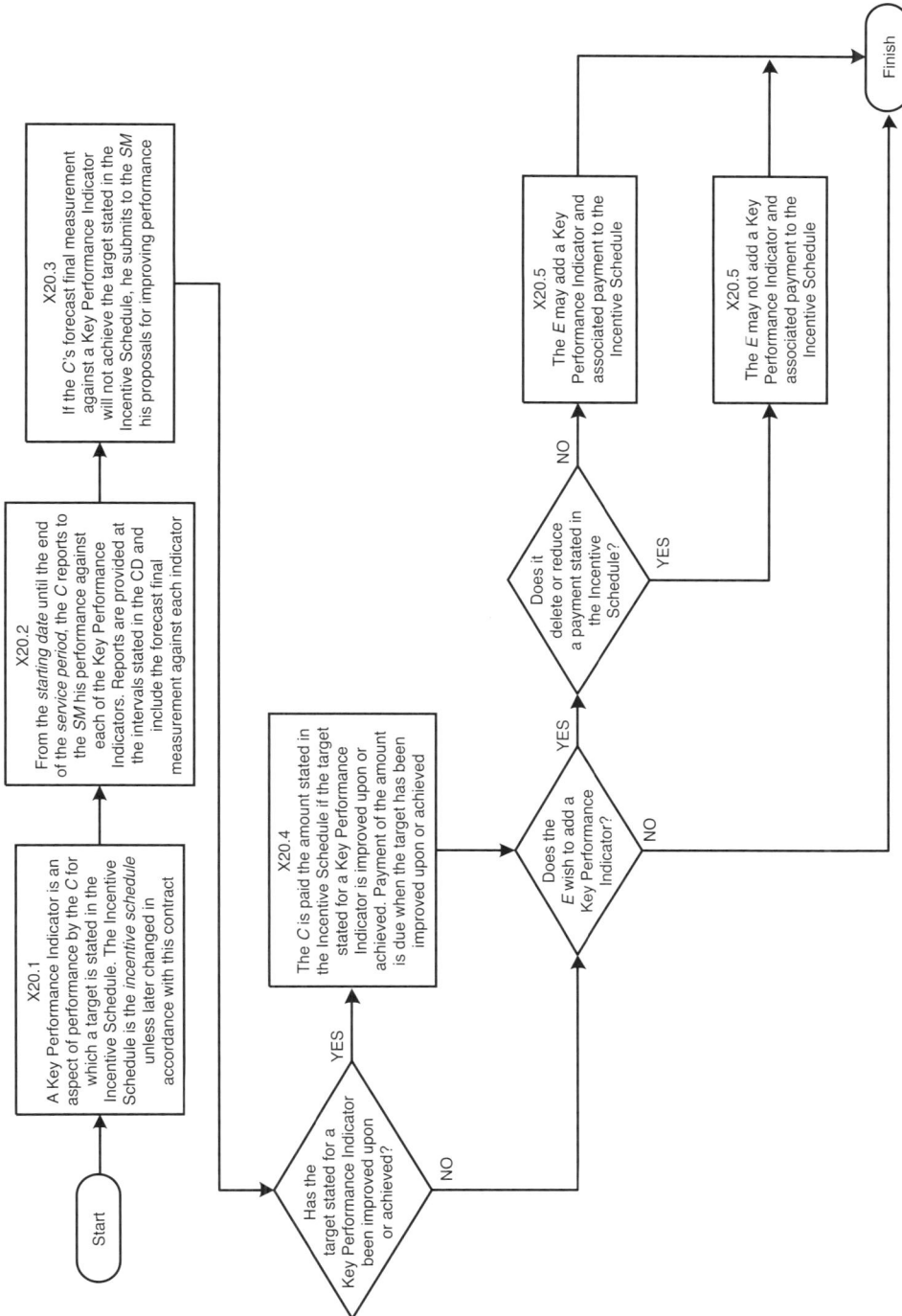

Flow chart X20
Key Performance Indicators (not used with Option X12)

AUTHORISATION

Start

Y1.1(1)
The Authorisation is a document authorising the *project bank* to make payments to the C and Named Suppliers

project bank is identified in the CD

NAMED SUPPLIERS

Y1.1(2)
Named Suppliers are *named suppliers* and other Suppliers who have signed the Joining Deed

Y1.1(6)
Joining Deed is an agreement in the form set out in the contract under which the Supplier joins the Trust Deed

named suppliers are identified in the CD

TRUST DEED

Y1.13
The E, the C and *named suppliers* sign the Trust Deed before the first assessment date

Y1.1(5)
Trust Deed is an agreement in the form set out in the contract which contains provisions for administering the Project Bank Account

Y1.1(4)
A Supplier is a person or organisation who has a contract to
• provide part of the *services*,
• provide a service necessary to Provide the Services or
• supply Plant and Materials for the *services*

PROJECT BANK ACCOUNT

Y1.1(3)
Project Bank Account is the account used to receive payments from the C and E and make payments to the C and Named Suppliers

Y1.2
The C establishes the Project Bank Account with the *project bank* within three weeks of the Contract Date

CHARGES & INTEREST?

Y1.3
Does the CD state the E pays any charges and is paid any interest made by the *project bank?*

YES

NO

Y1.3
The E pays any charges and is paid any interest made by the *project bank*

Y1.3
The C pays any charges and is paid any interest made by the *project bank*

Y1.3
The charges and interest by the *project bank* are not included in Defined Cost

REASON FOR NOT ACCEPTING

Y1.4
A reason for not accepting the banking arrangements is that they do not provide for payments to be made in accordance with this contract

Y1.4
The C submits to the SM for acceptance details of the banking arrangements for the Project Bank Account

Y1.4
Does the SM accept the C's submission?

YES

NO

Y1.4
The C provides to the SM copies of communications with the *project bank* in connection with the Project Bank Account

A
Sheet 2

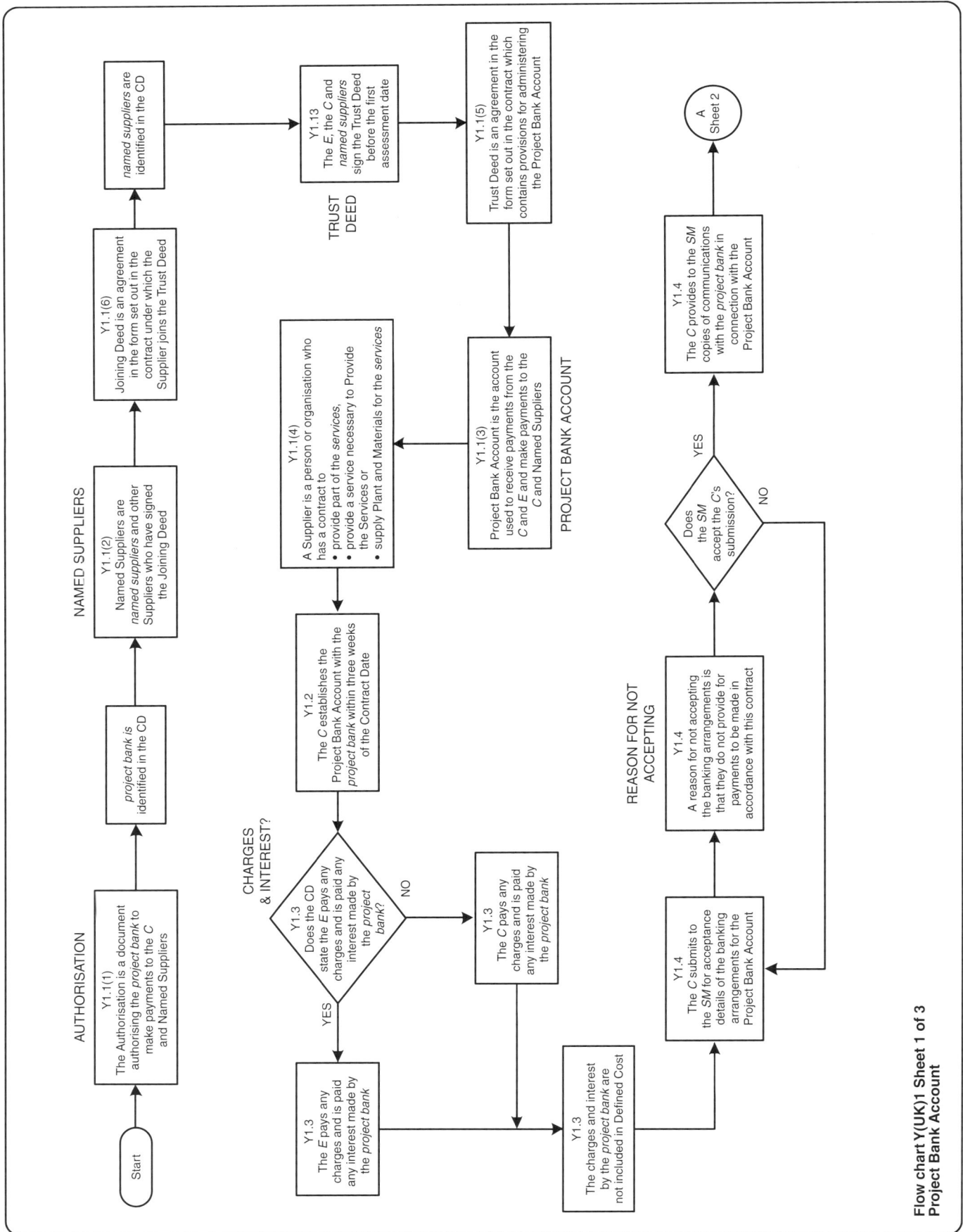

Flow chart Y(UK)1 Sheet 1 of 3
Project Bank Account

NAMED SUPPLIERS

A
Sheet 1

Y1.5
The *C* includes in his contracts with Named Suppliers the arrangements in this contract for the operation of the Project Bank Account and Trust Deed

Y1.5
The *C* notifies the Named Suppliers of the details of the Project Bank Account and the arrangements for payment of amounts due under their contracts

ADDING A SUPPLIER?

Does the *C* submit proposals for adding a Supplier to the Named Suppliers?

YES →

Y1.6
The *C* submits proposals for adding a Supplier to the Named Suppliers to the *SM* for acceptance

Does the *SM* accept the *C*'s submission?

NO →

Y1.6
A reason for not accepting is that the addition of the Supplier does not comply with the SI

YES ↓

Y1.6
The *E*, the *C* and the *Supplier* sign the Joining Deed after acceptance

NO ↓ (from Adding a Supplier)

PAYMENT

Y1.7
On or before each assessment date, the *C* submits to the *SM* an application for payment, and shows in the application the amounts due to Named Suppliers in accordance with their contracts

Is payment due from the *E* to the *C*?

NO → X Sheet 3

YES ↓

Y1.8
Within the time set out in the banking arrangements to allow the *project bank* to make payment to the *C* and Named Suppliers in accordance with the contract, the *E* makes payment to the Project Bank Account of the amount which is due to be paid under the contract.

Does the *E* notify the *C* that he intends to pay less than the certified amount?

YES →

Y1.8
Within the time set out in the banking arrangements to allow the *C* and Named Suppliers to make payment to the *project bank* in accordance with the contract the *C* makes payment to the Project Bank Account of any amount which the *E* has notified the *Contractor* he intends to withhold from the certified amount and which is required to make payment to Named Suppliers

NO →

ECC FC 51
Payment

Y1.9
The *C* prepares the authorisation, setting out the sums due to Named Suppliers as assessed by the *C* and to the *C* for the balance of the payment due under the contract

Y1.9
After signing the authorisation, the *C* submits it to the *SM* no later than four days before the final date for payment. The *E* signs the authorisation and submits it to the *project bank* no later than one day before the final date for payment

B
Sheet 3

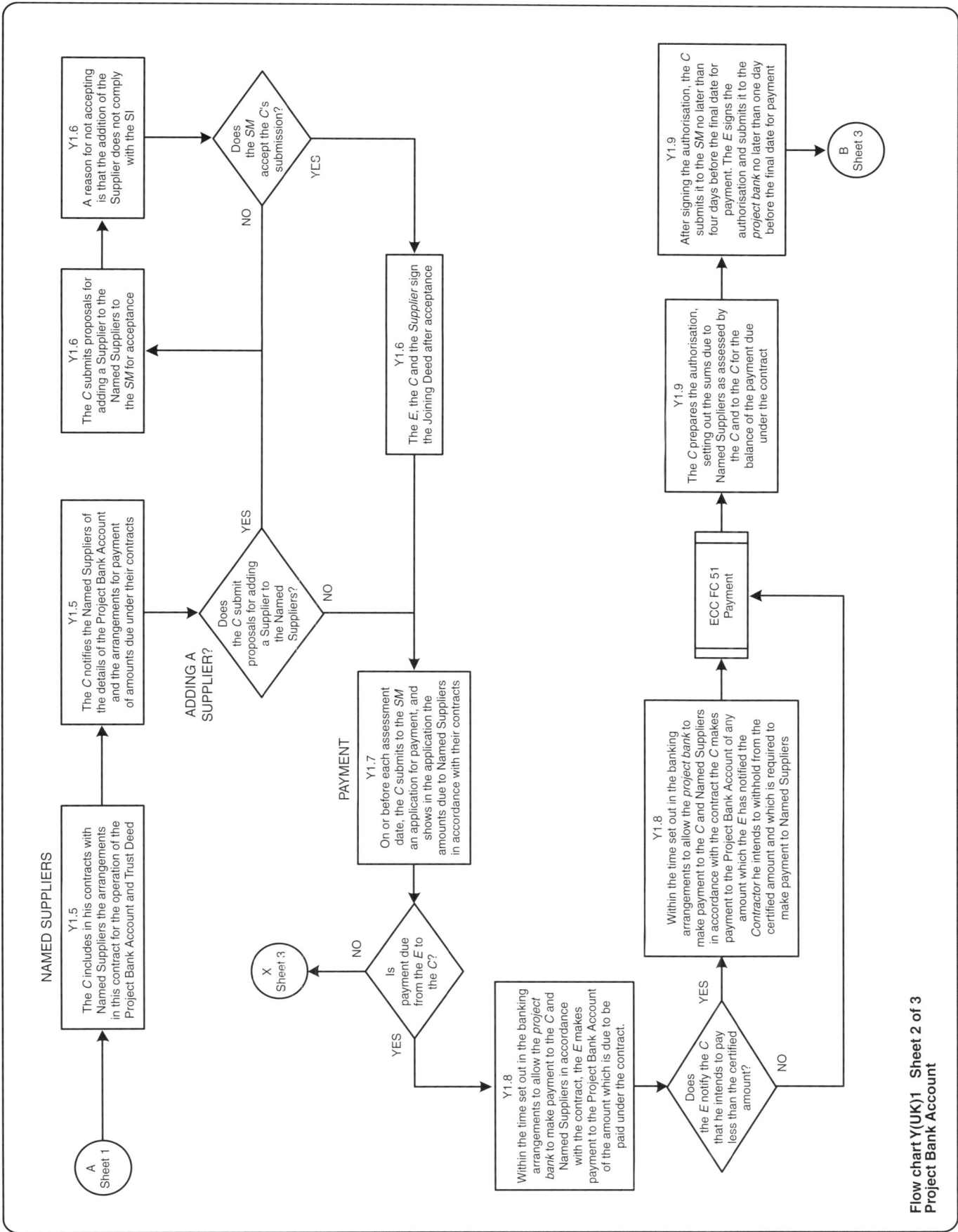

Flow chart Y(UK)1   Sheet 2 of 3
Project Bank Account

PAYMENT

Y1.10
The *C* and Named Suppliers receive payment from the Project Bank Account of the sums set out in the Authorisation as soon as practicable after the Project Bank Account receives payment

EFFECT OF PAYMENT

Y1.12
Payments made from the Project Bank Account are treated as payments from the *E* to the *C* in accordance with this contract or from the *C* or *Subcontractor* to Named Suppliers in accordance with their contracts as applicable

Y1.12
A delay in payment due to a failure of the *C* to comply with the requirements of this clause is not treated as late payment under this contract

PAYMENT DUE FROM CONTRACTOR TO EMPLOYER?

Is a payment due from the *C* to the *E*?

YES → **Y1.12** A payment which is due from the *C* to the *E* is not made through the Project Bank Account

NO

X
Sheet 2

B
Sheet 2

TERMINATION

Has a termination certificate been issued by the *SM*?

YES → **Y1.14** If the *SM* issues a termination certificate, no further payments are made into the Project Bank Account

NO

Finish

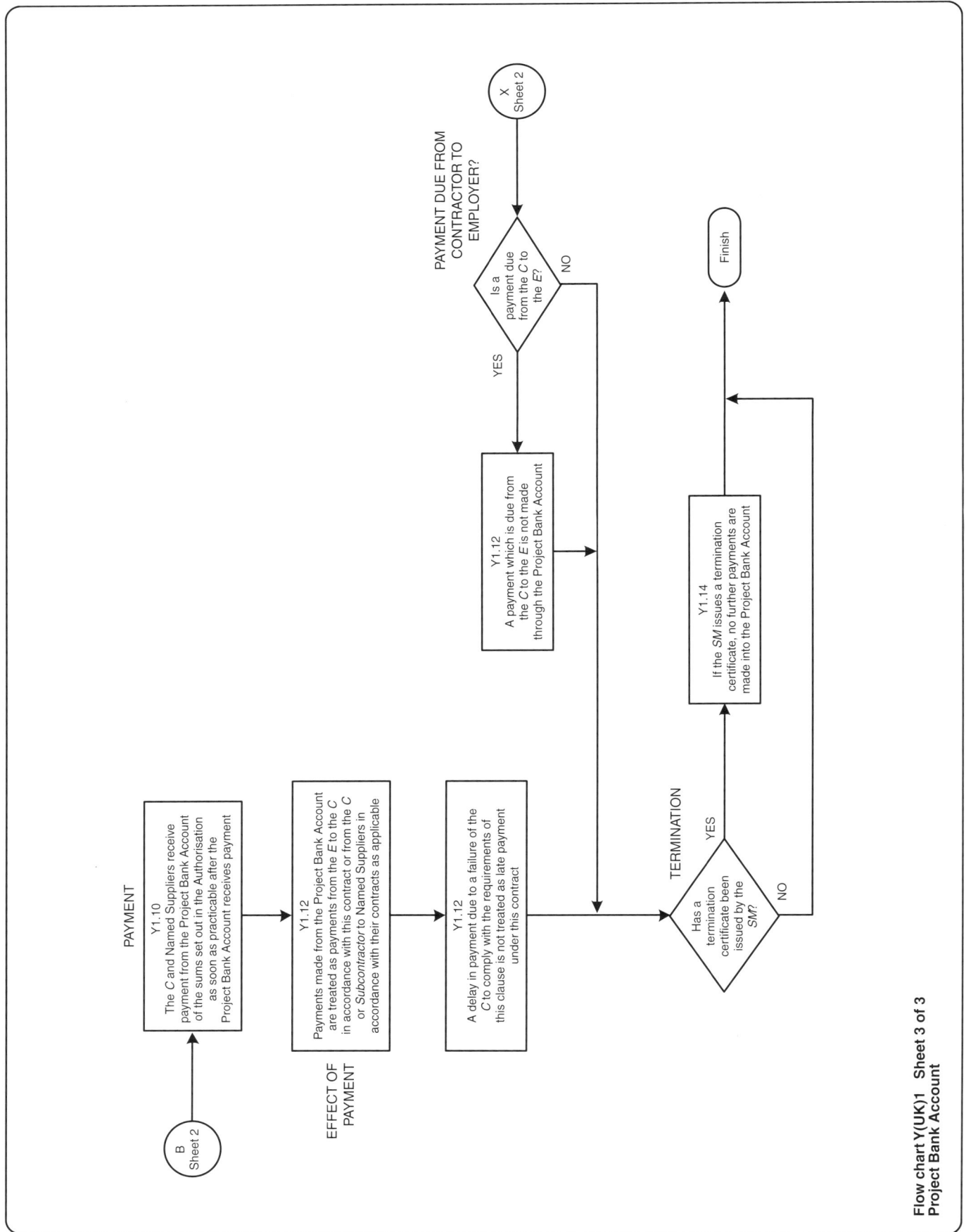

Flow chart Y(UK)1   Sheet 3 of 3
Project Bank Account

Start

DEFINITIONS

THE ACT

Y2.1(1)
The Act is the Housing Grants, Construction and Regeneration Act 1996 as amended by the Local Democracy, Economic Development and Construction Act 2009

DAY TIME PERIOD

Y2.1(2)
A period of time stated in days is a period calculated in accordance with Section 116 of the Act

DATES FOR PAYMENT

Y2.2
The date on which a payment becomes due is seven days after the assessment date

DUE DATE FOR PAYMENT

FINAL DATE FOR PAYMENT

Y2.2
The final date for payment is fourteen days or a different period for payment if stated in the CD after the date on which payment becomes due

SERVICE MANAGER'S CERTIFICATE

Y2.2
The SM's certificate is the notice of payment to the C specifying the amount due at the payment due date (the notified sum) and stating the basis on which the amount was calculated

INTENTION TO PAY LESS

Y2.3
If either Party intends to pay less than the notified sum, he notifies the other Party not later than seven days (the prescribed period) before the final date for payment by stating the amount considered to be due and the basis on which that sum is calculated

FC 13
Notification

PAY LESS NOTICE

Y2.3
A Party does not withhold payment of an amount due under this contract unless he has notified his intention to pay less than the notified sum as required by this contract

SUSPENSION OF PERFORMANCE

Y2.4
If the C exercises his right under the Act to suspend performance, it is a CE

COMPENSATION EVENT

FC 63
Assessing CEs

Finish

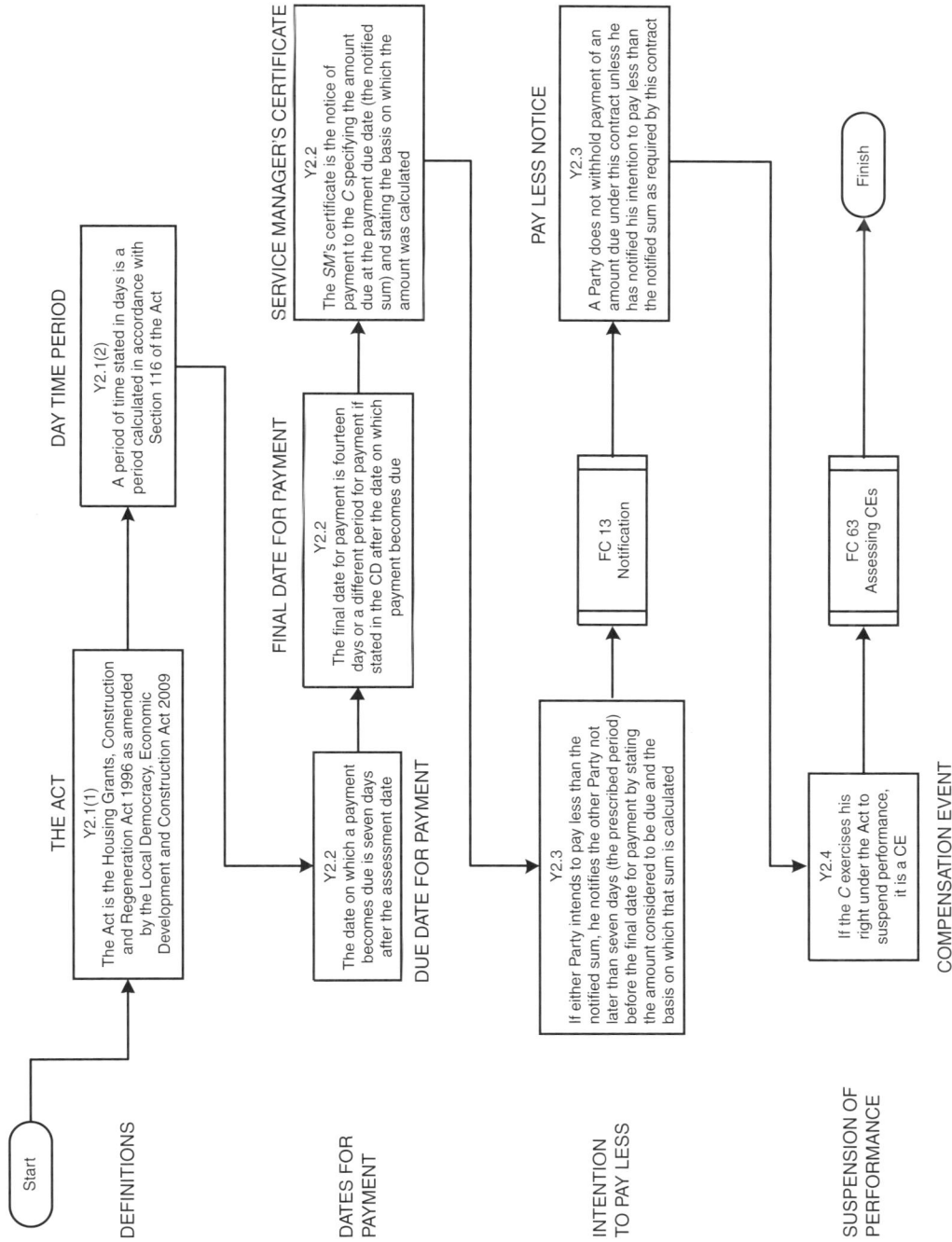

Flow chart Y(UK)2
The Housing Grants, Construction and Regeneration Act 1996

RIGHTS OF THIRD PARTIES TO ENFORCE CONTRACT TERM

THE PARTIES

Start

11.2(10)
The Parties are the *E* and the *C*

Y3.1
A person or organisation who is not one of the Parties may enforce a term of this contract under the Contracts (Rights of Third Parties) Act 1999 only if the term and the person or organisation are stated in the CD

IS THE PERSON OR ORGANISATION ONE OF PARTIES?

Y3.1
Is the person or organisation a Party to this Contract?

YES

NO

IS THE TERM AND THE PERSON OR ORGANISATION STATED IN THE CONTRACT DATA?

Y3.1
Is the term and the person or organisation stated in the CD?

YES

NO

CAN ENFORCE CONTRACT TERM

Y3.1
Term of contract can be enforced under Act

CANNOT ENFORCE CONTRACT TERM

Y3.1
Term of contract cannot be enforced under Act

Finish

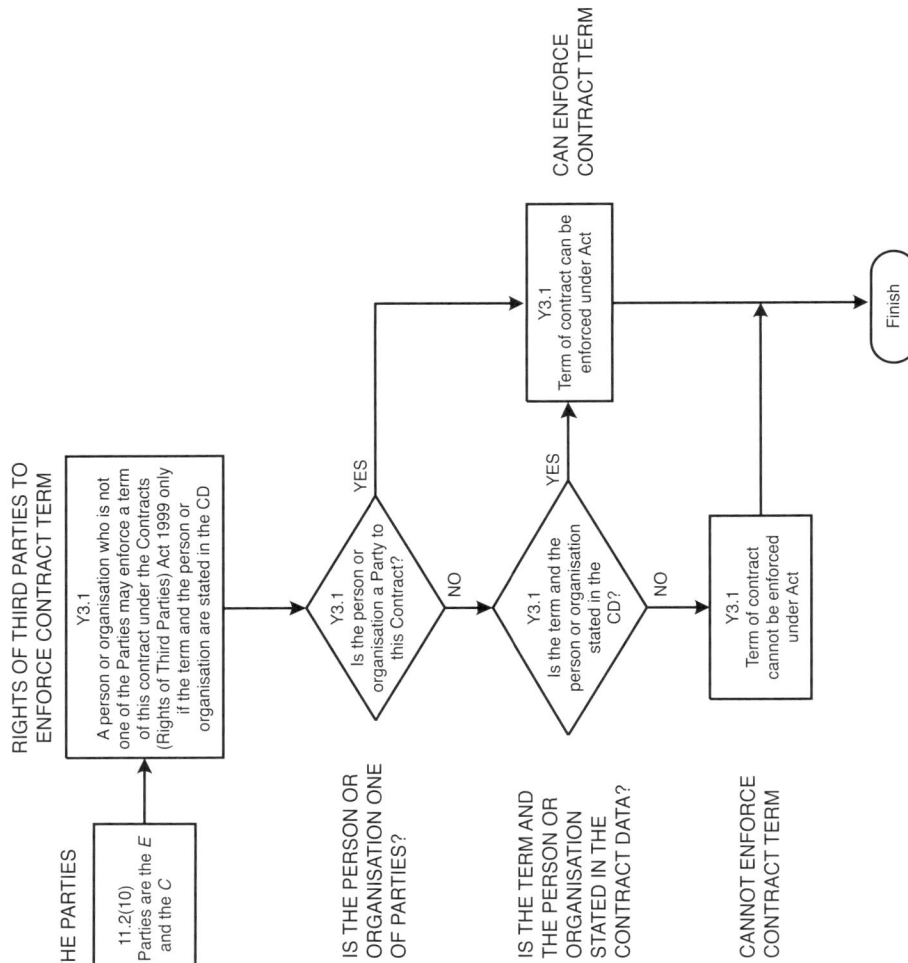

Flow chart Y(UK)3
The Contracts (Rights of Third Parties) Act 1999